loose**women**

Here Come the Girls!

Also by the Loose Women

Loose Women: Girls' Night In

The Little Book of Loose Women

loose**women**
Here Come The Girls!

HODDER

First published in paperback in 2010

1

Loose Women is an ITV Studios Ltd Production
Copyright © ITV Studios Ltd 2009
Licensed by ITV Global Entertainment

The right of *Loose Women* to be identified as the Author
of the Work has been asserted by them in accordance
with the Copyright, Designs and Patents Act 1988.

ISBN 978 1 444 70017 6

Typeset in Adobe Caslon by Hewer Text UK Ltd, Edinburgh
Printed and bound by Clays Ltd, St Ives plc

Hodder & Stoughton policy is to use papers that are natural, renewable
and recyclable products and made from wood grown in sustainable forests.
The logging and manufacturing processes are expected to conform
to the environmental regulations of the country of origin.

Hodder & Stoughton Ltd
338 Euston Road
London NW1 3BH

www.hodder.co.uk

To Loose Women everywhere

Acknowledgements

It has been a wonderful opportunity for us to have the chance to produce a second book following the success of *Girls' Night In* and we would like to say a big thank you to our talented writer Rebecca Cripps for taking the time to work with us on all our many stories and experiences!

A lot of work goes on behind the scenes of the show and so we would also like to thank the *Loose Women* production team for their daily support and all their help on *Here Come The Girls!*; in particular Fiona Keenaghan, Karl Newton, Dona Gower, Emily Humphries, Jacqui Saunders, Melissa Jacobs, Kevin Morgan, Jane Devane, Sarfaraz Hussain and Jane Robinson.

Last but not least, every good book needs a great publisher and we have been very lucky once again to have had the incredible support and talents of Hodder & Stoughton, in particular our editor Fenella Bates and her team Sarah Christie, Emma Knight, Susan Spratt and Ciara Foley.

CONTENTS

Introduction

The Loose Women Survival Guide

It's that time of year again, the kids are going back to school, the nights draw in, you've ditched the bikini diet and it's starting to get a little bit blooming cold!

Life can be bleak but fear not, we're here to help get you through it!

Here Come the Girls! is packed with everything you need to survive till Spring.

 Our first book went down so well, and thanks to you folks out there it went to Number One in the charts, and since it was so much fun to put together last time, we thought we'd be silly not to do it again. We wanted to do it a bit differently this time though, so we've based the book on lots of dilemmas we've found ourselves in, or friends of ours have gone through, and we'll do our best to advise, given our admittedly shambolic life experiences so far! It's packed will all-new content – we've spent hours discussing all our favourite topics and they're all right here. We know you'll love the results!

We've got toe-curling confessions of disgracing ourselves at the office party after one too many; we'll share our secrets for dressing to impress and how to look hot when then weather definitely is not; our tips for coping with bonkers family members; broken New Year resolutions and a stocking full of saucy confessions.

There's nothing like a good chuckle so we've crammed in as many wickedly funny stories and anecdotes as we could manage.

We wouldn't forget of course two of the subjects closest to our hearts – love and sex – and this book is brimming with tales of hearts-a-flutter and heartbreak. Carol and Jane will open up for the first time about their new relationships – Carol with her hunky toy boy and Jane rediscovering a long lost love. And Denise is still on about one day becoming Mrs Enrique Iglesias!

So curl up on the sofa, pour yourself a mug of hot chocolate (or a hot toddy if you prefer!) and set aside some 'me time' to be reminded of all the things that really matter in life.

About us…

As you probably know, we're all very different, which explains why we offer such a wide range of diverse opinions and pointsof-view. Here's a little bit of background about each of us.

SHERRIE HEWSON

Sherrie has been an actress for forty years and is best known for her roles in *Coronation Street*, *Emmerdale* and *Crossroads*. She won the prestigious Olivier Award for Best Newcomer at the age of fifteen and her varied television career took off in the 1970s, when she appeared in *Home to Roost*, *In Loving Memory*, *Love for Lydia* and *Russ Abbot's Madhouse*. She has acted alongside many of the greats, including John Thaw, Jeremy Irons, Thora Hird, Harrison Ford and Richard Chamberlain. But there's more to Sherrie than acting and last year she published her first crime novel, *The Tannery*, after winning the BBC show *Murder Most Famous*.

A true original, much-loved for her quirky outlook and self-deprecating sense of humour, Sherrie's a self-confessed eccentric with a surprising take on practically everything. For instance, did you know that snakes are her favourite creatures in the world? Whenever she's near a snake she wants to wrap it around her! Sherrie separated from her husband of twenty-five years in 2004, but today she couldn't be happier, because her daughter Keeley and grandson Oliver are the loves of her life and make her complete.

DENISE WELCH

Denise is currently in the BBC drama *Waterloo Road*. Despite being nominated several times for Best Actress awards, playing flirtatious French teacher Steph Haydock, Denise is filming her final scenes following a decision to leave the drama and concentrate on *Loose Women*. Her first TV break came in 1986 with *Spender* and she went on to appear in *Byker Grove*, *A Kind of Living* and *Soldier Soldier*. She became a household name when she joined *Coronation Street* playing vampish barmaid Natalie Horrocks, who soon began an affair with Sally Webster's husband Kevin.

Endearingly honest, upfront and funny, Denise is never afraid to reveal her most personal experiences; she happily opens up about everything from saucy frolics in the snow to chaos in her cupboards. Married to fellow actor Tim Healy for twenty-one years, she has two sons, Matthew and Louis.

ANDREA McLEAN

One of the show's two main anchors, Andrea keeps the ladies in check with warmth and charm, calming ruffled feathers during heated debates and adding quips to the more lighthearted conversations. Andrea has been a regular on the show since 2007 and loves every minute of it, especially when it's live. A trained journalist, she is best known for presenting the weather on *GMTV*, but after eleven years of getting up before dawn, she hung up her barometer and left the early-morning breakfast show to concentrate on *Loose Women* and enjoy the benefits of a full night's sleep.

In 2006 she took part in ITV1's *Dancing on Ice* and went on to co-present *Dancing on Ice Extra* with fellow ex-contestant Andi Peters after being eliminated in week three. She has also co-hosted *Loose Lips* on Living TV and presented *Our House* for UKTV Style. She still works as a journalist and has written for the *Daily Record* in Scotland, *TV Times*, *Woman's Weekly*, *Bella* and *Woman*, among other publications.

Andrea was born in Scotland and raised in Trinidad and Tobago, which explains her distinctive Scots/Caribbean accent. After her partner Steve proposed to her in a hotel room in his underpants in early 2009, they married in August. Andrea lives in Surrey with Steve and her two children Finlay and Amy.

CAROL McGIFFIN

Unstintingly honest, and achingly funny with it, Carol says and does what no one else dares. She first learned to voice her opinions fearlessly when she co-hosted a Saturday morning show with a certain Chris Evans, who went from being her lodger to her colleague and then her husband (and after that ex-husband!). Other radio highlights include an award-winning evening show with Moz Dee and a breakfast show with Paul Ross. Carol also loves writing and crams as much scribbling as she can into her busy life. She has written for the *Sunday Mirror*, *Daily Mirror*, *Daily Mail*, *Guardian*, *Daily Express* and *London Evening Standard*, as well as *Hello*, *Woman*, *Woman's Own* and *Best*, among others.

Carol used to love being single, not least because it gave her the opportunity to snatch snogs on *Loose Women* with the likes of Russell Brand, Danny Dyer, Gary Rhodes and Dougie McFly. But since her fiancé Mark Cassidy came into her life (and proposed not once, but twice – the second time in front of the Eiffel Tower) she describes herself as 'a proper one-man woman'. Expect wedding bells next year!

JANE McDONALD

This charismatic diva combines glamorous star quality with a forthright sense of humour and girl-next-door modesty. Who could fail to be charmed by her sparkling wit and down-to-earth frankness? Jane cut her teeth as a cabaret singer in the industrial north and her big break came when she was featured on the BBC fly-on-the-wall documentary *The Cruise*. Fourteen million people watched her tie the knot with Henrik Brixen on the show in 1998 and she went on to present BBC's *National Lottery* and ITV's *Star for a Night*. She joined *Loose Women* in 2004 'feeling very fragile and insecure' shortly after a very public divorce. Looking back, she says it was one of the best decisions of her life.

Singing remains Jane's first love, although she's finally considering living a more settled life so that she can spend more time with her other first love, Ed. Until now she's never been happier than when touring with her band and singers, and her popularity is such that her eighth album, *Jane*, reached number seven in the UK album charts. So is she really serious about slowing things down? Watch this space!

COLEEN NOLAN

Coleen is a member of The Nolan Sisters, who chalked up two Royal Performances, achieved huge record sales in Britain, sold more than nine million records in Japan (that's more than The Beatles, she'll have you know!) and recently reformed and are touring to packed audiences. As well as being a regular *Loose Women* panellist since 2000, she also writes columns for *Woman* and the *Daily Mirror* and wrote a bestselling autobiography, *Upfront & Personal*. This year she took part in *Dancing on Ice*, apparently her partner Stuart touched her in places she didn't even know she had!

Naturally warm and open, Coleen has a perfect sense of comic timing and can always be relied on to end a debate with what's known in the business as 'a funny'. Never short on strong opinions, she can be fearlessly controversial too, but her wit and charm seem to keep her out of trouble, (although she's been known to grab a headline or two!). An adoring mum and wife, she lives with Ray, their daughter Ciara and her two sons from her first marriage to Shane Richie - Shane Jnr and Jake.

LYNDA BELLINGHAM

Until she joined *Loose Women* in 2007, bringing her special blend of no-nonsense views and witty one-liners to the show, Lynda was probably best known as the mum in the OXO gravy adverts. Although she looks back on the ads with great affection, she's very glad that her career has moved on! Her first break came in the early 1970s with a role in the first daytime soap, *General Hospital*, and she went on to star in *All Creatures Great and Small* and *Faith in the Future*; she also appeared in *At Home with the Braithwaites* and *Bonkers*.

On stage, she earned critical acclaim in *Vincent River* in London's West End in 2007 and starred as Chris Harper in the stage version of *Calendar Girls* in 2008, which toured the UK in 2008/9 before moving to the West End in April. It was a tough run, but she made it through, because you have to be 'dead or dying to be allowed off a performance'. A true pro and a champion of the over 50s, she will doubtless be gracing stage and screen for many years to come.

LESLEY GARRETT

Britain's most popular soprano, Lesley has thirteen solo CDs to her name. After studying at the Royal Academy of Music, she won a prestigious Kathleen Ferrier Award in 1979 and went on to join English National Opera in 1984, where she won acclaim for a variety of comic and serious roles. Over the years she has performed throughout Europe and Asia, in the USA, Australia, Russia, Brazil and sung with Bryan Ferry, the Eurythmics, Mick Hucknall, Katherine Jenkins and Sarah Brightman, among many others. Her TV appearances include hosting the BBC series *Lesley Garrett . . . Tonight*, which continued as *The Lesley Garrett Show*. Lesley was appointed CBE in 2002. From autumn 2008 to summer 2009, she performed the role of Nettie in *Carousel* in London's West End.

Fun, bubbly and frank, Lesley is a poster girl for feeling – and looking – fabulous at fifty and beyond. A welcome addition to the *Loose Women* panel, she brings glamour, vitality and good old Yorkshire common sense to the show, whether she's discussing her phobia about colds or recalling being sick in the bins at Heathrow airport! Lesley lives in north London with her husband Peter and two children, Jeremy and Chloe.

LISA MAXWELL

After seven years playing Detective Inspector Samantha Nixon on the ITV1 drama *The Bill*, Lisa handed in her badge on 20 March 2009, appearing as a new presenter on *Loose Women* six days later. Smart and funny, she is refreshingly honest about her experiences and adds a mischievous warmth to the panel, where she offers forthright views about everything from infidelity to finding an ex-boyfriend in a compromising position with a tea towel.

Lisa grew up with her mother and grandparents in the Elephant and Castle, London. She won a scholarship to the Italia Conti Academy and played her first role on TV in a schools programme *A Place Like Home* and had her West End debut at the age of 14 as an orphan in the original cast of *Annie*. To say she has had a varied career is something of an understatement – from being the voice of a muppet in *Dark Crystal*, a presenter of kids shows *Splash* and *No Limit's*, starring in *Grease* on the West End, coming last in the Eurovision Song

Contest with her group Unity, to doing impressions alongside the likes of Les Dennis, Russ Abbott and Jasper Carrott. This led to her own series in 1991, BBC1's *The Lisa Maxwell Show* which took her to Michael Aspel's 'big red book' and a contract with Paramount Studios in Hollywood. Now she has more time on her hands, Lisa is looking forward to continuing her work as an Ambassador at her chosen charity, Centrepoint. She lives in London with her fiancé, Paul Jessup, and their daughter Beau.

Get by with a little help from your friends . . .

Chapter 1

The Highs and Lows of Long-term Love

Pet names and matching slippers

We're romantics at heart (yes, even Carol!) and there's nothing we love more than a happy ending.

We've all been through lots of ups and downs in our love lives over the years – shed a few tears; had lots of laughs; been proposed to a couple of times; some of us have had affairs; others of us have been cheated on – but whatever we've gone through, we've always come back to love. Or sometimes love has actively sought us out and found us!

There's no denying the fact that you need to feel loved and if most of us are honest, a long, happy relationship is one of the things we most want to achieve in our lives.

So here are some happy tales to warm you up and make you feel fuzzy . . .

The path of true love . . .

JANE: Falling in love again hit me like a sledgehammer!

ANDREA: Ah, you old romantic, you! Tell us how you two got together.

Alfred and Rose are as happy today
as they were when they married 50 years ago.
It made their dog sick.

JANE: It was meant to be – a sequence of events – and I'm a great believer in fate. OK, here's what happened: I was in The Ivy with my sister and a friend when this guy came up and said, 'One of your exes is now in our band.'

'Oh yes?' I said.

'Yes, Eddie Rothe.'

'Oh my God!' I said. 'How is he?'

'He's fine,' he said with a smile. 'He said he used to go out with you.'

'What band are you?'

'The Searchers.'

'Please give him my regards,' I said.

DENISE: The wheel of fortune begins to turn!

JANE: Thank you, Denise!

DENISE: How did you feel hearing his name again?

JANE: Well, that night when I got home, I thought back to what had happened between Eddie and me and wondered how he had changed. When I knew him, he was the drummer in a group called Liquid Gold – their song, 'Dance Yourself Dizzy', was a massive hit. I was nineteen and working at this fantastic pub/club called Pussycats, which was run by two gay guys. It was the campest place you've ever seen in your life – it was absolutely brilliant – and I was a barmaid, as well as being one of the dancers.

Well, Eddie spotted me from the stage and asked the owner if he could set him up with a date with the girl on the bar. I thought the owner was having a laugh when he told me. After all, this guy was in Liquid Gold! Still, we did go out with each other for quite a while and I moved down to Buckinghamshire to be with him.

He was often on tour, funnily enough. His career had just taken off, he was really busy, and eventually somebody took me to one side and said, 'Look, I don't think this is going to work, because he's got to go away to Europe now.' It would never have worked, back then.

I can't do this any more, I thought. I need to go back up North and work. I'd always been a very independent girlie. So he went off to be this massive star, and after that he joined Mud. Although I didn't know it, he was in Mud for around twelve years. And that was it – we lost touch.

DENISE: Until . . .

JANE: Three months after I bumped into his friend at The Ivy, I was at *Loose Women* having my makeup done when I looked up at the TV monitor and saw The Searchers on *This Morning*, talking about their new album. And there he was, the drummer! Wow, he still looks exactly the same, I thought. He's still got a full head of blond hair, piercing blue eyes and the most lovely face. 'I used to go out with him,' I told Donna, the makeup girl.

'Well, you've got to go and say hello,' she said.

'I can't just turn up like that!' I said. 'What if he doesn't remember me? What if he's married?' I was really worried that he wouldn't recognise me, but Donna dragged me over there just the same. She literally made me go and see him.

ANDREA: Good for Donna!

JANE: When I saw him, I said, 'Oh my God, how are you?' Towering over me (because he's six foot four and I had my little flat shoes on that day), he bent down and lifted me into his arms. Everybody in the room went, aaah!

It turned out that he'd just got divorced. He gave me his number and said give me a call, but within two hours I'd rung him. When we met up, it was like we'd never been apart and we've been together ever since.

It was such a shock, for both of us! He didn't want to meet anybody else; he'd just gone through a divorce. But now we couldn't be apart, although we are apart a lot! When we are together, it's just so natural. It sounds boring, but he's lovely and it's great. He's a very kind man with a very kind face. It's freaking me out a bit that I've met someone so nice, because normally I go for complete gits! I don't really, but I just seem to have picked the wrong men for most of my life.

ANDREA: They haven't all been bad, have they?

JANE: No, you're right. I'm being very unfair to my past partners because there's only been one love in my life and that's been my job. They've always had to be in second place to that, every one of them, which is very difficult for a man. But of course this one is in the same industry and doing the same job, so he understands it fully.

It's just lovely. It's completely different to anything I've ever had before. There's no pressure, we laugh a lot, we get on. He's the person I want to be with in twenty years' time, discussing the papers. So he's my mate, and I think that's the difference. It's like having a cashmere jumper on in a way – or does that sound really pathetic?!

It wouldn't have worked the first time round, but now we're absolutely perfect for each other. We've both changed – him particularly. He was really wild in his early days. He drank a lot and smoked constantly, whereas now he doesn't drink or smoke at all. He's grown up. It took him a long time to grow up, because he was a pop star in a rock band with a wild lifestyle, whereas now he's got different priorities. And so have I.

ANDREA: Does he have any children?

JANE: He has a nine-year old daughter, but at the moment I don't play a role in her life. I think it's still important that she has quality time with her dad. She knows I'm around; she talks to me on the phone and it's great; but I'm taking it very slowly and I hope it will work that way.

ANDREA: That's so wonderful, Jane! It sounds like you've found the love of your life – or rediscovered him, anyway. We're all really happy for you.

DENISE: Your path to true love wasn't entirely smooth, was it, Lesley?

LESLEY: No, that's right. Until I met my husband, I'd always struggled with men who wanted to dominate me. They saw a lively, positive, self-determining woman and they somehow want to capture that and contain it. That was my general experience. It wasn't until I met Peter that I found somebody whose only ambition was to be my equal. His entire

17

preoccupation was with us sharing everything: the bringing up of children, earning a living, and the responsibility for a home. He wanted it all to be entirely fifty-fifty. He is a great feminist, my husband. He was the first man I met who I could honestly say was an 'equalist', who genuinely believed in absolute equality between the sexes. So I married him in a minute! I'd been on my own for some time, actually.

JANE: Were you beginning to worry that you might never find the one?

LESLEY: Well, I was beginning to have my doubts! I got married to a lovely man when I was in my early twenties and the break-up of that marriage was very painful. Then I didn't meet Peter until I was thirty-five. I felt as though I'd auditioned the world and just couldn't find the right guy. I think part of the problem was that I kept falling into relationships with men in show business – in the opera world particularly – and that didn't ever work for me. There was always too much of a conflict of interests.

One reason I think that Peter and I have been so successful is that he's in a completely different profession. We have a great deal of respect and regard for one another's professions. He knows more about opera than I will ever know; it was his passion and his hobby well before he ever met me. So I fitted into that part of his life, and I always loved science and medicine. I was doing science A levels before I chucked them in at the last minute and decided to do music, because I couldn't face a life without singing.

Many doctors are good musicians. In the opera house, there's a running joke that if you do the famous 'Is there a doctor in the house?' line from the stage, half the audience will stand up. For that reason, I think we go together really well. There was a fabulous moment just after we met when we were in bed together and he was reading *Opera Magazine* and I was reading his *British Medical Journal*. I love the *BMJ*, especially the back page and all the readers' problems.

He is always asking me, 'How do you do that?' 'How do you make that sound?' 'How does that work?'

I say, 'I don't know!'

I will always say things like, 'What about viruses? How exactly are they spread? Do they die? If I've got a virus and I touch that table, is that virus still there ten minutes later?'

He'll say 'I'm not really sure!'

It's endless! He is a very intuitive doctor and I'm a very intuitive singer, which is why we often don't know the answers to each other's questions, but we know what's right.

ANDREA: It sounds like the perfect match. How did you two meet?

LESLEY: As I say, I'd auditioned the world and the right guy just wasn't out there. So I bought myself a little cottage up in Yorkshire and planned on living between my cottage and my little flat in town. I was no longer going to be bothered with finding Mr Right, getting married and having my own family; instead I was going to be the world's greatest auntie and sister and daughter. I felt very comfortable with the decision and wasn't in the slightest bit needy.

I was very happily working at English National Opera as a principal soprano; I was in an opera called *The Love for Three*

Oranges by Prokofiev and at one point I had to step out of a huge orange.

SHERRIE: An orange?

LESLEY: Yes, opera can be a mad world!

ANDREA: When was this?

LESLEY: It was coming up to Christmas 1989. Some very lovely friends of mine, who happened to be Peter's patients, decided to set me up with a fabulous bloke they knew. 'We've got this gorgeous man lined up for you!' they said. 'He's perfect. We're bringing him to the opera and we'll take you out to dinner afterwards.'

'Really?' I said.

'Yes, and he even knows lots about opera.'

'Get stuffed!' I said. 'There's no way I'm going on a blind date at this time in my life.'

They were very crestfallen about this but, about ten days later, just before they were coming to see me in the show, they said, 'Look, the gorgeous bloke we were bringing has cried off, so we're fetching our boring old doctor. Will you please come? Somebody has to make conversation at dinner.'

'Go on, then,' I said.

Of course, I fell for this load of twaddle. It was actually the same guy, but they fooled me completely. Spookily, Peter has never, ever accepted a social engagement from a patient before or since – he just doesn't do it – but this one time, he agreed to go to the opera with them. They hadn't been his patients for very long, but he'd warmed to them when he met

them socially at a party by coincidence, a few weeks before.

After the performance, they very casually said to him, 'We're just going backstage to see the conductor and one of the singers.' He tottered along, unaware that he was being set up. Meanwhile, I was expecting some old crumbly GP to appear at my door.

In my dressing room, which I was sharing with some other girls from the cast, I disrobed and put on my oldest candlewick dressing gown; I took off my wig and left my hair in pin curls, with a hairnet over them; and I put cold cream all over my face and started taking my makeup off. Obviously, I wasn't expecting my future husband to walk in!

ANDREA: Surprise!!!

LESLEY: Exactly! There was a knock at the door. My two friends came in first; then they stepped back and said, 'This is Dr Peter Christian.'

Our eyes met and bells started to ring. Before we'd even spoken, I thought, It's him! He's arrived, at last!

We shook hands and said hello, and it was like the whole room stopped. All the other girls in my room noticed it as well; they could hear the bells ringing as well!

My friends also saw what was happening between us and said, 'We'll let you get yourself dressed and we'll meet you in the restaurant in ten minutes.' Peter tore himself away from me and went off with them.

When he'd gone, all the girls in the dressing room screamed.

'How gorgeous is he?' they exclaimed. 'How fantastic was that moment?' I was dizzy and reeling from it all.

Then it turned into a scene from *Little Women* as they all gathered round me, fussing about what I would wear. All I had was an old woolly frock, because it was the middle of winter, so each in turn said, 'Let me lend you a scarf!' 'Let me help you do your hair!' 'Borrow some of this makeup!'

I've stayed in touch with these girls and we sometimes reminisce about this, because they remember it to this day. It was so wonderful! I went out to dinner transformed and Peter and I talked all night; it was immediately clear that we were very, very smitten with one another.

ANDREA: It was love at first sight!

LESLEY: It was! The next day, Peter went into work and said to his partner, Rosemary, 'Do I look sick?'

'No, you look all right. Why?' she said.

'I'm either sick or I've just met my future wife.'

'What?'

'Yes, I went to see this opera last night and my wife stepped out of an orange!'

ANDREA: It's certainly an unusual image.

LESLEY: Isn't it? What's also spooky is that in the same week that I met Peter, I did my first piece of television and got my first record deal. These three major events that changed the rest of my life happened in the same week.

JANE: There must have been something in the stars!

LESLEY: I wonder, I must say! We both went home for Christmas, and I frantically began to decorate my cottage in Yorkshire, with my mum's help. 'What's going on?' she said.

'I think I've met the father of my children,' I said. Mum sat down quickly.

Meanwhile, Peter went home to his parents and said to his mum, 'You've got to watch the *Bruce Forsyth Christmas Special*, because the woman I'm going to marry is appearing on it.'

I'd only met him two days before! It was really silly. His mum was only half listening and I don't think she quite took it on board. 'Oh yes, dear?' she said.

We met up again with the couple who had introduced us, at their house, and we watched some episodes of *The Singing Detective*, snuggled up on the settee, which was fabulous. The next week, which must have been the end of the first week of January, he asked me out to lunch. Afterwards we went back to his flat and he said, 'Now, you are going to stay, aren't you?'

'Yes, I am, actually,' I said.

Thinking that I might have thought he meant for the afternoon, he said, 'No, no, you do know what I mean, don't you?'

'Yes, I do know exactly what you mean,' I said.

'So is it OK if I pick you up next Saturday? Will that give you enough time to pack?'

'Yes, but I've got this cat . . .'

'Great, so I'll need to put in a cat flap. Oh, and I'm seeing this other girl at the moment, so I'll need to end that relationship properly. Is next Saturday OK, then?'

'Yes, that's absolutely fine. And I'll need to find a tenant for my flat.'

'Yes, so if you could be getting on with that in the meantime.'

It was as simple as that. Twenty years ago, he came and picked me up and we now live with children, rabbits, hamsters and a piano. Yes, we've had our ups and downs, but we're still here, still very much together and still very much in love.

ANDREA: It sounds like the perfect match. Hooray! But sometimes falling in love isn't the answer to all your problems, is it? Sometimes, your first years together can be the hardest, even when you've met your true love.

COLEEN: I would certainly agree with that. My first two years with Ray were really hard. I'd just come out of a very high-profile marriage, I had two kids, and straightaway I got pregnant with him, so there was a lot going on, especially for him. He met me, we moved in together, he became a stepdad, I was pregnant, my ex-husband was still a very big part of our lives because the boys were still young, and he had also to accept that Shane and I were still friends.

Friends and family were worried about me, because of what I'd already been through, so they were initially a bit cynical about him. And he had to find his way building a relationship with the boys. Then I had Ciara and was offered *This Morning* and we all moved to London! So it was a tough couple of years, with lots of adjustments to make. I think that, if I'd been him, I'd just probably have thought, Sod it, I'm walking away! Because it would have been easier for him. That he didn't walk away meant a lot to me with every hurdle we crossed – and each obstacle we got over just made us even stronger.

JANE: Ah, isn't that lovely!

ANDREA: What about you, Lisa? How soon after you met Paul did you know he was the one for you?

LISA: I moved in with Paul three weeks after meeting him! I knew I would, as soon as I saw him, because I think I knew what sort of man I was looking for, or at least I knew what sort of man I didn't want. I was in my early thirties and I'd been in a relationship for thirteen years with someone I had no intention of marrying or having children with. There wasn't that much wrong with the relationship that it warranted me leaving, though. It all kind of worked. It was just never really amazing and I kept thinking, There's got to be something different. Whatever it is, I don't think this is it because it doesn't feel like I imagine it should feel.

I know physically what sort of man I find attractive and Paul was absolutely it. I was doing *Grease*, the musical, at the Dominion Theatre at the time, and the cast were invited down to a party in a bar in New Burlington Street. I was being chatted up by some annoying photographer friend of Paul's, who it turns out wasn't actually a friend but somebody he'd hooked up with that night. He was really hitting on me and I was constantly being vile to him and taking the mickey, although not in a nasty way. I did it so that he didn't realise, but everybody there who knew me knew what I was doing.

Paul found it very amusing. We ended up chatting and then we went to a nightclub, stayed out and ended up having breakfast together. We just talked the whole night. I gave him my phone number and we arranged to meet for dinner that night.

JANE: It all happened so fast!

LISA: Yes, that's why, before we met up, I rang a gay friend and said, 'Look, I've met this guy and I think he's really amazing, but I was quite drunk, so I might have got it wrong. I'm going to meet him tonight in a cafe in Soho later, can you accidentally on purpose turn up, just in case he's a bit of a weirdo? Even though I'm sure he won't be.'

Well, when I saw Paul waiting in the cafe, I thought, Oh my god, he's gorgeous! I've got it completely right.' When my gay friend arrived, I said, 'It's all right. You don't have to stay.'

'Oh, I might as well sit down, have a drink and introduce myself,' he said. The next thing I knew, he spent the whole night flirting outrageously with Paul. I couldn't get shot of him. 'I think he rather likes me,' my friend said at one point.

'Don't be ridiculous,' I said. 'You can go home now. It's fine.'

'Wait, I just want to ask him about his intentions towards you,' he insisted. It was like having your mother there.

JANE: Did you fall in love that night?

LISA: I think I was already in love with him, actually. And I knew that he was the right person for me, because after about two weeks of being together, I told him I loved him. Normally, I like to be in control and I've always had this theory that if you surrender to somebody, then they will take advantage. You have to check out how the land is lying before you do that. But we were on a cheeky weekend abroad just two weeks after we met and I just said, 'I love you. You can take the

mickey out of me or do whatever you want, but I just want to say it.'

'Well, I think I love you too,' he said. It was really sweet. At that moment I realised that there has to be somebody that you have to surrender to in life, because you will never truly love anybody if you don't. I'd never really been hurt by anyone, because I didn't allow myself to be vulnerable in a relationship – until that point. To this day, whenever I've taken a chance on him or entrusted him with my feelings and my vulnerability, he has never taken advantage of it. He is a good man.

A couple of days later, he went off to Thailand on business. 'When I get back, I would really like you to have moved in,' he said, giving me his keys. So I did, and when he came back, that was that.

ANDREA: Wow, that's a real whirlwind romance! What a lovely story.

Brian's proposal came as a complete surprise.
It was only the second time she'd met him.

How do you win the hand of a Loose Woman? Let us count the ways . . .

COLEEN: When Ray proposed on my fortieth birthday, I didn't have a clue that it was coming. That morning when I woke up, he brought me a cup of tea in bed and I did wonder if there would be a little ring beside it, because I knew that if he were to ask, it would be in private. But there was no ring there and I thought, Oh shit, he hasn't proposed! I spent all day thinking, Will he do it now? Every time he was around, I thought, He's going to ask! But he didn't.

That evening, he threw a party for me. It wasn't a total surprise, because I knew I was having a party, but I didn't know who was coming or where it was. I just knew it was a black tie event. He organised the whole thing.

So I turned up at this do and there were two hundred and fifty people there. I don't even know how he'd got in touch with everyone, because people I'd known from years ago were there. He did it all himself. There was even a fifteen-piece orchestra playing. By now I was thinking, Well, it's definitely not going to happen now, because he wouldn't do it in front of all these people. I completely lost the scent.

Later on in the evening, a huge projector screen was lowered to screen messages from the kids, my family and friends. Right at the end, Ray came on the screen and said, 'Well that's it, love. I hope you had a great night. There's just one more thing to say, but I need to get down on my knees to do it.' The next thing I knew, he was kneeling and saying, 'Will you marry me?' on screen. It was so romantic. He couldn't have done it better.

Ray's shy, so he would never have had the courage to make a speech in front of everybody there, but he knew that once it was on the screen, he could hide behind the pillar while it was playing. The only people he had told were the two boys, because he felt he should ask them first. They were the only people who knew.

It came as a complete shock to me and I burst into tears. At the same moment, all two hundred and fifty people in the room went mental, cheering us. It was such a lovely atmosphere with all my friends and family there. When I eventually stopped crying, I looked up to see that Ray was in front of me with the ring, which was exactly what I wanted – just a solitaire diamond ring. It was perfect, fantastic. He's not actually very romantic and, for me, this was the most romantic thing he could ever have done. That's it – he doesn't ever have to be romantic again!

After that, we were caught up in a whirl of people coming up and hugging us – until, about an hour later, Ray said to me, 'I'm not being funny, but you haven't actually said "yes" yet.' Whoops!

I absolutely loved it. 'If you'd had the priest there, I would have married you there and then,' I told him later. The party was so good: everyone was there who I'd have wanted at my wedding, so it would have been good to do it on the spot.

JANE: It was lovely when Eddie proposed. We were in a restaurant having dinner and suddenly he cleared his throat and put his hand in his pocket. What's he doing? I thought. What's the matter with him? He'd been a bit funny all day and I'd been wondering what was wrong. Then he said, 'I should have done this twenty-seven years ago. I just want you to know that you are definitely the one for me and I'm so glad that you're back in my life.' It was beautiful. He'd obviously not prepared anything, he just wanted to let out whatever he had to say. 'Will you marry me?' he said. 'I know it's twenty-seven years late . . .'

Well, that was it, I was just a heap on the floor. It was so lovely and romantic. I burst into tears and so did he, and that's how I knew that it was different this time. Of course, no one in the restaurant realised that we'd just got engaged. Everybody thought we'd split up, 'Oh no, he's dumped his girlfriend! What an awful thing to do on Christmas Eve!' They all looked really concerned, because I was weeping like a baby, so in the end we had to say, 'Don't worry, we just got engaged!'

ANDREA: What about you, Lynda? How did Mr Spain propose?

LYNDA: Well, he asked me a couple of times, and I scoffed rather rudely and said, 'Don't be so stupid!' I wasn't sure how much of it he meant. Then we went to see a lawyer about doing my will, because I like to have all these things sorted. I had a flat and he had a flat and I wanted to make sure that everything was covered if we moved in together.

The solicitor said, 'Of course, if you were married, you would get tax relief on this and that.'

'Oh well, we'd better get married, then,' I said.

The solicitor looked pained. 'Please don't!' she said. 'That's not what I meant at all.'

'Don't worry about it.' I looked at Mr Spain and smiled.

As we were driving home, he said, 'Do I take it that you'd be prepared to marry me?'

'I don't know. You'll have to propose,' I said coyly.

'I've asked you already!' he protested

'I know,' I said. 'That was different. But should you feel the need to propose, I might not be averse to it.'

So he invited me to dinner and we went to The Ivy, where he arranged to put the ring in a glass of champagne. Which was unfortunate, because we weren't drinking by then! 'I think we should have a glass of champagne,' he said.

'No!' I said. 'We're not drinking. We're not having a glass of champagne.'

'Go on,' he said coaxingly.

'I don't want a glass of champagne,' I insisted.

He tried again. 'Well, just let's have one for the hell of it.'

'Is this what I think this is?' I said.

'Well, yes, it is.'

So we ordered the champagne and I drank a glass and my ring was at the bottom of it.

I had already shown him my idea of a perfect ring, based on an art deco dress ring that a friend had given me. But I hadn't intended it to be as big as the one he gave me! He did well.

JANE: You got a rather nice ring as well, didn't you, Carol?

CAROL: In the end, yes! Mark proposed over dinner when we were in Thailand on Christmas Eve last year. Afterwards I thought maybe I'd bullied him into it a little bit. Well, not bullied exactly, because I think he wanted to ask, but he didn't want to ask if he wasn't sure that I was going to say yes, so I let it be known that if he did, I would definitely say yes. It was the first Christmas I'd been away while I was seeing somebody and it was nice that he could come as well. He wasn't originally booked to come, because I had already booked my holiday when we got together in August. So when he booked it at the last minute and came along, it was brilliant.

There was no ring at the time, but when we went to Paris at the end of January, he went out secretly and bought a ring and proposed again in front of the Eiffel Tower, because he wanted to do it properly. So I actually got two proposals and I said yes both times! It was lovely. We'd talked about what would it be like if we decided to get married, so it wasn't really a surprise the first time, but I had no idea it was coming the second time.

I'd actually said that I didn't want an engagement ring, that I'd rather just have a nice wedding ring. But he ignored that! He got it a hundred per cent right – the size, design and everything. It's quite modern, a white gold band with two rows of small diamonds in it.

ANDREA: It's amazing, isn't it, Carol, because you were single for so long before you met Mark?

CAROL: I've always said I was very happy being single. I never complained about being single; in fact I loved my single life and had no problem with it at all. I wasn't looking for anyone. It just wasn't on the agenda. I wasn't even dating. But when I met him, it just seemed right.

SHERRIE: Do you miss your single life at all? I know I'd find it hard to get used to having a man around again.

CAROL: My life is different now. I used to have nice long weekends on my own, not speaking to anyone and I quite enjoyed the solitude. I don't have that now, but I don't miss it and I don't want it back. I much prefer having him around. That's because he's right, not because I'm forcing it or thinking, I'm dying to be with somebody! Anyone will do – and then trying to get rid of them whenever I possibly can. It isn't like that at all. I think that's how you know it's right.

LESLEY: Does the age difference matter to you?

CAROL: The age difference is a big issue for a lot of people and I think about it more than he does. It doesn't concern him in the slightest, but obviously it concerns me, because I'm the old one. Everyone has a problem with getting old. On the other hand, he's very mature and I'm very childish. So I see myself as being ten years younger and he acts ten years older than he is, so we kind of meet in the middle.

ANDREA: You certainly seem very happy together. It's so nice to see.

SHERRIE: How did Steve propose to you, Andrea? Was it very romantic?

ANDREA: Actually, Steve proposed in his pants while we were watching *Forrest Gump*! It took me by surprise, I have to say: I wasn't expecting it at that moment! It was romantic all the same, believe it or not.

SHERRIE: What happened?

ANDREA: Well, last year, our Christmas present from my parents was to baby-sit for a week, so Steve and I went on holiday to Egypt.  On our first night there, we were so demob happy with the fact that we had no kids with us that we got off the plane, got to the hotel, said, 'Yeah, let's go for margaritas!' We ended up getting completely squiffy within hours of arriving at the hotel. Inevitably I crashed and said, 'I need to go to bed! I'm really tired.' So we went back to the hotel.

I put my nightie on and we were watching *Forrest Gump*, which is one of my favourite films. Because I was a bit drunk, I became very emotional at a particular scene between Forrest Gump and Jenny. 'Oh, that's so lovely!' I cooed. 'He really loves her.'

'And I really love you,' Steve said.

'I love you, too,' I said, and went on watching the film.

He disappeared off the side of the bed and went to a cupboard and the next thing I know, there's a bit of a kerfuffle and he's kneeling down at the side of the bed, holding a box with a ring in it. I burst out laughing. 'I can't believe you're doing this now, in your pants!' I said.

'It just seemed really right; it's a nice moment,' he said, doubling up with laughter. So we just absolutely roared laughing and that was it. He put the ring on and asked me to marry him.

LYNDA: Did he get it right with the ring?

ANDREA: Yes, because months before, shopping somewhere, I'd pointed to a ring and said, 'By the way, if you're ever going to surprise me, I like that one.' I didn't realise it at the time, but he went back and bought it! I love it.

Despite being divorced and all the hurt that brought, I still believe in a happy-ever-after. The difference now is that I've realised that the only time you achieve perfection is when you stop looking for it. It's quite a profound thing to realise. So I've got to stop wishing everything was perfect and thinking that when everything's perfect, everything will be great, because nothing is ever perfect, although it nearly is. It's so much more relaxing! So I feel very positive and very relaxed about being married again.

My first wedding took place in the Masai Mara in Kenya, because my parents lived out there. We had a very small but wonderful wedding and I still look back on it with real fondness. I got married in a very simple dress, on the grass, in the sunshine in the Masai Mara, with wild animals walking past, which was amazing. But the second time was in England, and much more traditional, in a very pretty hotel. It was very different, but also just wonderful.

LISA: I've always said I don't do marriage. I've always maintained that, because I think men find it more desirable if you say that you don't want to get married. I've always said that I'm a career girl. I'm not particularly hung up on marriage, anyway. It's not something I really want to do.

But I've been engaged since 2000. Beau was born in 1999 and the following year, we got engaged. We talked about getting married. We had one conversation about it and started arguing about who to invite. Sod this, I thought. We'd already had a baby, moved house and had a house-warming, so at the time it seemed like one event too many to organise.

Now it's got to the stage where I just could not spend that sort of money on a white frock and a party. I'd rather pay off the mortgage!

SHERRIE: That's very sensible. I probably should have done the same!

ANDREA: How did your husband propose, Sherrie?

SHERRIE: He didn't. I did!

ANDREA: Really? So you took destiny into your own hands, did you?

SHERRIE: Yes, as soon as we started living together, I thought, Right, I'm going to marry him. I can be quite a domineering, strong woman; I was thirty-one and just determined to be married.

When I told him I thought it was a good idea, I think he just saw it as a fun day out, without understanding the consequences of marrying somebody. If he'd taken it seriously, I'm sure he wouldn't have done it. Don't forget, he was five years younger than me, which means that he was far too young to live with somebody, let alone get married.

I did it all without consulting him. I booked the cars and organised the food and drink; I even bought palm trees for the hall where the reception was. I sent out all the invitations myself and simply told him not to forget to ask his mother and father. 'Is that OK?' I said. 'Yeah, whatever,' he said. Then I told him where the church was, what time to be there and what to wear; he turned up and we got married. It was a very nice day out, as it happened!

ANDREA: Did you have a honeymoon?

SHERRIE: No! He went back to work and so did I. So it was doomed to failure, right from the word go. It was never, ever going to work, because it was done entirely in the wrong way. I really don't think he should have got married. He should have stayed single all his life, like a lot of men should. There are some men who shouldn't marry, because it's not who they are, and I think it certainly wasn't who Ken was. He didn't want children. And back then he just wanted to be free and single.

When we first met, he said, 'I am not a faithful person. I can never be faithful.' He said it to me many times.

Being a woman, I said, 'Don't worry about that. I'll sort that out. I'll change you.' The problem was that he meant it and I didn't listen. How mad is that?

ANDREA: You were in love. That explains away all kinds of madness.

SHERRIE: Ah, but there was once a man in my life whom I truly did love. He lived in Nottinghamshire, where I come from. He was a Paul McCartney lookalike, which meant that he was my ideal man, because I was only ever attracted to Paul McCartney lookalikes back then. I was very young and I was desperate for him to ask me to marry him.

One day, he said, 'I've got a fantastic job. I earn good money . . .'

I thought, Oh my God! He's going to ask me to marry him, and I felt so embarrassed that I changed the subject, so he didn't ask me, even though I was absolutely crazy about him. Then we drifted apart, because I went to drama school. He went on to marry somebody else in the end, because he thought that I didn't want to marry him – and that anyway he wouldn't see me, because I was going to live in London. In turn, I thought he didn't want to marry me. Yet he did, and I did, but we never got together. So it turned into one of those lost moments in life. It's a really sad story.

Through my marriage and his marriage, we always stayed in contact, and every now and then we spoke on the phone, for hours at a time. How much we meant to each other remained unspoken for all those years, although we felt compelled to talk to each other and were always thrilled to make contact again. When I phoned, I'd hear an intake of breath before he said, 'Ah, hello!'

Then suddenly a friend of mine said, 'I have the most terrible news. He died from a heart attack this morning.' So we never really got to say what we should have said to one another, which makes me sad even now, although he's been dead for fifteen years, maybe more. Death is so final.

ANDREA: Oh Sherrie, that's so sad!

SHERRIE: It is, but of course, the truth of the matter is that I was supposed to marry who I did, because I was supposed to have my daughter Keeley and my grandson. So that's how I look at life. On the other hand, by the time Keeley was two and a half, my marriage was a disaster. Had we had time to get together then, who knows what would have happened? Yet this man was married and had two children, so he obviously did the right thing in his life too, because he loved his wife. Fate takes its hand. It's just one of those things.

ANDREA: You nearly married Robert Lindsay, didn't you? How did he propose?

SHERRIE: You know, I can't remember! I think we just decided that we were going to get married, because we were both very young and foolish and silly. What a good idea, we thought. But of course it never happened. Funny to think of it now, but I was heartbroken at the time.

Is fifty a dangerous age for a woman?

DENISE: A few of my friends have sadly separated at about fifty, or maybe a little bit younger. Unlike me, they didn't have a second child at ninety-seven, so all of their children have left. That's when there's a process of weighing up to see if there is enough to keep you together without the presence of children. Unfortunately, I would say that maybe three of my friends have decided that there isn't.

SHERRIE: The problem is that when the children have gone, what's left? If it's just you and him, and you realise that the children have taken everything out of that door with them, it's the saddest thing.

DENISE: Yes, it's not always the 'life's too short' syndrome; it can be that life's too long. At fifty, you might have thirty years left and you've got to think about whether there's going to be enough to keep you together.

One of my friends is the happiest she's ever been and she

 doesn't have a man in her life. She said that she'd felt lonely for years when she was married, because you can be lonely in a marriage. What she was worried about was losing the 'couple' status, because it's always 'Bill and Sue' or 'Ted and Ange', or whatever.

SHERRIE: Strangely, men can't live without a woman, but women are beginning to be able to live without men.

JANE: We don't need men like we used to. In my mum's day and back into my gran's day, the only time you could really live alone was when you were widowed. Women in those days couldn't afford to leave the house, because they had nowhere to go and they had no jobs; they were kept. Whereas now women are very much career women and they can survive on their own.

SHERRIE: Women have altered completely, even in the last ten years. A lot of the time, we're the earners, which I've always been, and that puts men in a very strange position, because they no longer have the power. But I don't think re-evaluating or choosing to live alone is to do with age. I think you re-evaluate all the time. I certainly do.

ANDREA: Is it the women who make the big decision, in your experience, Denise?

DENISE: It's the women who instigate it, but that doesn't mean that the men aren't now thinking, I didn't want this to happen to me but now I'm glad it is! I don't think the men involved would ever have made that decision, but they almost always get someone else straight away, whereas the women don't. The women aren't bothered about whether they're still getting a bit of jiggy-jigs or what not.

JANE: I've gone the other way now, because I've always concentrated on my career, but for the first time in my life I want to spend some quality time with my other half. We're both so busy that I'm constantly looking at our schedules and thinking, No, this has got to stop! I would never have even questioned it before, but now I want to think about spending time together. So it's quite the reverse for me, because I'm looking forward to settling down a bit.

DENISE: Fifty used to be an over-the-hill age, so people didn't think so much about finding another partner and starting again. But fifty is different now.

LESLEY: Yes, it's only dangerous because it's so exciting. Fifty is an amazing age for a woman, actually. I've felt extremely free in my fifties. It's as if everything is a bonus. And as you're suggesting, Denise, ours is almost the first generation where the fifties have been such a liberating time. Jackie Collins and all those wonderful women who used to be on *Dallas* and *Dynasty* were probably the founding mothers of the fabulous fifties club and now women in society in general are a part of it. Now we can be who we want to be: sexy, glamorous, youthful and fit. We also in addition have opinions! We're powerful and autonomous; we're self-sufficient.

JANE: And people outgrow each other, don't they?

DENISE: They do! That's just the way it is.

COLEEN: I'm looking forward to growing old with Ray. I can't imagine things will change much. I expect when I'm eighty I'll still be trying to get him to be romantic and he'll be telling me to stop being an idiot!

DENISE: There comes a point when you realise you're glad you've stuck with someone. Tim and I spend a lot of time apart because of our jobs, but it's when we spend time together that I'm thankful we've managed to make it last.

ANDREA: Ahhhhh!

LESLEY: But don't you think men seem to be catching on and catching up? There are wonderful older men – and younger men, actually; look at Carol! – who have great respect for older women and see us in a very different way. You meet men who want to match you and understand how you've come to be so strong. A lot of men don't want women who are needy and weak, especially the kind of men that we'd be attracted to.

ANDREA: How true! So does your husband keep you feeling fabulous?

LESLEY: He certainly does. And my children keep me younger too; having teenage children in your fifties is lovely. I had one of the most enjoyable days of my life a few months ago, because I found I had a day free and I said to the kids, 'Let's do something different! What shall we do?'

To my delight, they said, 'Let's go and see the Banksy exhibition in Bristol. Can we bring our friends?'

'You can bring anybody you like,' I said.

We filled the car with their friends, took sandwiches and flew down the motorway to Bristol with wonderful pop music blaring. The great thing about my kids and their friends is that they've got really wide-ranging taste in music, so we had Jethro Tull and then Lily Allen, Eminem and then Fleetwood Mac. It was fantastic. After spending the whole afternoon at the exhibition, we piled in the car and came home. It was a really lovely day.

ANDREA: That sounds like fun. Can we all come next time?

LESLEY: Yes, let's hire a coach!

*Sandra couldn't believe what the vicar and
his wife got up to behind closed doors.*

Chapter 2

Sex

A stocking full of saucy confessions!

Birds do it, bees do it, but does anyone really want to do it when it's minus 10 outside?!

Well actually yes! We've got some very saucy stories of secret shenanigans to share, so get ready to blush!

Between us, let's just say we've had a few, and we like to think we picked up a few tricks along the way . . .

One thing you can always count on a group of girlfriends to have a natter about when they get together is sex, and in this chapter we'll discuss one of the topics that is closest to our hearts and try to answer some of the big questions, including:

- Is sex better when you're in love?
- Would you ever have an affair?
- How do you get out of sex if your partner is feeling frisky and you're just not in the mood?

And lots more too.

We can't promise to have all the answers (give Carol a chance, she only ended her seven-year dry spell last year!) but we can guarantee lots of laughs and one or two shocking confessions too.

So close the door, pour yourself a glass of wine and prepare to have a giggle with us. We know you want to!

It's snowing. You're on a long walk with your lover/ husband/partner. Do you or don't you?

CAROL: No, too cold!

ANDREA: No, no, no, no! Too cold!

LISA: Oh, I so want to be the woman who would do that. I really want to say yes. But I'm also thinking that it would be really cold! If we were away somewhere and the sun was shining and it was just the two of us, then yes, perhaps I would. But if my daughter was around, I know I'd get down on the coat just as she called out and I'd have run off with my knickers round my ankles in the snow to go and do something for a nine-year-old girl right that minute!

JANE: Well, I bloody wouldn't! I can't stand the cold – and, knowing my luck, the *News of the World* would be just round the corner.

ANDREA: You'd rather be inside in front of a roaring fire?

CAROL: I don't go for all that contrived stuff. That's the stuff you just see in films; it doesn't really happen in real life.

Try as she might, Miranda just couldn't compete with his first love.

DENISE: I'm not a winter lover, I'm not one of these romantic winter people; I don't really like it. I've had frolics in the snow, though, when Tim and I went to Lapland a few years ago with my sister and her husband and all the children. We were all really sozzled one night and the kids were all in bed, and we did that typical Scandinavian thing where you have a sauna and then jump naked into the snow outside. It was blooming awful!

JANE: I like the roaring fire bit, just don't put me out in the cold. It's the same on Bonfire Night; I like to watch it from the window. Don't leave me to stand out in the cold!

LISA: I love an open fire. If I feel warm, I feel sexy. I would probably be more inclined to do it by a fire than in the snow.

COLEEN: I'm a real romantic fool and I'll fall for anything that is romantic, so the idea of winter in the snow, going back to a raging fire in a log cabin and looking out of the window at snow-covered mountains are all very appealing. Or even just being indoors at home, with the curtains closed, a great film on the TV and the fire roaring. I love being cosied up.

I want everything to be like a film and I get so frustrated when it isn't.

I spend my life saying to Ray, 'You're so not Cary Grant!' I'd love our life to be like Cary Grant's and Doris Day's in all of those films. I say to Ray, 'Cary Grant wouldn't say that.'

'That's because he's a knob,' he says. But Cary Grant wouldn't even know the word 'knob'!

DENISE: Wait, I've just remembered that I have had sex with

a ski instructor in the snow, but that was a
long time ago!

JANE: How could you forget a thing like
that?

DENISE: As I said, it was a long time ago!

ANDREA: Go on, then. Tell all!

DENISE: I'd just split up with my first husband and I went to
Klosters ski resort with two of my gay friends, one of whom
was very wealthy. I'd never been skiing before and I had no
desire to ski, because I'm not an adventurer or adrenalin junkie
in any shape or form. Still, I was in need of something to do,
so I said I'd go along, but I wouldn't ski.

When we arrived, I just fell in love with Klosters. Some
of the places I've been to since then are just rubbish, but
at Klosters the resort was beautiful, the hotel was fantastic and everybody was attractive. My friend Martin said, 'If
you change your mind about skiing, I'll pay for you to have a
private instructor all day long.' So I did, for the whole five or
six days that we were there. I can't imagine how much it must
have cost! So off Florian and I went up the slopes! I learnt
how to ski really quickly, but it took two days to persuade him
to come 'après-skiing' with me.

JANE: Two days? Slow work! I went skiing on my honeymoon,
would you believe? My husband instantly took to it and within no
time he was a master skier; he was in the Olympic team after
his first lesson. Well, it wasn't the same for me; I was still in

the baby class at the end of the week, which was embarrassing. After a full day's skiing, I'd get up at eight the next morning feeling like I'd been hit by a boat, and by eight in the evening I was dying. I'd say, 'I'm going to bed, bye!' So I didn't see him for the whole day. I should have known then that the only way was down after that! I hated it, absolutely hated it.

ANDREA: That sounds miserable, you poor thing. I can't see the point of cold holidays. I'm cold here, so why would I want to go somewhere else and be cold? I've been skiing once, but that was with work and I was absolutely rubbish. I'm a very good tobogganer, but I don't think that counts, does it? You can't really go on a sledging holiday, so I have no interest at all really and everybody seems to go skiing in a cheerful mood and either come back in a cast or a bad mood, so I can't really see the appeal.

Having said that, I loved it when we were snowed in for four days last year, even though Steve had gone away for a week and I was completely on my own with the kids. If I'd known it was going to happen, I'd have been really worried about coping alone, but luckily I'd gone to Sainsbury's in the morning and done a massive shop, so we had loads of food in. It was brilliant, so much fun. We made loads of little snowmen and went to the park and joined in with building a big communal snowman with other kids in the village. The fifteen-minute walk there took us about two hours, because Amy kept plonking herself down and star-fishing, with her mouth wide open trying to catch snowflakes. It was really cute; I was out every day with them and loved it.

SHERRIE: Yes, I loved it when I was a little girl, but I'm not a snow person now. I've gone skiing twice and I don't like it. The ski instructor said I was good, but I was always falling over and getting cold and wet and I'm convinced I would break a leg if I went again. In fact, I'd break two legs!

My real problem with snow is that it reminds me of my ex-husband. I went skiing in Courchevel with him, so maybe that's why I didn't like it. If I'd gone with somebody really romantic, like Johnny Depp, I'd probably have really good memories of it. Or if I'd gone with Robert Redford in his day, or Clint Eastwood or Cary Grant, who was the most beautiful man in the world, in my view, then I'd probably love skiing and being in a log cabin. But it was boring, dreary and painful with my ex-husband. All he wanted to do was show off all the time. So I have bad memories of that holiday and I would never go back to Courchevel or any other ski resort.

CAROL: I don't know about skiing, but last year I went to Lapland with Denise and a group of sick children on a little trip for a charity called Wish Upon a Star. It was a great trip actually. Lapland was so naturally beautiful, it was amazing. I haven't seen snow like that since I was a kid and it made me feel very childlike. I'd do it again in a flash.

DENISE: Yes, we had a great time, didn't we? So much fun. And lovely to see those children forgetting about everything and just being kids.

A friend says that her partner is unadventurous/ boring/repetitive in bed. What do you advise?

LYNDA: My first question would be: 'Do you ever kiss him?' Because you'd be amazed how many people don't kiss.

People say, 'Well, what's that got to do with it?'

'Try kissing him,' I say. 'And you might be surprised.'

Kissing often gets lost in a long-term relationship, and yet it's so lovely. Amazingly, you get turned on by kissing, even though you think, Oh, I'm not going to get turned on, because how many times have I done it? But you do, because something in your brain tells you to.

My second question would be: 'Do you always do it at the same time in the same place? Try catching him unawares.'

If she said, 'My husband is boring in bed,' I'd say back to her, 'Are you sure it's not you who's boring?'

Because I do feel sometimes that women, especially after childbirth, say, 'Well I wasn't ready and he's got to understand. How can he possibly be thinking about sex?'

You really do have to compromise, because it's different for him, and it's a bit like falling off a bike: if you put it off too long, it can become a big deal. So better to do it than not, even if it's a bit sore initially, or you think it's going to be a bit sore, because you've had stitches.

If you're thinking, But I've got to feed the baby and my head is somewhere else, then let him start, and you might find you want to join in, eventually. Even if you're not in the mood, rather than berate him, poor man, because he's in the mood, try and go with the flow. You'll come round to it.

Bless him! In his way, he's trying to show you another

side of your body that you might have forgotten about. In this situation, your body will often let you down, of course, because you may think you're not in the mood when your body actually is in the mood if you let it be in the mood. There's a lot to be said for compromise.

CAROL: I'm not very good at giving advice. Anyway, there's no point in complaining to somebody else about something like that. You've got to grow up and have a conversation with the person concerned. I don't know why people find that so difficult. And if you suddenly realise that you're not compatible, then maybe you were lying to yourself about being compatible in the first place. I mean, people don't suddenly turn into boring, unadventurous lovers, do they? They either are or they're not, and if you don't like them how they are, then you've got to put them right from the outset. Otherwise, what's the point?

A lot of women make a rod for their own back, I think, because if a woman wants something to continue, she'll make out that he's the best lover in the world for maybe a little too long. At that point, it's then difficult to turn round and say, 'Actually I think you're really rubbish in bed!' After you've pretended it's great because you wanted to go out with him, or you wanted him to be a part of your life. Women tend to lie about things like that and it's just not helpful to anybody. That's why there are so many old blokes about who haven't got a clue what they're doing, because a load of women have always said, 'Oh you're brilliant!' when they're not. We tiptoe around the male ego too much. Women are their own worst enemy when it comes to things like that. They shouldn't do it.

Maybe a book would help, or a diagram,

which, as you know, I once did for a bloke. Or if that's too bold, then why not have a conversation? I know it's sensitive and it's difficult. Maybe most blokes would rather not know. But if you really care about the relationship, then it has to be addressed, because it can only get worse.

ANDREA: What about taking him out of his usual environment and whisking him away on holiday?

CAROL: But if he's dead boring and unadventurous, just going on holiday isn't suddenly going to make him adventurous, is it? It might make him a little more liberated, but I don't think it will really help all that much.

LISA: I was once with a man who was boring in bed and I had affairs rather than say anything to him. It was a long, long time ago. The relationship worked on so many other levels, but on a purely lusty level it never really worked, right from the beginning. That animal feeling of really fancying him wasn't there.

It's hard to get everything from one person, but I think it's very important that you absolutely fancy your partner from the get-go, because that diminishes as time goes on. I went looking for that missing element with other people. There was even somebody who lived in a far-off country who I used to run off and see.

ANDREA: Naughty Lisa!

LISA: As I said, it was a long, long time ago! It's not something I would think about doing now, but I was young and foolish then. It almost feels like another lifetime.

Samantha was determined to inject a whole new meaning into the phrase 'quality time'

Your partner/lover wants sex but you don't.
How do you get out of it?

CAROL: That doesn't happen! Why would I want to get out of it? I've spent seven years not getting it, so I'm not going to start making excuses or getting headaches – not yet, anyway!

ANDREA: How about if you want it and he doesn't?

CAROL: That hasn't happened, either! The only time sex doesn't happen is when we literally haven't got time. If my car's waiting outside and I've got to go to work, then no, I can't; I haven't got time. Now stop it! It's not an excuse; it's just that life gets in the way of a lot of things. That's life!

LYNDA: I think that everybody knows their partner's turn-ons. Again it depends how much you want it and how much work you're prepared to put in, to the point where he gives it to you. But, if we're honest about it, it's really nice to lie back and have somebody nibble your ear and seduce you, if you're in the mood. The idea that you've got to work quite hard to get that other person up to speed tends to take the polish off it, doesn't it?

ANDREA: What would you do if you thought he was losing interest in sex?

CAROL: It's never happened, but I'd probably ask why and try and sort it out. But I don't want to think about it at the moment, because naturally I think, because I'm older, that he will lose interest in sex. He says he won't, but we'll see. It's one of those things; you cross that bridge when you come to it.

Is sex when you're emotionally engaged more satisfying than a quick roll in the hay?

LYNDA: Some people think that having lots of sex means that it's good sex and you enjoy sex, but that's not necessarily true at all. It's not about how long it takes or how many partners you have, either. There are women who are able to be completely detached and have sex with a stranger and think it's fabulous, but that doesn't mean that the sex is fabulous. The fantasy of that close encounter is great, but if you actually pin them down and ask them how good it was, you might find that it wasn't very good.

LESLEY: That's just like a trip to the gym, isn't it? You just go in there for the physical experience, the thrill and to work up a bit of a sweat. It doesn't actually mean anything. It's not the great integrated, meaningful experience that true lovemaking can be.

LYNDA: I think great sex has a lot to do with trust. I can honestly say that for the first time in my life, I trust my partner, completely, and so it's fantastic. I can be uninhibited and it's fine, whereas in my youth, I've been very inhibited, because I didn't want to give away something that was deeply a part of me. Hence, I think, I used to have a glass of wine for courage. After a glass of wine, your insecurities become something that're quite exciting, rather than something fearful.

SHERRIE: But the next day, when you remember . . . oh dear!

LESLEY: I used to get emotionally engaged very quickly and then I used to get hurt. Mr Whoever-it-was really wasn't on my wavelength at all. It wasn't until I met Peter that things changed – and, for me, the key word is respect. We had complete and utter equality and mutual respect and then the trust comes and the real experience of lovemaking follows.

SHERRIE: But I find that I get more inhibited as I get older . . .

LESLEY: Do you really, love?

SHERRIE: . . . so have I gone wrong then? I probably have had uninhibited sex in the past, but it was so long ago now that I can't really remember if it was good. It's like Lynda said, you can have as much as you want, but it's whether it's good or not. Actually, it was good at the beginning of my married life; otherwise I wouldn't have stayed. But it then just died into nothing.

LYNDA: I feel very sorry for young men these days. I think it's up to young women to use their emotional intelligence to make young men feel better about themselves, women should tell them what's good, what's comfortable and what's rewarding. Women are always ahead on this anyway. Women today seem to think that if they're good at it and they offer it quickly and go wham, bam, thank you ma'am, the bloke will be pleased. Obviously, it's a more external thing with men. It can be here today, gone tomorrow. But it's up to us women, because we're more in touch with our emotions, so we need to think beyond that external side: What does he really want? *He* feels inhibited; *he* feels unloved; *he*'s not comfortable about his body. Maybe that's how emotional intelligence really works: you make him feel good about himself, if only for a brief period, and you'll get a lot more back from the boys. As a result, they'll feel a lot better about themselves and they'll in turn treat girls better.

SHERRIE: As long as everything's tucked away in a drawer and locked!

LYNDA: Um, yes, whatever that means!

Your partner's away and tries to initiate phone sex. Do you reciprocate?

ANDREA: I'm not saying, in case my mum reads this!

CAROL: Oh no, I can't be arsed. Phone sex seems a bit silly to me. What's the point? I don't miss him that much. Anyway, we've never really been away from each other long enough.

JANE: Well, yes, I have done, while he was away in Australia. Oh God, have I just admitted that? I get embarrassed talking about it. But our flirty texts kept us going all those weeks apart. Once again, the fantasy is so much better than the reality, sometimes!

SHERRIE: How did it unfold?

JANE: It would start off with a bit of a flirty text, and then I'd reciprocate, and then he'd come back again. There was lots of suggestiveness; you know, what I was going to do to him when I saw him again – and when he got home, I kept my word!

LYNDA: It could be brilliant fun, couldn't it? You start texting something like, 'Come next Thursday night' or 'I've got my new knickers on' and you can build it up, build it up, build it up, so that by the time he's back, he's really up for it!

LISA: I've never done it, but I've had some fairly saucy conversations about what one would like to do if one was in the same room and stuff like that!

ANDREA: That sounds like telephone sex to me!

LISA: Well, almost, but not quite, if you know what I mean!

You catch your partner watching porn, or he asks you to watch it with him. Do you have a fit?

CAROL: I wouldn't mind if he wanted to watch porn. I honestly don't mind it. I think it can probably help people sometimes. We don't really watch it now, we don't need to, but I imagine if I'd been married as long as Denise has, you might need a little help, with a few images and a bit of action to watch on the TV. I can see the reasons for it and I can see that it does have a purpose, so long as it's not gross.

LYNDA: No, it wouldn't bother me, as long as we had a reasonably good sex life. It would bother me if he couldn't get it up and he was watching a lot of porn, though, because that means there is a problem there. Also, if he's watching porn and it's not translating onto you, then I would say there is a problem.

LISA: I caught an ex-boyfriend watching porn and I remember being absolutely horrified, because he was on the living room floor watching telly with tea towels round him. My tea towels!

We were living in an open-plan house; the bedroom was downstairs and the living room was upstairs. So as I was coming upstairs from the bedroom one night, the first thing I saw was this bare bottom in front of me. He hadn't taken his trousers off completely, just pulled them down enough, if you know what I mean. Next, I saw the people on the telly doing it. So I knew exactly what he was doing, but I still said, 'What are you doing?' in a really accusatory voice, like I was the police or something. I don't know why.

'Oooh!' he said, like he'd been caught with his hand in the cookie jar. 'Oh, nothing, er . . . er . . .'

As I came closer, I noticed the tea towel in front of him. 'Just pull yourself together; sort yourself out!' I said, and I went back downstairs again.

Back in the bedroom, I started to think it over. It felt like some weird sort of betrayal. It wasn't like he had another woman, but I was thinking, Why is he doing that when I'm in bed downstairs? He could just come to bed, couldn't he? I've since gathered that the two things are very different for men, but at the time I thought, What's wrong with me, then? I'm lying in bed on my own and he's up there with a tea towel, *my* tea towel, from *my* kitchen.

SHERRIE: What happened to the tea towel?

LISA: It went straight in the bin, as you can imagine!

SHERRIE: I should think so! It makes you wonder how many times he'd done it before. With the tea towel, I mean.

JANE: Cup of tea, anyone?

Which would you prefer: a marathon session or a quickie?

CAROL: Well, it was quiet in my bedroom for quite a long time and now things are waking up and getting a bit noisier, so I don't actually mind it going on for a bit! But I've got nothing against a quickie. I quite like the idea of a quickie. Then again, it's quite nice to talk about it for thirty minutes first, and then, you know . . .

ANDREA: What do you mean by 'talk about it'? He says, 'Shall we?' You say, 'Yeah, in a minute.'

CAROL: No, no! You might do that now; after all, you've been with him for a while. But when you first get together, you like talking about it, and it can be quite exciting.

JANE: Isn't the question really: 'Which would you prefer: a Marathon or a quiche?' Chocolate or egg pie? I can't do with quickies: forget it! You know, if you're not going to make the effort, then don't call me! I like the acting part of sex. I think that part of it is more exciting than the actual deed. You know, the fantasy aspect and building up to it all day. I like to flirt all day, if I've got the time. If I know it's going to happen that night, I'll send texts, get myself organised and get it into my head that it's going to happen.

CAROL: You want to make an occasion of it?

JANE: I do. The problem is that by the time they've finished, I'm thinking, Well, I've only just got going! I want the whole nine yards. So I always think it's going to be much better than it actually is. I might as well confess − I don't have it very often, so when I do have it I like to make it an occasion.

CAROL: So, have you never been taken by the moment?

JANE: Taken by the what?

CAROL: By the moment! Have you never felt like just, you know, Quick! Let's do it now!

JANE: Ummm . . .

ANDREA: When you've got young kids, it's often a quickie. I've said it before and I'll say it again – it just depends how long an episode of *Peppa Pig* it is. 'We'll just put *Peppa Pig* on, quick!!' If it's on satellite, they'll sometimes show three episodes in a row, one after another, so you get about twenty minutes!

LISA: I've got a switch-off mode when my daughter is around. I've got used to switching from sexy partner mode into mother mode and never the twain shall meet!

ANDREA: If the kids are away and you've palmed them off for a little while, I think the best way to do it is have a quickie first and get that stress out of the way; then you can take your time. So then everybody's happy.

CAROL: Have you ever done it anywhere naughty, somewhere you shouldn't have?

JANE: What are you talking about now?

CAROL: So it's just me, then?

ANDREA: No, just you owning up to it!

JANE: Tell us about it, Carol.

CAROL: Well, once I was on holiday and there were these canvas changing tents next to the swimming pool. And, you know . . .

JANE: Quickie?

CAROL: It was quick, but it was quite sexy, actually. I enjoyed it.

JANE: Canvas?

CAROL: And chlorine! Yes, it was a very nice location. Come on, don't tell me you haven't . . .

ANDREA: Jane McDonald and I are maintaining a dignified silence.

JANE: We certainly are!

Could you have sex five times a day, like former Spice Girl Mel B claims she does?

LISA: Cor, that takes some multitasking, doesn't it! Dear, oh dear! Is that five times a day, *every* day?

ANDREA: It could be done if you multitasked during dinner and hoovering, I suppose!

LISA: Well, it would have to be, because where else would you fit it all in? So to speak . . .

ANDREA: Are you envious?

LISA: No, and what I don't understand is that she has children, so what does she do with them while she's having sex five times a day, every day?

LESLEY: They must nap a lot!

LISA: Yes, because children normally walk in on things. Anyway, I can't see how anybody can want it five times a day.

ANDREA: They say it's important to get your five a day!

LISA: Lovely stuff! You know what, it would have to be your job to get it done five times a day, every day, in my view.

ANDREA: Either that, or your children have to watch a lot of episodes of *Peppa Pig*! 'Do you want to watch more *Peppa Pig*? All right then!' I don't think I'd like it. It's all right if you're on holiday and the kids aren't there and it's all really exciting, but – well, no. Not for me!

LESLEY: What about anticipating the moment, savouring the fact that you might be about to do it? They're all going to run together, these 'events', aren't they?

LISA: You can understand if it's an affair, but not with your husband!!!

LESLEY: I admire her for wanting it five times a day, though. Don't you?

JANE: Is this with the same man?

LESLEY: Is it without a man at all?

JANE: Good point! So when would you do it? You'd do it with dog breath on a morning, wouldn't you?

LESLEY: No, actually!

JANE: And then elevenses, maybe? After lunch? Oh, I couldn't cope with that!

Can you be 100 per cent sure that you wouldn't have an affair?

CAROL: Obviously, there are no guarantees in life and everybody is human, but I think you've got to take that position if you're married to someone. Personally, I don't believe that monogamy is a natural human state, but I do think it's possible for exceptional people, even though it's really hard. It's very difficult to stay faithful to someone for your whole life.

COLEEN: Even for three weeks in your case!

CAROL: You have to believe that it's possible; otherwise you would never start a relationship.

SHERRIE: You believe it all when you're young, don't you? I'm going to sound very cynical now, because I am, but when you're young, you believe that dream, and when I was first married, I totally believed it. I wanted to believe it. When I was proved wrong, it really knocked me back and I don't know if a person can ever come back from that. In a fantasy world, you  think, Wouldn't it be wonderful if we were all faithful? But now I would never trust anybody a hundred per cent again; I would go into a relationship now with a totally different outlook.

CAROL: But what's the point of going into a relationship that you're almost expecting will go wrong?

SHERRIE: Well, I suppose that in the back of your mind, you're thinking, If this one goes wrong, it goes wrong. I just wouldn't go into it with all those wonderful, dreamy expectations. At the end of the day, women don't need sex, but men do; that's always in my mind.

COLEEN: Women need sex.

CAROL: Of course they do. We do!

SHERRIE: Not in the same way; I don't think it's the same thing.

COLEEN: You mean, men would have sex just for sex's sake, whereas for women it's more emotional?

ANDREA: If you go into a relationship thinking that neither

one of you will ever be unfaithful, are you being foolish and naive?

COLEEN: I'd understand someone thinking that, but to me it seems slightly dangerous, because when I was married to Shane, I was blissfully unaware that he was seeing other people. I had no reason to mistrust him: he was always attentive; he was always where he said he was going to be; he was phoning me ten, even twenty times a day. What I hate and what I would hate anyone else to go through is that feeling of knowing that you've been sitting there with MUG written on your forehead, because everybody knew and you didn't. Still, I do think there are people out there who can be faithful for ever.

SHERRIE: Are you glad that you didn't know? Is that what you're saying? So you had ten years of happiness in ignorance?

COLEEN: Absolutely, I didn't know and I didn't need to know. But, obviously, when you split up you find everything out; it affects you. I always think that I'm not affected and then something will happen with me and Ray that allows that little bit of doubt or insecurity to creep in, and then he has to reassure me.

CAROL: Still, you can't carry the past around with you.

COLEEN: I don't, but when something happens, you realise that the past has affected you. Because you're frightened of being that person again, of going through another ten years with someone who you trust a hundred per cent and then they betray you. I really, really trusted Shane; I thought we were forever.

CAROL: But that's what human beings do!

COLEEN: That's why I don't believe it a hundred per cent. I've always said it: we all make mistakes because we're human beings. I don't want Ray to trust me a hundred per cent. I'm quite a feisty girl. You never know what I might get up to!

SHERRIE: You have to keep excitement going in a marriage. My ex was always jealous of me until he knew I wouldn't stray; as soon as he knew that, he lost interest. So you have to keep the interest there.

COLEEN: That's right. Keep 'em guessing, just a little bit. It keeps them on their toes!

Chapter 3

Beauty Secrets

Because you're worth it

Like most women, we like to feel attractive. We don't always love our God-given features and some days we feel good, but on other days, we wish we could crawl under the duvet with a bag over our face! That's when you need your friends to gather round and remind you that a) there are more important things in life than the spot on your chin and b) you can't even see it and remind you that you're gorgeous anyway.

It's a bit of an eye opener when you read that the average woman spends the equivalent of a small house on beauty products during her lifetime. But then we always think that if a new lipstick or an eye cream is going to help you feel good about yourself, then it's worth it. Just don't believe everything the adverts tell you!

A friend tells you that she's thinking of having cosmetic surgery. What do you say?

CAROL: I would never tell someone not to have a face-lift and I wouldn't judge him or her. It's your face and your body, so do what you like. Even if I had a friend who I thought was going too far with it and was beginning to look weird, I still wouldn't say anything, because she must have a mirror so she must know what she looks like. People always know when they've got a problem; mostly you don't need to tell them – and if you do tell them, it just winds them up. People have got to admit to their own shortcomings and failings. It doesn't help to be telling anybody what to do, or to highlight their problems. What's the point? I'd probably be sympathetic if she ever admitted that she'd gone too far and looked like a weirdo, but people tend not to do that.

DENISE: You're absolutely right. I know someone who has had too much work done, unnecessarily so. What's weird is that she seems to have a reverse body dysmorphia, because she thinks she looks fabulous, whereas in reality she looks like she's been in a road accident! You can't take your eyes off her big swollen lips and she insists on wearing the brightest lipstick. It's like she's saying, 'Look at my collagen implants!'

COLEEN: It seems that too many people have a bit done and then go on to have too much done. They become obsessed and keep going back and back and that's when they start to look just weird, like androids.

DENISE: Yes, and this woman I know is now talking about having a thread lift done, where threads are inserted under the skin and then pulled to lift a sagging chin, brow, neck or eye area. I've not seen much evidence of it, but it sounds horrendous. Still, necks are the giveaway, aren't they? Necks and hands.

SHERRIE: The papers have reported that the latest celebrity trend is to have a thread put under your skin to hold your face up. I didn't like the look of it, because they have to thread it all the way through your face. There are quite a few people I know  who've had a thread lift and you can always tell, because they have a little protruding chin. It isn't permanent, though. It has to be pulled up again.

Some people get really horrible wrinkly necks, don't they? Fortunately, I haven't got a bad neck for my age at all. I might have a little iron, as I call it, sometime soon. I've come to a point where I've been thinking that I might just have a little tiny bit of help again. I don't know what I'd have done, but I'm very aware of not losing my identity and changing. I don't want anything touching my eyes, but you can always lift your neck slightly. So I may do a little bit – but not much and certainly not to change my face. It's just a little incision.

It's difficult growing older. As Carol said earlier, it's especially hard when you are on telly, because you have to keep trying to look good to keep your job. There are always other girls coming through. You have to keep looking as good as you can and if it means having a little tuck, well that's the way it is. I know it's awful. My mother hates it when I talk like that. She keeps saying that I mustn't do things like that to myself. But it can help a little, as long as you only do a little and it doesn't change your face completely. To some extent, you've just got to accept that you are getting older.

LESLEY: I'd advise someone to look at the dermatological angle before going under the knife, although I don't have an ideological objection to it. My worry is that it's irreversible and that it may not end up representing who you are. My biggest fear would be to look in the mirror and not to recognise myself. So I'd advise them to look at what can be done before taking that last step, because to me cosmetic surgery is very much a last step and should be put off as long as possible. That's not to say I wouldn't do it; I just wouldn't do it yet.

There have been enormous strides in what is achievable now in the science of skincare and makeup. So I would also recommend that they go to a makeup artist and have a makeup lesson. It changed my life when I started to have professional makeup done. I thought, My God, I can look fabulous every day! Show me how you do that? I never looked back after Lawrence Close, my makeup artist of choice, gave me a makeup lesson.

DENISE: I agree with everything you're saying, Lesley, but I'd probably still say, Go for it! I know a couple of people who would really benefit from a face-lift. I'm very into the subject of cosmetic surgery; I'm fascinated by it, plus I had my eyes done and I've had fillers. I do the voice-over for *Ten Years Younger*, which is my favourite programme. I've watched it so often that I can see the difference a face-lift can make.

I think it was Helen Mirren who said, 'Little and often,' and I think that's what my policy would be. If something's really making me unhappy and I can do something about it, then great. But as Sherrie will attest, if you're in trouble emotionally, changing your physical appearance won't necessarily make you feel better inside.

SHERRIE: That's right. I thought I would wake up a new person. Instead, I was still the same person and my face was swollen up like a turnip! When the swelling went down, I looked fine. But inside I was just as unhappy.

DENISE: And I would definitely discourage someone who in my mind didn't need a face-lift, because I agree it can become an addiction for some people.

SHERRIE: Yes, you only have to look at someone like Heather Locklear, who seems to have turned into somebody else. Sharon Osbourne is the perfect example of somebody who has had work done and looks stunning.

COLEEN: Yes, Sharon Osbourne was a great advert for cosmetic surgery, initially. She looked fabulous. I always said that if I was to have it done, I'd try to get her surgeon, because I thought she looked amazing.

SHERRIE: But if you go that one stretch too far, you can't come back. In America they can actually take your face off, stretch it and put it back. If I had that done, I'd want Julia Roberts's face instead of my old face back, thank you very much!

DENISE: *Ten Years Younger* makes you think twice about smoking, going in the sun and drinking sweet fizzy drinks, because lots of the people who come on the show look like that character in *Benidorm*. They nearly always have just one tooth – we've named that 'central eating'! And their wrinkles are incredible – you just want to iron them – and they readily admit that they've spent days on end lying in the sun covered in olive oil, or at the very least without sunscreen.

With people who are very wrinkled, the doctor usually does

a really intense chemical peel. It literally burns several layers of the skin off over the course of three weeks and it makes people look like something out of a Hammer horror film. During those three weeks, they have to pull the layers of skin away, but the effect is fantastic. It's a massive improvement for these women and it lasts quite a while, as long as they never go out in the sun again.

LYNDA: That's quite a sacrifice to make, isn't it?

SHERRIE: But it works! When you look at Joan Rivers, her skin is actually quite good, because she has face peels. Face peels are fabulous because they take away the damage done by pollution. It comes back because we live in pollution, but it's fabulous to have beautiful new skin for a while.

COLEEN: I'm not against anyone having surgery if that's what they want and it's going to make them happy: each to their own. But I don't think it looks right when men have surgery. I'm just thinking about the Mickey Rourkes and David Gests; you wonder why on earth they did that to themselves. I simply don't understand it with men, because they get away with ageing so much more easily than women. They don't get judged so much and they don't tend to lose jobs as much for getting wrinkly, so I don't know why they put themselves through it. It's an age phobia with me, I think. It is a fear of getting old. But I like a rugged, kicked-in-looking face, which my husband is not particularly happy about me saying.

LISA: In principle I'm not against plastic surgery at all. If, for example, you've always wanted bigger breasts and you know that you are going to be happier if you have bigger breasts, then do it. Personally I'm not sure whether having bigger breasts can have that much of a psychological difference; it wouldn't make me happier, I don't think. But each to their own. I work in an industry where so much importance is placed on how you look that sometimes it is practical to make sure you look the best you can.

Personally, I wouldn't cut myself open, but then I'm a coward. I hate operations. I hate the thought of having an operation just because I wanted to change the way something looked. And once you get one thing fixed, it makes everything else look really old. You've got these young breasts and a tired forty-year-old bottom, so where it is going to stop? You're going to have to get your bottom lifted, aren't you? You might have the top of your eyes done and it looks amazing, but then suddenly the bits under your eyes look about two hundred years old, so it can open up a huge can of worms.

I look after myself. I use proper skin stuff and I quit the fags five years ago, which made quite a difference to my skin. But I wouldn't cut myself open. I don't have a problem with people having injections and fillers; I've had Botox once before and I should have more of it, because there are a lot of lines around my eyes. But I don't like needles. I'm a bit paranoid about injections.

Still, having injections isn't like having an operation and going under an anaesthetic. Putting yourself under an anaesthetic for a beauty reason seems too far to go to me. But if I was single and I was still trying to pull the man of my dreams, who's to say what I would do? I'd probably want to try and make the best of myself.

SHERRIE: The trouble with getting older is that you lose your muscle. But I don't agree with having fillers and I don't agree with injections. Everybody I know has had fillers and they're all walking around with their faces puffed out. I can't bear it. Botox doesn't work on me – I don't know why – and if I had fillers, I would look like a fat chipmunk, just like so many other people do. I don't really want that look. Fillers give you big baby faces. You don't have any lines, but you've got this big baby face. I would hate that.

LISA: Yes, I don't like the sound of that much, either! My partner is into his aesthetics – he had an interior design company and he's a sculptor – so he's very much into things looking beautiful to the eye. But he likes the lines around my eyes. When I laugh, my whole face screws up and he thinks that it's beautiful, and I believe him, although sometimes I find it hard to accept that he means it. I know it's how he feels, but how could somebody love all those faulty bits? Still, I think it's a shame that when you get to your forties and fifties you start thinking about cutting bits of yourself open. It's a pity that you haven't arrived at that place in yourself where you think, I'm all right, really. I know who I am now.

LESLEY: My general message is that if you don't look how you feel you should, do something about it if you can. That can mean smiling, getting a bit more exercise or looking at your diet. I think that all of those things affect age.

LYNDA: Yes, we all know that when you get up and have a good day, you just feel good-looking. Now if you could only bottle that . . .

Uh Oh. Mum's trying to look like Madonna again.

On average a woman spends £185,528 on beauty in her lifetime. Is it worth it, or would you rather have a small house?

JANE: I look better when I've had a bit of grooming, I have to say. So I do think it's worth it, because it gives you confidence. Whether you've got a bigger house or a smaller house, it's important to feel good in it. Just having your brows done, a waxing job or a facial can make you feel better about yourself. So I never feel guilty about the money I spend on beauty. I don't just do *Loose Women*; I'm also in concert about three nights a week, so that takes a lot of maintenance. Think of all that makeup!

LESLEY: I agree with you, Jane. I think it's worth every penny, especially if it enables someone to express how they feel about themselves in a positive and creative way.

DENISE: I no longer spend money on creams or potions, though: I'd rather save it for surgery and go straight for the kill. My skin seems no better or worse for it if I fall asleep in my makeup, which I regularly do. I'm openly admitting that I'm a complete slut at night-time! I'm often so tired that I'll fall asleep on the settee and stagger up to bed later. But I can honestly say that my skin is no better when I'm using expensive potions and lotions, cleansing, toning and moisturising, than when I fall asleep in my makeup.

I haven't got good skin; I get break-outs, I go through phases where it's very dry and I certainly don't drink enough water. I hate that pressure to drink water. I'd always rather have a cup of tea, or a vodka!

CAROL: A hundred and eighty-five thousand, five hundred and twenty-eight pounds? I find that a bit depressing, really. It's sad that women buy into the idea that if you use this cream, you're going to look like Andie MacDowell or whoever's doing the commercial. It's hard not to think that women are a bit stupid, sometimes.

LISA: There was a time when I would have said, 'Is that all?' But nowadays I believe in good skincare, not makeup.

COLEEN: I like face and body moisturiser, but I haven't got a lot of makeup. I'll try anything out if it's free. But if I'm buying it myself, then I stick with what I know and it's always under twenty quid. Fifty quid for a pot of face cream? You're having a laugh. I'd want you to give me a face-lift for fifty quid!

CAROL: I'd rather have a lot of flash holidays and some first-class travel than spend all that money on beauty. I'm quite low maintenance: I don't buy expensive creams and I don't buy a lot of makeup. I hate makeup. I never wear it unless I have to, for work.

I wore it a lot when I was younger. You know, when you're fourteen and you think it's such a grown-up thing to do? You're so desperate to grow up when you're a teenager that you plaster on tons of it: blue eye shadow and everything. You look completely hideous! I went off it around about my early twenties and I've never really worn it since. Well, maybe a bit of mascara or blusher occasionally, but that's all. I can't bear foundation. It feels like it's suffocating my skin. The first thing I do when I finish work is take it off. Urgh, it's just horrible!

COLEEN: I don't have a lot of makeup, but I love it. Even when I'm not working, I'll always put on mascara, blusher and lipstick. Otherwise I look ill.

SHERRIE: I think we are all obsessed with makeup. I certainly am. I hate myself when I go in and buy yet another foundation. The problem with foundation is that, as you get older, nothing is right, because your face isn't right. Whatever you put on, you see more and more lines. But it is a constant battle with me to not go in a store and buy another foundation. Why? I ask myself. Why do you keep doing this?

I'll also go to every single counter in a department store and say, 'Have you got a moisturiser that will make me look twenty years younger?'

'No,' they all say. 'But we have got one that's really moisturising.' Yet again I went in last week, and the woman said, 'Try this one!' and so I bought it. Not long afterwards, another guy was serving me at another counter and he said, 'We have really nice moisturiser.'

'Don't worry, I'll buy it,' I said. But, please don't tell me that it will actually do anything, because I know it won't. Every cream is exactly the same. If you put Nivea on it's exactly the same.

'Well, not quite,' he said. 'Ours has got this and that in it and it does this and that.'

I said: 'I'll buy it, but I can't bear all of you people saying your creams do these things. If they did do what you told me, you'd be worth trillions!'

ANDREA: Those companies *are* worth trillions, Sherrie!

SHERRIE: But they don't do what they say they do!

ANDREA: I know, and I'm like you. Every time I stand at a beauty counter, I can hear Anita Roddick saying, 'It's all crap. Just buy moisturiser. Nothing else matters.' But I can't help myself! I'm a marketing man's dream. When someone says, 'This latest potion will work wonders,' I'll always try it. There's a part of me that knows it's wrong, yet I also think, 'Ah, but if it costs that much money, it must be really good.'

I'm always convinced by the TV adverts, where you see someone put a cream on and their wrinkles magically shrink. Wow, that's amazing, I think. I'll have some of that. So I'm what you might call a moisturiser slut. Day cream, night cream: I'll try anything, although I can't be bothered with eye cream. Actually, I use an oil at night-time and I've found that really works for me, even though it's a bit greasy.

SHERRIE: I've got a friend who says you should never put night cream on because it will settle into the wrinkles and when you get up in the morning, your face will crease into those wrinkles. But I don't see how that can be true. Still, I do wonder if she's right, but I couldn't cut out night cream because I always think you have to moisturise your skin. I know people who use avocado skins. They're very good for your complexion, apparently. But you smell rather green and I'm not sure I want to smell like that, even though I live on my own.

LYNDA: And that's your choice, Sherrie! I find that when you're in a career where you have to dress up, put makeup on and be aware of what you look like every day, it's quite tedious to have to do it at home. So you tend to fall into the trap of not trying very hard at home – not putting makeup on, for instance – and I hold my hand up to this. So it really does look as though you're taking someone for granted, whereas if you put on a rather attractive outfit, you're making an effort in a way, without making an effort! Also, if you put on a rather attractive outfit, it doesn't look as though you're angling for him to come and give you one – you can see about that later if he's in the mood or not. So I'm always looking marvellous; otherwise it weighs rather heavily if you suddenly make an effort. It's like wearing a flag.

Which item of makeup couldn't you do without on a desert island and how fiercely would you fight to defend it?

SHERRIE: Mascara and foundation!

LESLEY: Tinted moisturiser, with an SPF, closely followed by mascara. I'd have to have sun protection and I'd fight to the death to keep it!

COLEEN: If I were on a desert island I'd probably choose to take some blusher with me, because I'm pale. How hard would I fight to defend my blusher? Well, if it was my blusher or my husband, I think the husband might have to go!

LYNDA: Mine would be mascara, but I don't have a problem with not wearing makeup. I don't wear it much and sometimes even my husband says, 'Can you not put some makeup on when we go shopping, so you look a bit glamorous?'

I definitely wouldn't spend that much money on makeup in my lifetime! I'd much rather have a villa in Spain, thank you very much! I suppose the one thing I couldn't live without is some kind of moisturiser. Even when I was young, I always craved some kind of cream when I washed my hands. I wouldn't mind what it is – Vaseline, whatever – as long as I have something moisturising.

JANE: Mine would be this fantastic mineral powder out at the moment called Bare Minerals. It makes you look so healthy. It works as a concealer as well, with a different brush. Since my skin breaks out a lot, it's a heaven-sent thing. I look flawless now! I would fight very fiercely to defend it.

I'm usually very placid and happy. But, by God, I've got a vicious temper if somebody attacks me or mine. You might not think that about me, but it's true. I'm very good at defending myself. I'll try to do it with wit and humour first. But if I'm not getting the point across, then I will definitely shout. I'm a fire sign, you see, Aries.

ANDREA: Do you believe in astrology, then, Jane?

JANE: A little bit. My partner's an Aquarius and he's a dreamer,

very happy-go-lucky, which is typical Aquarius. I seem to be very typically an Aries, the ram rather than the lamb. I would tend to avoid Geminis and Scorpios. They're very passionate and I can't be bothered with all that. It's awful, isn't it? I sound like a right wet weekend.

What about you, Andrea. Which item of makeup would you choose?

ANDREA: I can't live without lip salve; I can't stand the feeling of having dry lips! I have about a thousand lip salves dotted around the house, so that there's one in every room, handbag and coat pocket. I always have to try the latest one on the market and I find myself feeling irrationally jealous of anyone who pulls out a new brand of lip salve that I haven't tried. Eyeliner is pretty important too, because at least you can see your eyes then. I can do without most makeup, though. I don't wear it if I'm not working, unless I'm going to a do.

LISA: If I were on a desert island, then I'd probably choose eight-hour cream, because you'd just shrivel up and die without any moisture, wouldn't you? Otherwise, I'd go for eyelash curlers. I've always had quite small, fairly heavy-lidded eyes, so eyelash curlers open them up a bit. It's very tragic, because some days I'll sit chatting while I use them and when I take them off it looks like my eyelashes are trying to turn a corner. If I could have two items, I'd take mascara as well. But false eyelashes don't suit me, because I've got such a small face; they make me look like Ermintrude off *The Magic Roundabout*!

CAROL: Makeup would be the last thing on my list. I don't know: women are just mad! When they're on *I'm a Celebrity, Get Me Out of Here!*, they do their utmost to smuggle in mascara or eyeliner, and you think Why??? You're in a bloody jungle! I don't get it. Maybe I should make more effort, but I don't.

ANDREA: Not at all. We love you how you are, Carol!

When you see a new wrinkle or grey hair, do you panic or take it in your stride?

CAROL: These days, I notice my wrinkles, obviously, but I don't feel any different as a result. Whenever I point them out to him, my fiancé just tells me to shut up, which is nice. I don't have a *real* problem with getting older or ageing. It's only because of what I do: there's just so much pressure on women, especially women on TV, and even more so on women who are going out with younger men. Everybody else piles the pressure on you.

JANE: It's true: we're all under pressure. But like you, I had a lovely experience of going out with a younger man. He was very lovely as a partner. I do like a partner who allows me to feel that I don't have to breathe in the whole time. I can't bear that. In the past, there have been times when I've woken up and thought, I must get up, clean my teeth and put my makeup on before I get back into bed. But those relationships don't last very long.

I've got an older man now and I know it sounds daft, but I'm always going to be young to him, so I don't really mind about ageing as much as I did. What's more, I live with my mum, so I see her every day and she looks fantastic to me. She's got great skin, even at seventy-eight. She doesn't dye her hair and she's only just going grey now.

ANDREA: Speaking of grey hair, it's really irritating that Carol's got no grey hair and I've got loads. I think that's wrong! She's constantly laughing at me because, being tall, she'll stand above me and say, 'Ha! I can see a grey hair.' I know everyone says that you shouldn't yank them out, because ten will grow back in its place, but mine seem to grow in patches right in the crown and as soon as I see them glinting in the light, they're gone.

LESLIE: I've never had an issue with grey hair, because I've always been very inter-ested in colouring my hair and being creative with my hair. There wasn't a day when I thought, Gosh, I'm going grey, so I'd better colour my hair. Many years before that, I thought, I'm so bored with my hair! What can I do with it today? So I've never particularly noticed whether I have grey hair or not, although I think I do have some. I go to Trevor Sorbie and have done for fifteen years. He is extra-ordinary and he and his staff really look after me. I adore his colourist Nathan, particularly; he experiments with my hair all the time.

COLEEN: I don't worry about ageing. I feel that age is a state of mind. My mother-in-law is very inspiring – she's eighty-four going on twenty. She's still very with it and loves life. Physically there are many things she can't do, obviously, but mentally she is great. I like seeing people age. I like seeing life on people's faces. I think I've earned my lines. They really don't bother me.

JANE: Me neither, but I'll keep saving up for a bit more surgery, though – what the heck!

LESLEY: Wrinkles are interesting things. I really like some of my wrinkles. I'm happy to own the wrinkles that represent the laughter that's been in my life. I'm also quite fond of wrinkles that represent curiosity in my life. And there aren't that many wrinkles that represent sadness, because I've done something about those!

So I've done something about getting rid of the wrinkles that I don't feel represent me. More than anything, I want my face to represent the person I am. There is nothing sad about me, so I don't have those wrinkles. I was famously quoted as saying, 'Botox? Yes, of course I have Botox. Even my cat has Botox!' A little goes a long way, in my opinion.

But I think the best way to combat wrinkles is to look after your skin in the first place. I really do fundamentally believe that skincare is the answer. If you put your sun block on and exfoliate like a mad thing and use really good-quality skincare products, then you can mitigate the effect of wrinkles. I'm not talking about silly price skincare products, but good-quality skincare products: I use my dermatologist's own range. But if you do have a wrinkle that you don't like, then do something about it.

LYNDA: I cleanse and tone really hard. I use a range that's recommended by cosmetic surgeons for people after surgery because it's got a lot of healing stuff in it. I use a moisturiser with a high-factor SPF, and my husband uses it as well. You still get a suntan through it and it's really good for skin damage.

People make this terrible mistake of thinking you can hide your lines. Well, you can't. You can do something about broken veins, though: I put on a little layer of makeup over mine, but no powder. Lots of good brands now do makeup that doesn't need powder. It's just so much nicer. I don't know why women think powder is going to hide anything. Well, I suppose it's because the makeup industry tells them it will.

LISA: And we believe them! I've got to the stage in my life where I just worry about the bits that are on show. You know, the tired baggy face, the neck and the arms. If I get the odd dimple in my bum – well, I've pulled anyway; I'm with the bloke I'm with – he's seen my bottom dimple and he seems all right about it.

LYNDA. Quite! It's very comforting, isn't it? I don't feel old yet, but I'm quite conscious of 'mutton dressed as lamb', and I'm perfectly aware that there are parts of my body that are best left covered up, unless I can lie down, breathe in and put my hands above my head!

LESLEY: I think that each stage in your life has clothing that is appropriate for it or that you feel comfortable in. That doesn't mean it won't be glamorous, sexy or interesting as you get older. On the contrary, the older I get, the more confident I feel to explore all the things that are possible. There are some things that I would just feel silly in now, but I would have felt silly in other things when I was younger. You've got to wear what expresses who you are at that particular moment in your life.

That's the point of clothing: it's all about freedom of expression and expressing how you feel at that time in your life. I don't feel the same as I did when I was twenty. I dress to suit my contemporary feeling. I feel powerful now and confident and I've achieved a certain status in life. I feel that I can dress in a way that expresses that. It's interesting.

Sometimes I dress in clothes I used to wear, because I'm feeling nostalgic that day. Sometimes I dress in clothes that are possibly more appropriate for an age that I'm yet to reach, because I just want to experiment with the future. I love the way Vivienne Westwood takes tweed and turns it into a party, into an art form. I just worship that woman. I've got lots of her dresses in my wardrobe. I suspect that she feels that clothes are a wonderful, creative art form and that's the way it should be for all of us.

When I was a child, the shops that kids have nowadays didn't exist. I revel in that for them; it's wonderful. I shop on the high street all the time; all the *Loose Women* girls do. We're all sitting there in Top Shop, H and M, Warehouse, River Island and Principles. There's so much choice now and nobody cares about high street versus couture any more. We mix it up and that's how it should be.

I'm also loving what they now call the vintage movement, but we used to call it charity shop shopping when I was a kid. They used to be second-hand clothes, but now they're called vintage. In north London, where I live, we are so blessed with our charity shops, because they are well served by the local community and the north London women have very good taste on the whole. So my daughter is having a great time in Sue Ryder, as I did thirty years ago.

ANDREA: I'd love a peek inside your wardrobe!

LISA: Around what age did you start worrying about the whole 'mutton dressed as lamb' problem, Lynda?

LYNDA: You start feeling that way around thirty, but you move through that period and then you get over it and become quite brazen about it. You defy it. Later, you just become realistic about it. I mean, there's no question that your body has changed.

That's the interesting thing about plastic surgery: you can have your face done, but where do you stop, ultimately? Are you going to have operations on the tops of your arms and the tops of your thighs, too? You can't ultimately stop your skin getting old. So you have this perfect wind-tunnel face and you cover yourself up to the top of your neck, but then somebody's going to have to see the rest of you eventually and say, 'Oh blimey, there's a difference!' Whereas at least if you introduce the world to it gradually and get old graciously, they kind of don't notice.

CAROL: Everybody seems to be having something done all the time. It's just not acceptable to look your age any more. It's hard, but you just have to fight it. You have to think about it a lot and accept that this is what happens to everybody. You can have a load of work done, but eventually you're going to look old; it's going to happen whatever you do. Either that or you're going to end up looking like Joan Rivers.

LYNDA: Absolutely. I totally agree. I'm lucky, I guess: I've got good skin, olive skin. I do look after it, though. And I'm not thin. If I became really thin to get my body to a size ten now, it would show on my face and probably not be very pretty. I think there is a point where you need to keep a bit on the old face.

SHERRIE: Yes, when you get older you have to make a choice: it's either your face or your body. If you want your face to stay not too bad, it has to be at the expense of the waist and the tummy, I'm afraid. If you want to stick to a size eight, your face will  go. So, do you want a very thin, gaunt face or do you want a bit of weight on it? When I lose a lot of weight, I become very gaunt. So I would keep weight on my face as much as I can, at least until I can have another face-lift.

LYNDA: All those Hollywood stars look drawn, except on camera. To look good on camera, you have to walk about like a scarecrow. But then people say, 'God, is she ill?' In Hollywood they're used to it, so they don't ask if you're ill, but here, if I became thin enough now to do a film, people would think I was seriously ill. It's chicken and egg: should I bother in case I got that film? Highly unlikely, the way the world is at the moment, so I'd rather people said, 'You look much nicer than you do on the telly!' than the other way round.

CAROL: You get to a certain age and you can't help but notice things changing physically, and I think a lot of people then suddenly hanker after their youth. Maybe they start to realise that they didn't make the best of what they had, when they had it. They say that youth is wasted on the young, because you don't appreciate how many wrinkles you don't have when you're twenty-eight! So when you start to get them, you think, I want to be how I once was again! But you can't.

Yet a lot of people don't have a good time, even in their twenties, because they're too worried about what they look like. Many people are very insecure when they're young, and that's why I think they don't like to accept that they are looking older in their forties, because they didn't appreciate their youth and were always fussing. Everyone's confused in their twenties anyway, because they don't really know what they want. They go out with the wrong people; they have the wrong friends; they listen to music they don't really like. It isn't until you get to your forties that you're honest with yourself about who you are and what you want, and then you're covered in wrinkles! So you start stressing about that, but you've got to try not to stress about it.

There's no point stressing about things you can't do anything about. People say that you *can* do something about it, but actually I don't want to go down that road. I wouldn't have anything done because I don't want to not look like me. Of course I'd love to wave a magic wand and look exactly like I did when I was in my twenties, but you can't! People try and they start to look deformed.

I wasn't particularly happy in my twenties, but there's no point in stressing about what happened back then, because it's gone. There was nothing wrong, but it was just a decade of confusion. That's just the way it was.

LESLEY: Yes, I remember my twenties as being a time of enormous chaos. I would definitely say my happiest, most creative times have been since I was married to Peter, since my mid-thirties.

LISA: It's funny, isn't it? Now I'm in my forties, for the first time I am completely happy with who I am. There are things about me that I don't like, but I accept them. But for years I tried to be somebody else; in my twenties and thirties I was a complete chameleon. Now I am who I am.

I was seeking approval, I think, looking for reassurance. I was this kid who went to a very posh stage school, but lived in a council flat at the Elephant. For a while I spoke like Princess Diana. There's a clip of me presenting a magazine show when I was twenty-one and I was 'terribly like that'. I thought that was the way stage-school girls who wanted to be actresses should speak.

When they showed it on *Richard and Judy*, both Richard and Judy said, 'Oh, everybody was posh then. We were really posh too. If you were presenting stuff, that's the way you had to speak.'

But at the time I wouldn't have had the courage to say, 'Actually, I don't really talk like that.' Then you'd meet my mum and she'd say, ''ello darlin', and you'd think I was adopted or something. I was so different from the rest of the family.

I was never embarrassed about where I came from, though. I was always very proud of my nan and my mum. But I think I would have preferred to come from a richer, more (what I considered to be) acceptable background for a stage-school girl – a kid at a fee-paying school.

I still speak with a completely different accent to my mum's. What's funny is that she worked as a receptionist at RADA for twenty-odd years and she'd answer the phone saying, ''ello, RADA', in a cockney accent. She even made tapes for people in a cockney accent, so that they could imitate her. Everybody loved her. Loads of students who have now become really well-known actors just love Val. She is just a really good, warm woman; I realise now that people can see past all of that class stuff.

The first year, my mum worked her lunch hours to send me to stage school and then I got a scholarship. When that ran out, I worked and paid my own fees. Looking back, I don't know if it was my own insecurity that made me wish I was a different kind of person from a different background, or if I was made to feel like that. Either way, I felt it quite strongly, to the point that I pretended to be somebody else who lived somewhere else and told loads of lies to match the persona I'd created. But now I don't. I'm happy in my own skin, wrinkles and all.

JANE: That's good to hear, love.

LESLEY: I still maintain that the best way to deal with wrinkles is to smile. An interested, quizzical expression and a smile can go a very long way, in my view. Fortunately, I don't have to make a conscious effort to do that, because I am naturally a very smiley person!

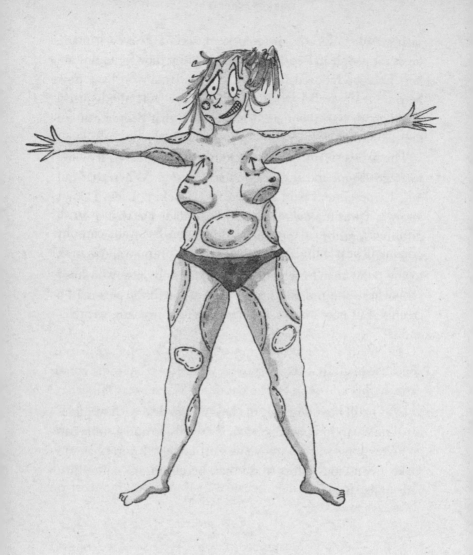

Tracy had only asked the surgeon to suggest
absolutely ESSENTIAL work to be done.

Do you let go and tuck into winter comfort food or try to restrain your appetite?

COLEEN: I suppose I'm more likely to put on weight in the winter, because that's when you need hot food to warm you up, whereas in the summer you tend to eat more fruit and salad. Also, you're not out so much in the winter, because it is too cold.

LYNDA: No, no no! Everyone says, 'Isn't it marvellous in the summer? You just want a salad.' Rubbish! I want carbohydrates all year round! Then they say, 'Isn't it marvellous in the winter: you can have carbohydrates because you need something warming?' It's all crap! I can put on weight any time, summer or winter.

JANE: Well, I think I am more likely to eat in the winter because of all that comfort food, whereas I'd eat more salads and barbecued food in the summer. We tend to hibernate in the winter in our house and my mother's always got a really big pot of soup going, or she'll serve up casseroles and food with lots of gravy. I love a Sunday roast, as well. We have that every week, but sometimes we have it on a Monday or a Tuesday, because I often have a concert on Sundays now.

ANDREA: I definitely eat more in winter because I love comfort food, unfortunately: stodgy things like pies, potatoes, sausages, mash and beans. I spent a long time as a weather girl standing around in the cold, constantly eating just to keep myself warm. So I'm used to refuelling more often in the winter.

I'm not fanatical about my weight, because I keep fit all year round and my weight stays more or less constant. I put a bit on over winter, but I work out three times a week, so that tends to burn it off. I don't enjoy working out: I hate thinking that I've got to do it and I hate it while I do it, but I love how I feel afterwards.

SHERRIE: I can put on seven pounds and take it off again just like that. I'm just one of those people who can juggle it if I want to.

ANDREA: Lucky you! If I even think about going on a diet, I instantly start craving chocolate, so there's no point to dieting for me. You know when you're eating rubbish and you know when you're eating well, so just try to eat more of the good stuff than the bad stuff.

Having said that, I'm thinking of going to a hypnotist to be weaned off chocolate and sugar, because I can't get through the day without having at least a couple of chocolate bars and then some chocolate biscuits at night. I'm hoping that hypnosis could just flip that switch off.

I used to be able to eat whatever I wanted, but now I'm older I put on weight more easily, so I would rather someone flipped a switch than I ended up feeling deprived in any way. Feeling deprived just makes you want something even more and life's too short to feel you're missing out.

I have a dairy allergy, so I'm not even supposed to eat chocolate. But I love it, even though it sometimes makes me ill and I get headaches. The sensible part of me is shouting, 'What are you doing? Stop it!'

but I can't help it. It's my one vice. I don't like expensive dark chocolate that tastes really rich, either; I'm just crazy about cheap chocolate from the local shop.

DENISE: I tend to put on weight in the winter, but I'm never going to put on the kind of weight I gained the Christmas before last, when I went on a cruise. The problem was that I knew I was going to diet heavily when I came back, so I kept thinking, Well, I might as well have another ten pies! But I can't really blame the winter for that, because I was in the Caribbean.

COLEEN: I'm very prone to putting on weight. Summer or winter, it doesn't really matter. If I even look at a bar of chocolate – let alone if I eat it – I put on half a stone. But sometimes I'll have one anyway, because the whole thing about losing weight this time was not to feel deprived, the way a lot of diets make you feel. Now I think, OK, I'll have a bar of chocolate, but that's all I'll have. I see it as a little treat, rather than thinking, Oh I've ruined my diet now. I may as well have another – and another. I've managed to keep the weight off for three years now, so it's definitely the right approach for me. I also work out with my own fitness DVD to keep on track.

DENISE: Well done! I know I won't put on that kind of weight again because it made me so miserable and it was really hard to lose. I could have dropped a stone quite easily a few years ago, before I was forty – certainly half a stone was not that difficult to lose – but now I feel I virtually have to go on a starvation diet. I'm not hung up on my weight like I used to be, though. I'm a size twelve and that's fine. I may sometimes dip a little bit, but I don't ever want to be the size I was. I felt unhealthy and nothing fitted me; everything looked wrong. Since my career is on television, which makes you look bigger anyway, it was like watching blooming Hattie Jacques!

The only successful diets I've been on are the eating-sensibly-and-exercising diets. That's really the only way to lose weight. Having said that, I went on a quick-fix diet about four years ago because I wanted to lose a few pounds very quickly. It's a radical five-day diet and it left me feeling famished, so you definitely couldn't survive on it long term. I'm not condoning it, but it worked up to a point. I think it's called the chemical diet now, but back then it was called the egg-and-grapefruit diet. You hardly eat anything, but the grapefruit is vital. If it says to have a steak and half a grapefruit, you can't think, Oh, I'll have the grapefruit later, because it's crucial for breaking down the steak in your stomach.

LESLEY: I hate diets! So I get bigger in the winter and I go down in the summer. I think it's quite natural. It's because I sit around more; I don't exercise as much in the winter. I also eat food that is appropriate to winter: I drink hot chocolate and hot toddies and eat mashed potato instead of salads. I love making casseroles; we have a really battered crock-pot that always has a stew in it.

It was particularly difficult last winter, because I was in *Carousel* in the West End and singing always makes me very hungry. A classically trained singer sings in an extremely energetic style. It's quite athletic, actually. It's an enormous effort to produce this huge sound that has to reach to the back of a two-thousand-seater auditorium without the help

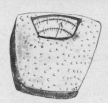

of a microphone and it uses up a lot of calories. Even though I had a microphone for *Carousel*, I didn't change the way I sang. I still sang with a very projected sound.

I don't eat much before I go on stage, because a singer's diaphragm is huge and the diaphragm presses down on the stomach, so if your stomach is full, that can cause acid reflux. It makes you feel sick if you sing on a full stomach. You wouldn't go for a run after you'd had a big meal, would you? Well, it's the same. You can't have an empty stomach either, so I will always eat something. Only something very light, though. Pasta is very good because it's carbohydrate, which means instant energy.

After a show, I always come home and end up with a great plate of stew and mashed potato and a glass of red wine, which isn't very sensible! This is why singers tended to have a problem with their weight in the past because, after performing, you are just so hungry! It's very common for an opera singer to go out and eat three bowls of pasta after coming off stage. Eating late is also very bad for acid reflux: it causes heartburn in the night and you wake up with a croaky throat.

I came out of last winter quite heavy. I could tell particularly by my bust, which had grown to a 32F. I'm very hampered by my bust: it's enormous, while the rest of me is very tiny. I'm a size eight to ten everywhere, but all my weight is in the front and I've got a very narrow back. It's a nightmare, because things never fit. Everything has to be taken in or altered in some way.

SHERRIE: I should be so lucky!

ANDREA: You win some, you lose some ...

COLEEN: Well, I sympathise with you, Lesley, because I know what it's like. It can be very inconvenient!

LYNDA: And I sympathise with you, Lesley, but for entirely different reasons! Eating around performances is a tricky one, I find. When I was in *Calendar Girls*, I planned to go on a massive diet before it started. I was going to have to take my clothes off on stage and I just couldn't get my head around it. Funnily enough, the more nervous I got about taking my clothes off, the more I ate the wrong things.

In the end, I discovered that I couldn't eat before the show, because I can't go on stage with a full stomach, or after the show, because I can't go to bed on a full stomach. So I cut out a whole area of eating and brought it all back to the beginning of the day. I had porridge and berries in the morning, some orange juice and a cup of tea, and then I had lunch, usually sushi, at about three p.m. That worked brilliantly. I was usually a little bit hungry by the time I went to bed, so I had a hot chocolate with skimmed milk, which is really filling. That's all I had and on average I lost two pounds a week while still feeling really healthy. The first month I lost about ten pounds!

I'm doing Pilates now, and I do think it really works, and I do the treadmill at home three times a week. In half an hour, I walk two and a half miles. Elsewhere, I try to walk as much as I can, by taking the bus part of the way to work and then walking the rest of the way. It really does make a difference!

Chapter 4

Tips for Feeling good
And coping with man flu . . .

 Our bodies have a tough time – they have to fend off coughs and colds on a daily, if not hourly basis; many of us suffer from the winter blues and the party season can really take its toll.

When you're feeling under the weather, how do you cope? Do you soldier on or panic and take your temperature every five minutes? In our experience, women are the ones who have to keep everything going, so we rarely have the chance to take to our beds. But why is it that as soon as a man has so much as a slight sniffle, suddenly it's flu and he'll be lying on the sofa for days while you wait on him hand and foot. Man flu strikes again!

In this chapter, we'll reveal our tips for feeling as good as you possibly can and share our stories of tough times we've gone through with our health.

You've got a cold coming on. What do you do?

CAROL: I completely ignore it. I don't even think to myself, I think I've got a cold. So what, it's only a cold! You've only got to blow your nose a couple of times a day, and you might have to take a headache tablet.

If I were ill, I probably wouldn't even tell anybody, unless I was really dying. I've had flu, proper flu, about three times in my whole life and I know how debilitating it is. It is absolutely hideous; no wonder people die from it. The last time I had it I was living on my own. I couldn't lift my head up, couldn't even get a drink of water; I could not even make it to the kitchen.

When you have real flu, your head's pounding, you're sweating, you're freezing one minute and boiling hot the next and you can't move. So when people come into work and say, 'Argh, I've got such bad flu,' I say, 'You haven't! Just be realistic about what's wrong with you!' It really winds me up, so I won't acknowledge a cold at all.

COLEEN: I agree! If you've got proper flu, you can't get out of bed, so it's annoying when people say, 'Oh, I've got the flu!' and you're thinking, 'No, you haven't, because if you did have, you wouldn't be standing there telling me about it.'

I don't tend to get colds, touch wood, and I'm definitely not a hypochondriac. But if I've got a cold, I won't moan about it all day. Once you have kids, you've got to soldier on. You've got to get up and do the school run with or without a cold, if your partner's not around. I'm one of those people who starts taking stuff once the cold is already in full flow, which is completely pointless. Then I take the usual over-the-counter stuff.

DENISE: I'm sure there's something to be said for things like echinacea, but I can never remember to take them until it's too late. I should, though, because there isn't time to get flu, which knocks you out for days.

LESLEY: I'm obsessive about not getting a cold. In fact, I would almost rather have a broken leg than have a cold, because I can't sing with a cold. If my husband goes down with one, he sleeps somewhere else; if the kids have one, we do hugs, not kisses, and they've known from an early age not to bring a friend with a cold home. I practise barrier nursing, which I've learned from my mum, who was a nurse. So I wash my hands until they're raw and we have bottles of antibacterial wash throughout the house; I won't travel on public transport in the winter; and I will wear a mask if I need to.

Having said that, I don't take vitamins, because I don't think they help at all. I don't bother with vitamin C or echinacea. I believe in my body's natural defences and they're really good, most of the time. Usually I get one nasty bug every winter.

LYNDA: I never take those things that dry up your cold, although they're quite a temptation during the run of a play, because I think they dry up everything, as in *all* the fluids in your body! There's something not right about them. With a cold, I think you've got to go through those two days where it all runs. It's not attractive and it's especially difficult on stage, because you constantly have your hand under your nose, but I think it's got to come out at quickly as possible. Steaming is good. Pineapple is good for a sore throat, but it's a pain to chop up, unless you have a minion to do it for you.

SHERRIE: My cold remedy is the best in the world: a very large whisky, added to boiling water or boiling milk, cloves and Manuka honey. One or two of those will kill any germ or virus that's in your body. It's really medicinal.

ANDREA: I ignore it and plough on. If I really feel a proper cold coming, I take some paracetamol, have a hot toddy made from honey, lemon and a little bit of whisky and go to bed. It really works.

LISA: I steam, because my voice is the first thing that goes when I've got a cold. I put my face over a bowl of hot water with Olbas oil in it. I'm a big fan of Olbas oil. I also drink lots of water, take a bit of echinacea and drink a Berocca. Oh my God, what would I do without Beroccca? It really does pep me up. It's a big old B and C boost and it works so well that most unit nurses on set go around giving it out to the crew. It's a good preventative if you have one every day.

COLEEN: Now you're just making me aware that I don't take any of these things! But I'm trying to give up smoking. Or at least, I've got as far as carrying Nicorette patches in my handbag next to my cigarettes. It is a start, isn't it? I'm mentally preparing myself. My kids are desperate for me to give up, but I'm a full-on addict.

LISA: I don't smoke, but I sound like an eighty-a-day girl. My daughter would go potpie if she saw me with a fag in my hand. If you asked my daughter to describe the devil, she'd say, 'It's Ronald McDonald smoking cigarettes.' That's partly because I told her about that bloke who lived on McDonald's for a month and his organs practically fell out of his body, or whatever happened.

Are you sympathetic when other people are ill?

JANE: Yes, if they're really ill, and especially if I've given it to them!

ANDREA: No, I'm rubbish, unless they're genuinely ill, in which case I'll happily drive across town for fresh soup, or to put someone to bed and look after them. But if someone's just being a whinger and a wimp, then I have no patience whatsoever and it makes me really cross. Man flu seriously gets on my nerves. I have to bite my tongue, though. It's not worth getting into a fight about, because in their head they're dying even if you know they're not! I tend to leave him alone and occasionally pop my head round the door to say, 'You OK? Do you need anything? No? Good.'

COLEEN: My husband gets man flu. If he gets a runny nose it's like, 'I've got the flu.'

And I think, No love, you've got a runny nose: now get up and put the bins out.

DENISE: I know, and have you noticed how men clutch the

furniture when they walk in the room, just in case they pass out? When all they've got is a cold?

JANE: Man flu does my head in!

COLEEN: I'm sympathetic up to a point. Initially I'll say, 'Do you feel bad? Do you want a Beecham's or a cup of tea?' But after a couple hours I say, 'Do you want a smack in the gob? Because you are getting on my nerves now.'

DENISE: I can't deal with other people's illnesses. I expect them to deal with mine, but I can't deal with theirs.

CAROL: Don't get me on blokes getting colds. Suddenly they've got the flu! Mark just has to sneeze and he's got swine flu! I'm like, 'Just shut up!' A cold's a cold. People have been getting them for donkey's years. Stop making a big deal out of it!

Still, I do understand that when you're ill, the only thing that you want is to be better. It's pathetic, but you do feel a bit sorry for yourself. You think, I'm never ever going to take my health for granted again! But then as soon as you're better, you forget all about it and take your health for granted again.

SHERRIE: That's just human nature, isn't it? What a funny lot we are.

Christine couldn't help but feel slightly resentful.

You've got an important event to go to but you're feeling really fluey. Do you try to get out of it?

ANDREA: In the old days, I've gone out to a do and sat there shaking and shivering and feeling like I was just going to die, but I wouldn't do that now. Apart from anything else, I would infect everybody and they're not going to appreciate it. When you're younger, I think, you're so much keener to please. You feel you would let the whole world down if you didn't go, but now I know that people will cope very well without you. Don't flatter yourself by thinking you're the centre of everyone's universe! You're not and they'll just get someone else. Obviously, I wouldn't just leave people in the lurch, though.

COLEEN: When I was touring with my sisters, there were many, many times over the years when we had to soldier on regardless. I remember a time when some of us had the kind of stomach bug where you're vomiting your guts up in a bucket in the wings. You sing a song and run off and vomit in a bucket. That happened when I was hosting *This Morning* once. They put a bucket behind the couch in case I threw up, and I had to lie down in every break.

LYNDA: Like you, I go on, no matter what's wrong with me. You'd really have to be dead or dying to be allowed off a performance. My worst-ever experience was when I had food poisoning during a production of the musical *Salad Days*. I was sick and had diarrhoea in a bucket at the side of the stage in between scenes! That was a Saturday night in Birmingham never to be forgotten!

COLEEN: When you grow up in show business – and by that I mean live performing – it really is a case of 'the show must go on'. In TV, on the other hand, someone only needs to have a slight headache to say 'I must have the day off!' You think: Oh shut up!

A few months ago, on *Loose Women*, I had the worst toothache. I was up all night the night before, crying with the pain of it, and I just couldn't concentrate in the morning meeting because I was in absolute agony. I was just eating painkillers, but you wouldn't have known it on the show. Then, straight afterwards, I went to the emergency dentist. It's just the way I've been brought up. Cancelling an appearance is really the last resort. As Lynda says, you have to be near death to cancel

JANE: That's the way the business works! About four weeks ago, I had a really bad cold. On the way to the concert, my brother said, 'I don't know how you're going to do this tonight.' I took two Sinutabs a couple of hours before I went on and all of a sudden Dr Showbiz kicked in and I sailed through the whole show. But when I came off, I went straight back to sneezing. It was amazing. The adrenalin rush when you go on stage is a cure for just about everything. But it's only temporary and when you come off you feel terrible!

Generally, I don't do ill. My mother's the same. I don't like it and it just doesn't enter my psyche. Nurofen is a wonder drug, too. I try and be aware of what I'm doing and eating, but I'm not very fit. I used to be; I used to swim all the time, but I just don't seem to have the time now. I know that's a real cop-out, though. Still, a two-and-a-half-hour workout on the stage, three times a week, seems do the job.

My backing singer once used a pedometer to count how

many steps she took onstage and by the end of the show she had done nine thousand steps in two and a half hours! She's doing dance steps and routines, whereas I'm up and down that stage like someone possessed, so I probably do eleven thousand, easy! Maybe that's why the weight drops off me as soon as I'm on tour. I'd waste away if I went to the gym! And living on adrenalin a lot of the time means that I've got very low blood pressure as a result, so it does have a positive effect. I'm very blessed to have a job that I absolutely have a passion to do. All the excitement before going on, when the orchestra kicks up, really gives you a buzz.

ANDREA: Do you still get nervous before you go on stage?

JANE: Luckily I've managed to transform my pre-show nerves into complete excitement. It's all about switching the vibration, isn't it? When I first started out, I used to throw up with nerves; I was literally vomiting in the sink before I went on, which is extremely bad for the throat! But now I just have a couple of Drambuies and go out there.

Drambuie is very good for the throat, because it's got honey in it. We have a ritual now: the backing singers and the musical director come in and we have a drink of Drambuie before we go on. It just really perks us up. Then, when I come off, it's a cup of tea!

SHERRIE: You and your cups of tea!

You hear that someone in your street has swine flu. Do you panic?

ANDREA: My first reaction would be to feel really sorry for them – and then just hope that they'll stay inside!

JANE: I'd just carry on. I tend to think: Well, if I get it, I get it. I would be very sorry for them, but I wouldn't panic.

COLEEN: I think the problem with epidemics like swine flu is that the media makes you panic. When it first broke out, someone only had to sneeze in front of me for me to think, Oh my God, swine flu! It was mainly because I've got kids, but it's hard not to overreact when the papers are telling you that it could wipe out half the nation. I'm a real punter when it comes to reading the papers. I'm like, 'Can you believe what so-and-so did?', and then it turns out to be totally untrue.

I still love reading all the gossip, though, even about myself. I'll read something and think, Really? I didn't know I did that! I don't mind. It just makes me laugh. In this business you have to accept the bad along with the good.

CAROL: Remember when bird flu was being touted about as being the next thing that was going to kill the entire population? To be honest, I was a little bit concerned about swine flu at first, because it wasn't like bird flu, which you could only catch from birds. So you literally had to be sleeping with a chicken or order to get it! But it's much more serious that swine flu is being passed from human to human. That's how pandemics occur. But then it was completely blown out of the water by MPs' expenses and didn't get mentioned for ages, so it's always hard to know when something's really serious.

LYNDA: I don't worry about it: I might if I were one hundred and ten or had a small child, but if you're reasonably healthy, you should be OK.

SHERRIE: It's so ridiculous how we always panic at the latest wave of flu. Yes, it will probably hit a few people, but they can cure it, as they keep saying. It's not like we are all going to die. You just need to have a positive attitude.

LESLEY: Well, my husband's a GP, so I'm on the front line when it comes to swine flu and I'm worried to death about it. When Peter comes home I immediately put him in the shower and wash him down with carbolic soap! By the way, it makes me apoplectic when I see doctors criticised in the press, because they're the hardest-working people I know. The fact that the government decided that they didn't want them to do after-hours service any more doesn't mean that they work any less hard. My husband often puts in twelve- or fourteen-hour days.

I also wish that people who go to the doctor with a common cold or anything else infectious would spare a thought for the doctor, because he will in all likelihood catch those germs and take them home to his family, who will in turn catch the cold. And if his wife happens to be an opera singer, it's even worse!

LISA: My reaction to swine flu has been a little bit out of character for me, because usually I'm the sort of person who thinks it's not going to happen to me. But I was really worried when I heard that a twelve-year-old boy had contracted swine flu and they started closing schools, because of Beau. I'm not in the least bit hypochondriac, but I think I responded more strongly than I usually would because no one seemed to know anything about it.

It broke out a few months after President Obama was elected, didn't it? Well, I got a funny text about that. It said, 'Someone once said that when a black man becomes president, pigs would fly. Sure enough, a hundred days later, swine flu.'

JANE: That's a good one!

Do you suffer from SAD or the winter blues?

ANDREA: I probably do. I think everybody does, but again I just put my head down and get on with it, thinking, It'll pass. I've thought about getting a UV light, but then I just forget about it. I've seen them in Boots now; you can get them all over the place.

SHERRIE: I do start to get depression in the winter, but I always make sure I get some sun somehow.

COLEEN: I've never suffered from SAD. I have blue days like everyone, but they can be in winter or summer. I'll be down one day because of a particular circumstance, not because the sun is not shining. It doesn't depend on the weather.

JANE: Yes I did suffer from SAD this year. I became very down, because I didn't take any time out and go on holiday, which I should have done. My other half was on tour in Australia during January and February and that depressed me, too. I felt really down. It was so grey and miserable here and he was in Australia, saying, 'God, it's baking hot here!' I could have poked his eyes out. I decided that next time he goes away at that time of year, I'll take some time off and go too.

CAROL: Make sure you do! I get a lot of sunshine over Christmas and if we have a particularly long dark period I'll go and have the odd sun bed, just to get some UVA and vitamin D. I know people say that that's a really bad idea, but five minutes every couple of weeks ain't going to do anybody that much harm. It's the people who have a sun bed every day for an hour you have to worry about. But I do not want to look like I've been dipped in cocoa!

LISA: I am happier when it's sunnier and brighter. But it's so difficult to define whether I suffer from SAD or not, because I think I've got so many different affective disorders, what with PMT and the rest of it. It's a bit hard to pinpoint which one you've got at any time, because they are so alike! So no, I absolutely don't have it and if I did I wouldn't know which day of the month to fit it in.

DENISE: I definitely suffer from SAD. I can't cope with the greyness. It was a side effect of my depression. I'm much better since I started taking hormones, as I've said before. But before my treatment, I'd get a tingling feeling in my hands whenever I saw black clouds in the sky, and I'd be overwhelmed with fear about the effect such a dark day would have on me.

Some people have SAD so badly that they just can't operate in the winter, but mine was a daily thing. There was a certain type of greyness that would change my chemical makeup. I have to go to the sun as much as possible in the winter. I don't like the cold, but I can cope with a cold and bright wintry day, whereas I can't cope with the greyness.

ANDREA: Have you tried using a UV light? They're supposed to help.

DENISE: I have actually, and there's quite a bizarre story behind how I came to get it.

ANDREA: I had a feeling you might! What happened?

DENISE: Well, I was filming *Down to Earth* in Henley on one of those awful grey days and I was really feeling awful between takes. That day, the series took a slightly odd turn: my fortieth birthday was approaching and out of the blue it was revealed that I was a big Chris de Burgh fan. This hadn't been mentioned in the previous three series, but apparently I was just mad about Chris de Burgh: all of a sudden 'Lady in Red' was playing in the background while I was doing my housework.

Ricky Tomlinson played my husband in the series and he hired a local lookalike called Chris de Bird to sing at my fortieth. A fairly random storyline unfolded after that: Ricky thought he had prostate cancer and went to a holistic healer, played by Paul Kaye. Ricky then found out that he wasn't going to die, he saved Paul Kaye from something, and it turned out that Paul Kaye had been to college with the real Chris de Burgh. So they flew Chris de Burgh in from Norway for one afternoon to be my surprise birthday present.

Now, I think I'm a pretty good actress, but the next scene was pretty challenging. I had to run down the stairs and be amazed to see Chris de Burgh singing 'Lady in Red', while at the same time someone was whispering in my ear, 'Your husband's got cancer.' I just didn't know how to play it!

It was just the most random day: it was pouring with rain, I was feeling SAD and Chris de Burgh was singing 'Lady In Red'. Anyway, in between shots, I started telling him about my SAD. How boring for him! I was saying that the bad weather does more than just piss me off; it actually really affects me. He was very interested in this and asked me whether I had a SAD lamp.

'No,' I said, 'but when I was filming *Soldier Soldier* in Germany, whenever I had the chance, I used to stand under the big halogen lamps that the crew used to create false sunlight.'

Chris de Burgh then told me that his friend happened to have a halogen/SAD lamp factory just down the road in Maidenhead. He asked for my number and very kindly organised for me to have a lamp from his friend's shop, which came next-day delivery.

ANDREA: Denise, that is the maddest story!

DENISE: I know! However, I think that my SAD might have been too severe to be helped by just one lamp, because it wasn't until I had hormone treatment that it started to get better.

ANDREA: Well, it's really good that you got it sorted in the end.

Chapter 5

Christmas

(How to cope)

Ah, Christmas time, mistletoe and wine . . . Or is *Nightmare at Christmas* a better description of what goes on in your home?

Christmas can be an incredibly stressful time. Well, we certainly think so. What with hyperactive kids demanding ever-bigger presents; bonkers relatives you see on that one day every year; queuing for four hours at the supermarket because you forgot the Christmas pud; cooking enough to feed 5,000 then feeling guilty when you scoff the leftovers and later being furious with your husband when he gives you an iron . . . again!

But however much you may dread it, Christmas can still be a magical time.

Seeing the kids' faces light up on Christmas morning makes it all worthwhile. Even the bigger kids can get surprisingly animated over an iPod or a pair of trainers.

And when finally, at the end of the day, you can put your feet up and dose happily in front of the Queen's speech with a glass of something lovely in your hand, and some chocolates on your lap, well, if you're anything like us, you'll already be feeling a tiny bit sad it's coming to an end and might even be looking forward to doing it all again next year!

Well no, she hadn't managed to pull off a Nigella Christmas…

Christmas is coming, do you cover your house in tinsel or hide in the garden shed?

LYNDA: I like hosting Christmas. It causes me grief and stress, but I love it. I want people to feel the excitement that I always had at Christmas: that tingling excitement and the prettiness of it all and the lights on the tree.

I just love Christmas decorations. Every year, I try to be good and use the same ones again, but every year I get led astray by some new light or table decoration.

Getting everything ready is more fun than the actual event, obviously, because everybody messes it up! For me, Christmas Eve is probably the most joyous of all. I play carols on the CD and get the candles going. All the anticipation is lovely. I try and make sure that everything is ready so that Michael and I can go to midnight mass. After mince pies in the church afterwards, we get back at about half past one. Then I take a last look at the tree and it feels like the world is waiting . . .

COLEEN: Ah, that sounds so lovely! I love the anticipation of Christmas too. We used to go to midnight mass when we were younger. It was so exciting to be up at midnight, although I used to fall asleep in the church, because it was so boring! I soon grew out of that excitement. These days I'm just so desperate for the kids to go to bed so that Santa can come.

LYNDA: Oh I know. I didn't think I'd go on doing it, but I still do stockings for the boys. Over the year, I fill up hidden carrier bags with presents for stockings and then I wrap them up on Christmas Eve, when everyone's out at the pub. I can no longer stay up, so I get up early and put them out instead. It's understood in our house that you somehow get to bed by six o'clock in the morning, because I'll be up at seven putting the stockings on the beds. If you're still out and up, you're not going to get your stocking! So they somehow manage to stagger in.

DENISE: I hate Christmas, I really hate it. Bah, humbug! I feel awful saying it, because I have children but they've never been aware of it. It's not Christmas Day I hate, anyway; it's the run-up to Christmas that I can't bear. You know, on the thirtieth of August I go downstairs into the basement of my local department store and the barbecue section is there, but then you go on the first of September and there are tinny little Christmas tunes playing! I'm in shorts still waiting for the summer to come and they've got the Christmas trees up!

You buy a wedding present for someone in September, and the shop assistant says, 'Started early?'

No!!! I have a life and I haven't started early! It's a blimmin' wedding present!

CAROL: That's what I don't like about Christmas here: it's become too commercial. In this country, a) it doesn't feel like Christmas as it's never cold enough, and b) people just go mad. People are such consumers now and children are so spoilt. I can't bear to go shopping and see people buying so much stuff or hearing about my friends' kids getting the latest five-hundred-pound computer, or a TV or games-playing machine.

DENISE: I hate the fact that, from November onwards, people are stockpiling at the supermarkets for what is in theory a Sunday dinner with an added sausage wrapped in bacon. It's a Sunday dinner! Sometimes it's for a few more people, but often it's just for the usual number! I get really hyper about it; I get a rash with Christmas anxiety, as you can probably tell!

I just want to go into the supermarket before Christmas and shout: 'WE ARE NOT AT WAR! THERE IS NO WAR! YOU DO NOT HAVE TO BUY EIGHTEEN LOAVES OF BREAD, TWENTY BAGS OF SUGAR AND ALL THOSE CAKES!' I mean, maybe Auntie Florrie might have a slice of cake if she pops round, but that's it.

I remember my cousin telling me that she'd gone to the supermarket at five a.m. on Christmas Eve morning and couldn't park. I just wanted to go and slay all the customers in that car park! Look, the shops are open on Christmas Eve; the shops are open from seven a.m. on Boxing Day; and on Christmas Day, if you forget your Paxo, the local Spar will also be open. People don't seem to have realised this. In their heads they're still living in an age when the shops used to be shut for the week in between Christmas and New Year. So that does my head in.

COLEEN: The build-up to Christmas is a bit ridiculous. It starts something like three months before Christmas. Then Christmas Day is over so quickly and you think, I've been planning this for months and now it's over! Still, I get a fuzzy feeling when I hear carols playing in the shops.

DENISE: Not me! City centres like London and Manchester are busy anyway, but from October onwards you can't park

 and that also does my head in. Maybe if I had the luxury of not working, I wouldn't mind so much, and if I didn't get invited to so many dos, perhaps I'd look forward to the Christmas season more. I'm very lucky that I do get invited out so much. But when people say to me in July, 'What are you wearing for the Christmas Eve do?' I just want to kill them! They've got it planned and organised, and I won't know what I'm wearing until the day.

CAROL: I'd rather go somewhere they don't have all of that. I mean, Christmas does happen in Thailand and they celebrate it big time. But it is literally a celebration, an event, a festival that everybody takes part in. People don't stay in their houses stuffing their faces like greedy gluttons like they do here: everybody's out celebrating and it's a proper party atmosphere.

Why would you want to sit there and eat so much that you end up wanting to be horizontal, not being able to breathe? I just don't see the sense in that. I'd rather be on the beach with a Tiger beer and a couple of chicken satays.

JANE: Well, I love it. Christmas is a big occasion in our house and we all dress up. I usually wear red and of course there have got to be sequins, because this is Jane McDonald we're talking about, darling! We're not bothered about watching the Queen's speech or anything else on television. We've got a big enough house for the younger members to go off and watch TV, if they want to, but we're much more likely to chat and tell jokes. We've got a piano in the lounge and we all sit down and have a singsong. It's very traditional in that way. It always turns into a big party, because I have all my crew over, and my management nip over as well. I'm very lucky to be surrounded by lovely people.

My sister-in-law is a brilliant cook; my sister's so good, she could have her own restaurant; and my mother is brilliant as well. Me? Well, I'm really good with the drinks! I'm the talker as well, so I'm the one who's networking out front, while they cook behind the scenes.

LESLEY: That sounds like fun, Jane! Christmas has become a movable feast in the Garrett household and we usually tour at Christmas. We like to have it at home in London first and then a charabanc will head north. We'll go to Peter's family in Lincolnshire and then we'll have several days at my cottage in Yorkshire, visiting my sisters' homes, and my mum and my dad's homes. That means we'll have several more Christmases.

It's a major feat of organisation, which I take upon myself. I create an instant Christmas in Yorkshire by bringing a tree from home in the back of the car, along with all my Christmas cards, which are on ribbons, so that I can hang them up on the picture rails. We usually have Christmas dinner at the cottage as soon as we arrive. I bring the food from London and do a Marks and Spencer Christmas lunch, which is all pre-packaged. I just stick it in the oven and the microwave and then everyone turns up to eat it.

ANDREA: So is there lots of music in your household at Christmas?

LESLEY: Yes! I often do a BBC television series called *Christmas Voices*, so there are always lots of rehearsals for the series going on in the house. The kids have masses of music at school, so we go to their carol services. We also go to midnight mass in London on Christmas Eve, which I absolutely love.

SHERRIE: Do you drown out the rest of the congregation when you sing?

LESLEY: Usually I'm so tired by the time I get there that I'm a tiny whisper at the back! Anyway, the kids get terribly embarrassed if they can hear me above anybody else, so I get kicked and poked if I'm singing too loudly. If I'm at their carol services and they can hear me, I get dagger looks from them! It is the uncoolest thing in the world to have a loud mother.

ANDREA: And do you gather round the piano on Christmas Day?

LESLEY: Yes, we do, and when we get up to Yorkshire, we quite often go to the pub for a singsong. It's a lot of fun and my dad especially likes it. We also get together at my sister's and have a wonderful singsong there: one nephew drums; my brother-in-law is a very good guitarist; another brother-in-law plays the banjo and squeezebox; my niece is a fabulous flautist; my daughter will play saxophone or pipes; my son drums as well; and my sisters are fabulous doo-woppers; I, of course, am lead vocals! Everybody will bring an instrument and play it and sing. And Peter's indispensable at these occasions because he pours the drinks, which are absolutely vital for oiling the Christmas voice.

SHERRIE: What's your Christmas tipple then, Lesley?

LESLEY: Well, it's the only time of year that I drink sherry – and I drink it most of the days through Christmas! I like old-fashioned drinks as well, festive drinks that I would never drink at any other time of year, like snowballs, with advocaat, lime juice, lemonade and a cherry. This year I'm challenging my husband to devise a Christmas cocktail, because last year the kids bought him a cocktail shaker and glasses. I'm imagining something garnished with a sprig of holly or mistletoe.

ANDREA: Very festive! Like you, Lesley, I've always loved Christmas. I love it, love it, love it! The brilliant thing about it now is that Steve cooks – because I am a terrible cook, or at least very average, but he loves it. He loves all the preparation and spends ages looking through cookbooks and watching Jamie Oliver. Last year he was obsessed with doing really good roast potatoes, so he did trial runs for ages building up to the big day, which was great, because I like roast potatoes and we got to eat lots of them.

COLEEN: Yes, Ray's done the cooking for the last couple of years and I've been his assistant. He really loves cooking and I really don't, so it works out well that way!

DENISE: In our family, if we're home for Christmas, we all go to my sister Debbie's house in Northumberland. There are usually about fourteen of us and Tim and Peter, Debbie's husband, do the dinner, because they're better at it, and they enjoy it. But that means that Debbie and I have to do THE SHOP in THE SUPERMARKET. Kill me now! It's a huge thing.

ANDREA: It does sound like there are rather a lot of you! Steve and I make quite a good team. He's really good at the practical side and I'm very good at set dressing. So I make sure that everything looks nice and he cooks the core meal. The dining table's in the kitchen, the tree's in the kitchen and the playroom is just off the kitchen, so the hub of it all is the kitchen.

There's a long-held tradition in our family that you have to play The Carpenters' Christmas album at Christmas. One Christmas I couldn't find it and I got really grumpy, because I couldn't put up the tree unless The Carpenters were playing. Another tradition is to buy someone a very special Christmas bauble. When I was going through a hard time about five years ago, I had a party to thank all the people who'd looked after me through it. I called it an 'angels' party', because I felt they'd really taken care of me like angels.

So I bought them all a Christmas tree bauble with an angel on it and wrote a little poem on it: 'Every year at Christmas time/When you decorate your tree/Hang this little angel up/ And know that you are one to me.' I often get texts round about Christmas time saying, 'Just hanging your angel up. Hope you're still good.' It's nice to know that they'll have this little thing to hang up forever, in the knowledge that they really meant something to me.

COLEEN: That's a nice story! I love Christmas too, and that's down to my mum and dad. They always made it magical when we were little, even though they didn't have much money. I love the Father Christmas aspect of it, the Christmas tree, Christmas carols and the presents under the tree: I just love everything about it.

ANDREA: Does Ray love it as much as you do?

COLEEN: Yes, once the shopping's done! One of our best Christmases together, especially for Ray, was probably our first Christmas. He comes from quite small family – it's just him, his brother, his mum and dad – and he couldn't get over our first Christmas together, because all the family came to my house in Blackpool. He couldn't believe the presents under the tree, because we still buy for each other, each other's partners and all the kids as well, so the presents stretch from the tree halfway across the lounge! When everyone arrived in the morning, he was so emotional, because it was like the kind of Christmas you see in a movie. 'What's up with you?' I said.

'I've never seen anything like it,' he said. 'It's just fantastic! I know now why you love Christmas so much.'

LESLEY: Like you Coleen, I absolutely love Christmas and I make a huge deal out of it. We have several trees and it takes us a week to trim the house. The kids join in; one of their favourite things to do is to wind Christmas lights around the banister rails from the top of the house to the bottom, so there are three floors of lights with tinsel. That's the magic pathway they follow downstairs to where their presents are on Christmas morning.

I always make a trail of sparkly bits and arrows and bits of debris, like mince pies for Santa, and spilt sherry, and carrots for Rudolph. I've done that since they were little. They still get wild with excitement as they follow the trail, even though they're teenagers now. I always hear them thundering downstairs on Christmas morning.

LISA: How lovely! Me, I'm like a big kid at Christmas. I decorate virtually every room in the house. I have a tree in the dining room, a tree in the living room and trees with lights outside the front of my house. I absolutely go to town. I love it. Everything looks prettier with fairy lights on and it's an excuse to shop, isn't it? 'We need some more napkins; we need another tablecloth; we need another wreath. We need. We need. We need.' It's an excuse for me to completely over-indulge and I do, I'm ashamed to say.

Since everybody comes to us on Christmas Day, I think we need to do it properly. I want to make sure that all my friends and family get that Christmas feeling. Doing it properly, for me, is to have a tree when you're sitting at the dining table, reminding you that it's Christmas, and another one in the sitting room, so that wherever you go, you know it's Christmas.

COLEEN: I'm like you, Lisa. I turn into a child at Christmas. I still look out of the window every single Christmas Eve before I go to bed to see if I can see Santa. I'm always the first one up on Christmas Day and I run around the house yelling, 'He's been! He's been!' My boys now who are sixteen and twenty say, 'Mu-um!!!!' And I always have to play Christmas carols when I'm decorating the tree.

My mum used to cook for about twenty-four every Christmas dinner so she'd be in the kitchen doing all the food and my dad would always have Christmas music on, normally Sinatra's Christmas album, so we'd always have Sinatra playing and we'd sing and play games.

We were a family of TV addicts and we had the telly on twenty-four/seven as kids, but Christmas Day was the one day the telly was never on. Ever. This was partly because the TV had to be moved to fit us all in the room around three trestle tables. I loved the fact that for one day of the year the TV wasn't on. Instead we talked and sang Christmas carols. We spent hours over Christmas dinner and playing with our presents.

It's funny because most people can't understand why I don't want to watch telly on Christmas Day. I've had to give in to my husband and kids, because they love all the Christmas programmes, like the Christmas *Dr Who*.

'Let's sit down and play games,' I say. But apart from Ciara, who's too young to get a vote, I've got one teenager, one twenty-year-old and a husband who thinks he's a teenager, so I'm outvoted. In fact, I love Christmassy films: *Miracle on 34th Street*; *It's a Wonderful Life*; *The Santa Clause*; *The Polar Express*; and programmes like *Noel's Christmas Presents*, where he gives out the most amazing things. Lots of people say it's not Christmas unless you put the Queen's speech on, but I don't watch the Queen's speech and I never have. I always try and dress up a bit on Christmas Day.

ANDREA: And I always wear red. That's another family tradition.

LESLEY: And our most important family tradition is wearing the family pyjamas, which are covered in reindeer. I bought two sets each years ago and we still wear them all day on Christmas Day and Boxing Day. If visitors come, they just have to see us in our pyjamas! It's what we do. The kids just love it.

COLEEN: I'm in my pyjamas for most of Christmas, I must admit! That's because Ray will stay up until four or five in the morning on Christmas Eve to make sure that everything Santa has bought is built and ready for when Ciara comes down. Sometimes I'll say to him, 'Let's go to bed. We can do that in the morning while she's playing with something else.'

'No, I want it all done,' he says.

Last Christmas it was half past four before we went to bed, because he insisted on building the bike and the doll's house. He wants Christmas to be absolutely magical for Ciara, so he always writes a letter from Santa and puts it up the chimney for her to find in the morning. Every Christmas, I sit there and think, God, this is what real dads do!

So by the time my kids have opened their presents, it's about three o'clock and I think, Oh, I'd better get dressed now. But I usually buy a little Christmas outfit, a new dress or something. I can't imagine just wearing my trackies on such an important day of the year.

Much as I love Christmas, though, there's a part of me that also finds it very melancholy, for some reason, and I always did. I love it, but there is a sadness to it as well. Some of those Christmas carols make me sad. My mum died two Christmases ago and the year afterwards was very sad. You really miss the people who aren't there.

You've dropped the turkey on the floor! What do you do?

SHERRIE: In the earlier, happier days of my marriage, there were always around twelve people for Christmas day lunch and I always cooked an enormous turkey; my husband didn't do anything, needless to say. One day I was getting the turkey out of the oven and my arms just seemed to bend the wrong way under the weight of it. I saw the whole thing topple off onto the floor; it felt like it was happening in slow motion.

It was all over the kitchen floor and I just sat looking at it for a while. Then I thought, Well, nobody saw that and there's no way after all I've done that I'm not going to serve that turkey. So I picked it up, wiped it down and put it back in the baking tray, just slightly crusty. I was the only one who didn't eat turkey that day. Terrible!

LESLEY: Didn't they suspect anything? I'm quite good at improvising in these situations. For instance, if an omelette goes wrong, I turn it into savoury scrambled egg; if I drop the turkey, I just rinse it under the tap and whack it back in on high for fifteen minutes to make sure I've killed all the germs. 'Now this turkey is sadly misshapen, because it was a deformed turkey,' I say. 'Nobody else wanted it, but I decided that we would have it because we are all-inclusive in this family.' The kids completely buy it.

JANE: I'd do the same and pretend it never happened. What the eye doesn't see... Anyway, it's like Marco Pierre White's *Hell's Kitchen* in our house at Christmas!

COLEEN: I haven't dropped the turkey, but I once cooked it with the giblets still wrapped up inside!

JANE: Yuk!

There's a particular relative you don't like very much. But neither does anyone else, and if you don't invite them over, they will be on their own for Christmas. What do you do?

CAROL: I probably would invite them. I wouldn't say, 'Come over to Thailand!' I wouldn't invite them on my holiday. But if they were just up the road and on their own, I'd invite them along.

ANDREA: My relatives live in Scotland and luckily I like them all. But if someone lived quite close and I knew that they'd be alone, I couldn't *not* invite them. I'd feel bad, even if they were totally odious. I think maybe I'd try to invite a neighbour, or somebody they'd get on with, and put them together in the corner. Then they would have a lovely time without noticing that everyone else was having a lovely time without them.

LYNDA: I've done it to a degree with certain people in the past, so I probably would, because a little kindness goes a long way. As you say, Andrea: you can lose them in the general Christmas melee; they can be absorbed. My mum, God rest her soul, was absolutely brilliant about having stray uncles for Christmas. There was a funny old uncle who nobody wanted. Dad couldn't stand him. But Mum invited him and we all rallied round.

JANE: Good for your mum! I've got a soft spot for anything connected with family, so we have everybody who's on their own at Christmas over to ours and we just always have, because it's a bit of an open house.

You can't pick your family, but you can pick your friends, so I tend to change the rules as far as family is concerned. Saying that, I get on really well with all my relatives. I'm quite lucky.

My auntie comes, because she's on her own; she's always staying over. The great thing is that I really like older people. They can help you out so much, because they're so wise and they've got so much experience. 'Oh yes, that happened to me once!' they'll say.

You just think, 'Blimey, it's not just me that's been through this, then.' They've all done it, several times probably! I suppose that's why I like living with my mum.

SHERRIE: I haven't got any relatives now who people don't like. Most of my relatives get on. On the periphery there are people who I don't have to deal with. That's a different thing, but if somebody was on their own, I'd ask them over, unless they were a nasty old bugger, in which case I'd say, 'I'm sorry, but you're a nasty old bugger, so you deserve to be on your own!' There's no need to be rude or difficult, no matter what age you are.

If they are on their own and getting older . . . well, we're all going that way, aren't we? I always think, That's going to be me sitting there one day. I hope to God nobody ever says, 'Don't invite Sherrie! She's a pain. She never stops moaning.'

Hopefully, I'll be sozzled in the corner when I'm eighty, or standing on a table, telling stories.

JANE: I'm sure you will be, Sherrie, if you want to!

*Having reached the age of 36, Sue had really hoped she might have
grown out of Great Aunt Marjorie's festive jumpers.*

Your mother-in-law has spent the last two hours lecturing you on why your mince pies aren't as good as hers. Can you ever get on with your mother-in-law or is it a doomed relationship?

ANDREA: I definitely think relationships with mothers-in-law can work, but that does probably depend on the mother-son relationship. If a mother has a very healthy love for her son and she'll happily let him go, then she can have a good friendship with her daughter-in-law and it can be a lovely bond. But if she's hanging on and still trying to control her son, then it can be disastrous!

LYNDA: Yes, I think it's only doomed if neither person stands down. The mother, as the elder, should be able to compromise and keep it on a certain level; she should be able to avoid engaging in any conflict. It can happen at Christmas, because alcohol's usually involved and all the rest of it, but I'm very lucky with my in-laws now: they're absolutely charming and my stepdaughter and my stepson are lovely.

At Christmas, I would always grit my teeth and make it work, because I believe in Christmas, so everybody's going to bloody well do it right, for the kids and for the family. If you don't see each other for the rest of the year, it's just good to remind some people of their sense of family. It can give them something to think about and they might need it one day. So I would insist that we did it.

JANE: In my relationships, I've always got on better with the mothers more than the sons, which is a bit sad! One of my mothers-in-law couldn't speak English though, so that

was a bit difficult to start with. She was a formidable character as well, very strong. She brought up three sons and so she was the only woman in a house full of men for years. They were all six feet five, these men, so she had to be a strong character.

You got the feeling from her that nobody was good enough for her sons. Strangely, every time I went over to Denmark, I fell ill and took to my bed. I'm sure there was something psychological in it! I was like, Oh God, don't make me do this!

LYNDA: That doesn't sound like a coincidence to me!

JANE: No, well, she lived in a different country so I didn't have much to do with her; I had to put on a thick coat and get on a plane to visit her! But she still managed to have quite a strong influence over my husband, even though he often defied her. It was a difficult relationship, because he was Danish and his mother was Danish, which was always going to be a problem, because there was a huge cultural difference between us.

Class was a factor, too, because he was very upper-middle class and I was a working-class miner's daughter. I married out of my class and that was very hard for me. I've always said that you can't buy class – you've either got it or you haven't – but I really did feel out of my league with all of them. They were very clannish, as the Danes apparently tend to be. So I didn't fit in, even after I became his wife. It was a combination of everything.

COLEEN: I used to love Shane's mother coming over, because she used to tell me what I was doing was all wrong and then take over. I'm very nonconfrontational: anything for an easy life. So if you want to iron his shirts and cook his dinner, that's all right with me. I won't bother!

It's Christmas morning. Would you rather start giving [and receiving!] presents or do you just want to crack open the bubbly?

JANE: I love my stocking. Yes, I'm forty-six and I still have a stocking. My mother does mine and I do hers. On Christmas Eve, my mum, my partner and I have a special moment and give each other a special present. Then we have the family round on Christmas Day and open the rest of the presents.

LESLEY: Peter's the elf to my Father Christmas and I have carrier bags full of presents for different family members. There's the Yorkshire bag and the Lincolnshire bag. One of my worst Christmases was the one before last, when I managed to leave all the Yorkshire presents at home in London. I cried big tears from Lincolnshire to Yorkshire, because it wasn't until we set out from Lincolnshire that I realised I'd left the Yorkshire presents behind.

SHERRIE: Did you have to send them all by post when you got back?

LESLEY: No, because my sainted husband dropped us all off in Yorkshire and then turned round and drove all the way back to London to pick up the presents, then drove all the way back again. That was taking his elf duty to the limit! He rescued defeat from the jaws of Christmas disaster! So you could say it was one of the best Christmases because it was the Christmas I most loved my husband.

ANDREA: Wow, that was nice of him!

LESLEY: Wasn't it?

COLEEN: Amazing! I love the fact that for one day of the year people have to think about somebody else other than themselves. Ray hates it. He particularly hates Christmas shopping, as most men do. He doesn't do any of it, though. He just gets my present.

DENISE: Tell me about it! Normally I'm really, really busy in the run-up to Christmas, either with television or pantomime work. So there is no leisure aspect to my Christmas shopping. It has to be done in the three seconds I have in between shows, and wrapped at some point later. I remember doing a panto in Darlington with the Krankies and it was a nightmare, because Darlington didn't seem to realize it was Christmas and the shops shut at half past four. So I would rush out between shows, literally as the grids were coming down! Somehow, it's always just a real scramble for me getting ready for Christmas. Then your husband turns to you and says, 'Why are you so stressed?' and then he says, 'By the way, what did *we* get Aunty Florrie?' What did WE get Aunty Florrie! That drives me mad.

COLEEN: And Ray always moans, 'I never know what to get you.'

'No, you've missed the point,' I tell him. 'It's not about what you get me. It doesn't matter if it's a pair of bloody socks, it's the fact that for that hour – or for however long you've spent – you've thought about me enough to make the effort and go out. Also, I'm a bit of a child about presents, so it really doesn't matter as long as it's wrapped, because I love ripping the paper off.

Having said that, he's never let me down. I've always had loads of fantastic presents from him on Christmas Day. It's never just a case of, 'That'll do her.' He's always really over the top, which means a lot, because I know how much he hates it.

ANDREA: Ah, that's lovely!

COLEEN: He's just very special. I'm a very lucky girl.

ANDREA: And he's very lucky too.

COLEEN: He's more lucky! He's a pain in the arse at times and I'm not!

JANE: Do you always have to pretend you like something when you don't really?

COLEEN: Yes! Always. I've had presents that I've opened and thought, 'Oh dear!' but I always say, 'Thank you very much. I really appreciate that.' I would never turn round to somebody and say, 'I don't like

your present.' The fact is that they made the effort to get you something or make you something, so they don't need to know if you've ever worn it or used it or not.

I would never open a present and say, 'Oh my God, that is awful!' not even to my husband, and I would hope that he would never do that to me. I'm brilliant at pretending I like something. Perhaps, a couple of days later, I might say, 'Do you mind if I change it, because it doesn't fit very well?' or 'Do you mind if I change it for something else?' but it would never be a case of: 'Because I hate it.' I just think that's cruel. There's no need. I can change it quietly. My husband would never know if I wore it anyway: he doesn't pay that much attention. I'd just tell him I wore it when he wasn't there. To be honest, he hasn't bought me anything that I haven't liked.

LESLEY: I love all my presents with all my heart because I love the people who are giving them to me. Then, perhaps after Christmas, I'll have a little rethink . . .

CAROL: I usually pretend to like presents I don't like, especially if someone's put a lot of thought and effort into something. If people make that sort of effort for you, the least you can do is appreciate it. But if someone buys me a candle because it's easy – well, thanks! I'm not going to say, 'Oh my God, it's brilliant!' I think the whole present-giving culture is just completely out of control.

COLEEN: You're right. It is out of control. When we were kids, we got one toy each from Santa, unlike today, when children get two sack-loads each. I remember playing with that one toy all day. Every time, I absolutely adored it. When I became a parent, I thought that maybe I should keep up the one-toy tradition. But then my mum pointed out that we would have had more presents if they could have afforded it. But with eight kids and no money, they didn't have the choice. I love spoiling my children, although as they get older, their presents get more expensive. When they're younger it's about quantity not quality, but when they're older, it's about quality.

CAROL: We had a great time at Christmas when we were kids. We didn't have any money, but my mum always managed to scrape together enough to make it look like we had loads of presents. They were all in big piles in various parts of the living room. They were mostly board games and selection boxes; we never got bikes or anything, nothing flash. But we were fine with that, really happy with everything.

DENISE: I don't like presents, to be honest. I'd much rather give presents – and I'm not saying that in a Mother Teresa way. I'm just not bothered about presents. Christmas is about kids, isn't it? We always have our dinner on Christmas Eve, which is apparently a Scandinavian tradition. My mother has no links with Scandinavia, but we've done that for quite a long time and actually, it works much better that way. So we have dinner at about nine p.m. with all the children, which means that nobody has to spend Christmas Day cooking the Sunday dinner. The plan is for the children to go to bed and hopefully go to sleep, which is always a bit difficult with kids, and then the grown-ups open their presents at midnight, so that in the morning it's all about the children. We put out their ridiculously big piles of presents on Christmas Eve. You say, 'I'm

not going to spoil them this year,' and
then the huge pile comes out.

On Christmas Day, we have the cold
turkey and ham with chips or potatoes.
Tim does the most fantastic roast ham
with crackling. Then if people want
to pop in, they're not interrupting.
But I hate that as well: I hate people 'popping in'. Knock
knock: 'Yoo-hoo!' You think, I've never asked you round all
year, probably because you're not really my friend, so why do
you think you can just pop in at Christmas? 'Yoo-hoo! It's us!
John and Lisa!' But I don't like you! You're not invited! And
of course they've been to the pub, so they've got that pubby
cheeriness going on . . . oh God!!!

So I'm just so relieved when it's all over, although the
children have never been aware, as I've said. I'm not saying
that we haven't had some fabulous Christmases on the day,
but it's just the whole run-up that gets me. This is why, when
I was given the opportunity to go on a cruise two years ago, I
just thought, Yes! People say, 'Oh, it won't be the same on a
beach on Christmas Day'. But actually, it's blooming ace on
the beach on Christmas Day!

COLEEN: I know I wouldn't like it, though. It just wouldn't be
the same.

DENISE: That's the point. It's a total escape! It was especially
good last year, because we took the whole family. We took
Mum and Dad and Debbie and the kids. I loved being away
for Christmas. Debbie and I were nearly crying with the joy of
being away for Christmas. We forgot it was even Christmas

Day, you know? We didn't have to spoil the children, because they knew that the cruise was their main present. The only downside was that I wasn't with Matthew for the first time: it was his choice, because he was doing too many things with his band.

Louis was the little 'un and he wanted a Subbuteo set, so Santa got him a Subbuteo set and another couple of little things. He did have some drums when he got back, but it was great, because he knew that Santa could only leave a couple of things on the ship. In fact, he was so delighted with what he had, it just made me think: Why do we give them so much stuff at Christmas? It reminded Debbie and me of how we used to want something all year and we got one thing from Santa, like a doll. That one present was so important, but now they rip wildly through a pile of presents, saying, 'Oh thanks, Mum, thanks, Santa, thanks, Mum,' when you've spent a fortune on it!

JANE: I'm very lucky, because my fans send me some beautiful things. They really do the homework on what I like, so they find out what my favourite perfume is and what my favourite chocolates are; they're so fabulous. I've got a great PA called Pete, who lets them know everything. He knows me better than I do; he really gets my psyche. So he always knows what I'm going to want and what I'm going to need. Wouldn't it be brilliant if all men were like that?

ANDREA: Do you have groupies then, Jane?

JANE: Do I have groupies? Oh you've no idea! There are about twenty hardcore fans and they're mostly women, which is a bit weird. I've no idea what I put out, but it's obviously something. I think a few of them might even be in love with me and I'm very honoured and flattered that both sexes find me attractive in a certain way. For me it's a compliment if another woman fancies me. I would never follow it up, though. I couldn't – and I wouldn't know what to do. Flipping heck, I don't even know what to do with a bloke!

Do you go on pretending about Santa to the kids, even when you know they only half believe you?

DENISE: Oh God, I remember having this dilemma with Matthew! One year we went to Lapland with my sister and her kids. Well, I hate winter; but, actually I like *going to* winter; I just don't like it coming to me in England. In Lapland, we stayed in a log cabin that was so beautiful that when my sister and I first walked through the door, we started crying. If you could have painted a Christmas log cabin to be in with your children, this would have been it. There was a massive log fire and an open staircase and beautifully wrapped pretend presents around the tree. It was like something out of *Hello* magazine. We had two local women who came and cooked for us, which was heaven. And there were reindeer on tap, and Santa was there, and we went on skidoos.

Matthew was about eleven and he still believed in Santa, because I kept it going until around then. But not long before we went, he said to me, 'Mum, I just want you to tell me that there isn't a Santa Claus, because everyone is taking the

Derek looked sheepish as his wife unwrapped her present. He suddenly remembered that a new iron hadn't gone down too well last year...

mickey out of me at school. I know there's not a Santa Claus and I think I'm old enough for you to just tell me now.'

Well, I dread anything like this! I said, 'OK, there's not a Santa Claus,' but unfortunately that just made him cry, so of course I had to start back-pedalling. It was just awful. He knew really, but he just didn't want to hear it.

A couple of days later, we wrote letters to Santa with my sister's kids. The other kids wrote theirs, but Matthew said, 'I'm not writing one!'

'Just let the kids see you writing a letter,' I said gently. So he wrote one and I went off and photocopied it; when I gave it back to him, he threw it on the fire. I then secretly copied his handwriting perfectly, because I'm quite good at that, exactly replicated his letter, and gave it to Santa when we arrived.

One day we went on skidoos to a log cabin, where the door was opened to us by the 'real' Santa Claus! Debbie and I started crying again, of course, and then I noticed that Matthew was looking hard at him, really checking him out.

'I have a lovely letter from you, Matthew,' Santa said, and Matthew nearly fainted! He really couldn't believe it, because you could see that Santa was wearing normal shoes, but there he was with Matthew's letter from home. So he had another year of believing after that, which was great. It's never the same when you don't believe in Santa Claus, is it?

COLEEN: We visit Santa every year. One year Shane and I took the boys to Lapland the week before Christmas. We came back on Christmas Eve and it was magical. Ciara is desperate to go. She's always saying, 'Are you taking me to Lapland this year?' It is magical while they still believe, so I need to organise it soon. This could be her last year because they seem to stop believing at a much younger age now.

LISA: I think my little girl still believes in Father Christmas, aged nine, but perhaps she's stringing me along. Some of her friends at school have started saying that he doesn't exist, but she says, 'I understand why they feel that way, because why would you believe in somebody you've never met? But I've met him. I've been to his house in Lapland. I know he is real.'

She's done the Lapland trip with me and she's met the weirdo out there who dresses up as Santa. Unfortunately, she hit a tree while she was going quite fast on a toboggan because the barriers weren't in properly. Afterwards, we went to see Father Christmas and he said, 'Are you the little girl who tried to take down one of my trees with your head?'

'Santa knows! Santa knows!' she said.

'Oh, he knows everything,' I said.

Santa did a ho-ho-ho and said, 'Next time use an axe to take down a tree, not your head,' and everybody laughed. Then he looked at me and said, 'What do you want for Christmas, Mummy?'

'Me?' I said, and then, off the top of my head, 'Oh, a pair of boots.'

'High heels?' he said, his eyes glinting. 'What sort of boots would you like to wear? Describe those boots to me.' As I say, he was a bit of a weirdo and I'm not sure if I believe in Santa any more!

Have you ever disgraced yourself at a Christmas party?

LYNDA: I could disgrace myself all year round – it doesn't have to be Christmas – and I've done lots of that.

ANDREA: I've never snogged a colleague or anything like that, but I do cringe when I remember one *GMTV* Christmas party. Their parties were legendary and I loved getting very merry and dancing the night away with all the crew and the behind-the-scenes people, because you don't generally get to see them very often. One year I got really quite drunk and, unbelievably, I thought that it would be hilarious to tip a whole bottle of beer over a female producer I was very friendly with at the time. Of course, in reality it was an absolutely terrible idea!

She was chatting to this guy and I thought, let's play instead! So I crept up behind her and tipped my beer over her head. What an awful thing to do! When she turned round, I thought she was going to kill me; I thought she was going to smash me in the face with her bottle of beer. But she just tipped it over my head, much to my amusement. For some reason, I thought it was the funniest thing in the world, although normally I wouldn't find that funny at all; I'd storm off home and have a real sense-of-humour failure about it.

She was so angry with me and everyone else was angry with me, because the dance floor was wet and people were skidding all over the place and going, 'Whee!' I felt terrible the next day. The producer didn't speak to me for a couple of days, either. I still feel bad about it, so if she reads this, I'M VERY SORRY, AMANDA!

It wasn't until the next morning that Liz realised that snogging the work experience boy at the office Christmas party might not have been a good idea…

You've been invited to two Christmas parties on the same night: one will probably be really fun, but you feel obliged to go to the other, less fun party because you accepted the invite ages ago. Which one do you go to?

ANDREA: I'd show my face at the one I felt obliged to go to and make sure that they knew that I'd made the effort to go. I'd be quite honest and say, 'I've been invited to two parties tonight: I'm coming to see you first and I hope you have a lovely time.' Then I'd go on to the other one. If I couldn't go to both, I'd go to the one I was obliged to go to, because otherwise I would feel too awful. If I went to the fun one, I'd feel guilty all night and not enjoy it anyway, so I might as well go to the other one.

JANE: I'd go to the fun one, absolutely. Life's too short to spend it with miserable folk. I don't go out socialising very often because I'm out working all the time, so I'd get out of the dull party and go to the one I wanted to go to.

LYNDA: I'd go to the one I was obliged to go to. If it was anything to do with duty, I'd go to that one, because I'd feel too bad if I didn't. The good fun one would obviously involve people I knew well, or was close to, in which case I could repeat it anyway. And trendy premieres and first-night theatre-type parties are never good fun, so I wouldn't worry about missing one of those. You think they're going to be good fun, but I've never been to one that was.

DENISE: I would probably go to one I felt obliged to go to, unfortunately. That's just the way I am. I'm constantly doing things that I'm obliged to do. People say, 'Why don't you just ring them and say no?' But I'm just not very good at saying no, so I end up tying myself in knots because I feel obliged. Also, I couldn't bear it if they heard that I'd gone to the other party, the sex, drugs and rock-and-roll party around the corner! So I'd end up going to the boring party and trying to liven it up a bit.

How do you feel about panto – good old-fashioned fun or a real chore?

COLEEN: Don't mention panto! I've had sisters in panto for the last thirty-odd years and I've a lot of sisters. I went to see them all once and then I said, 'OK, I've seen you all in panto and I'm never seeing you again.'

Luckily, Ciara's school go to all the local pantos, so she doesn't miss out. But Denise could not get over the fact that I didn't take Ciara to see her in panto. She kept saying, 'I can't believe you're not bringing your daughter to see me!'

DENISE: I couldn't believe it, that's why!

COLEEN: And what did I say? 'Well, believe it, because I'm not!' I think pantomimes are great and I'm glad they're still around; they're part of a great tradition. But, honest to God, I've seen so many pantos! They all share the same script, no matter what people say. I've only ever appeared in one myself and that was enough: I was in *Dick Whittington* about eighteen years ago; I played Alice Fitzwarren.

Never again! It ruined Christmas for me because it's full-on hard work and the only day off you get is Christmas Day. I was so knackered that I pretty much slept through Christmas. I missed the whole build-up to Christmas, too, which is the bit I love: the shopping and putting the tree up. I love Christmas Eve but of course I had the panto on Christmas Eve. Christmas Day I was knackered and then on Boxing Day I was straight back to panto. That's it, I've done panto. It's just not for me. I love Christmas too much.

ANDREA: Well, we love going to panto. It's a nightmare with Amy because she's so little and she just runs up and down the aisles screaming, but luckily no one seems to mind. I love panto because the kids don't get half the stuff that goes on, which is just great. It makes you feel really Christmassy when you come out of the theatre after a panto.

How do you cope when you're faced with a really miserable Christmas?

COLEEN: The last Christmas I spent with Shane was horrible. I already had suspicions that Shane was probably seeing somebody but I didn't have the evidence.

We were spending Christmas with my family in Blackpool and, during dinner, Shane said he wasn't feeling well and left to go back to where we were staying. A couple of hours went by and I tried to phone him to see how he was getting on, but he was constantly engaged. At first I was angry, but then I started wondering if he was all right. What if he was really ill and his phone was just off or something? Eventually I went back to the flat and he was sitting there watching the telly, absolutely fine. 'Who have you been on the phone to?' I asked.

'My manager,' he said.

What, on Christmas night? I thought. Deep down, I think I knew. I just didn't want to face it.

We split up not long after that. It was my worst Christmas, when I realised that he didn't want to be with me any more. No Christmas has ever been as bad as that.

 It was hard splitting up, but at least I knew why we weren't together. It was all the not-knowing that was so soul-destroying, all the constant questioning: What is it? What am I doing wrong? 'I can handle you not loving me any more but, after thirteen years, you should at least like me enough to not want to put me through this,' I said. 'Just tell me what's happening, because then at least we can sort it out,' I'd plead. 'But I can't sort out what I don't know.'

It was so difficult, because at the same time he was constantly telling me that he loved me. I didn't know what to think. I was a mess.

ANDREA: How do you get over something like that?

COLEEN: Well, I hate the expression, 'All men are the same.' I don't believe in generalising. No, all men aren't the same. No two people are alike really, so it's unfair to tar everybody with the same brush. I'm one of these people who trusts someone until they let me down and then that's it, I won't trust them again. That was how it was with Shane. I gave him a lot of opportunities to make it right and he kept letting me down. Then I woke up one day and thought, You know what? I don't love you any more and I don't want to be here any more. At that point, it's too late: you can't win me back.

I think you can take something positive from a traumatic experience if you make sure that you learn from your mistakes. I think this is what has made my second marriage much stronger, because both Ray and I know where the line is in our relationship, whereas I don't think Shane or I ever knew where the line was. When I found out about the affair, he said to me, 'But you'll never leave me.' I genuinely believe that he didn't think I would. I think that's why he was so devastated when eventually I did, because he wasn't expecting it. But from day one, Ray and I knew where the line was: if you do this, then this is what will happen. Shane and I never had that discussion.

The one good thing that came of it, if there can be anything good that came of it, is that I became a much stronger, more independent and secure person. That means that my relationship with Ray is much stronger, because I'm not needy. God forbid that anything should happen, but if it did, I know that I can be a single parent, because I've already done it. I know that it will hurt for many, many months, but I'll get over it, because I've got over it before. Ray knows that and I think that he finds it attractive to know that I am an independent woman who chooses to be with him. It's the same with him.

ANDREA: So you're in a much happier place as a result?

COLEEN: Yes, I definitely am. What happened with Shane seems a long, long time ago and although break-ups are always difficult, I never forget that he is the father of my boys and we were together for a long time. It may not always appear that way, but I do try to focus on the positives.

ANDREA: That's true maturity! How about you, Sherrie? Have you ever had a bad time at Christmas?

SHERRIE: I've had several miserable Christmases. My husband wasn't really a family man. If I'd been the person that I am now, I would have told him exactly where to go and what to do with himself. But I was a much weaker person.

I remember one particular Christmas. Keeley was only about six or seven and Ken refused to go anywhere. We lived in Surrey at the time and all my family were in the North, but he didn't want to go and have Christmas with them. I remember ironing on Boxing Day that year! My husband had gone out and I stayed at home crying and ironing, feeling desperately unhappy and lonely, with my little daughter watching me. He was probably seeing someone else and off with another girl.

JANE: That sounds awful!

SHERRIE: I was only telling Keeley about it the other day. She said, 'But why didn't you get in the car and drive up North, taking me?'

'I don't know, Keeley, I really don't know,' I told her. I was just trapped in my unhappiness and Christmas became a really awful, horribly, lonely time for me, especially as my brother and the rest of the family were having a lovely family time somewhere else. The more unhappy I became, the more desperate and helpless I was, until finally I did insist on taking Keeley to see my family for Christmas. I should have left altogether, but I didn't have the courage.

Now Christmas for me is joyous again. All of that unhappiness is behind me and I make it a big occasion. It's always fun, a wonderful family time for those three days. There's no fighting; no television goes on; and I never iron on Boxing Day!

My brother lives in Wales, my mother lives in Nottinghamshire and my daughter is in Lancashire, but I make sure that everybody gets together. We all have busy lives, but I have my mother for the whole of Christmas and New Year and I make sure she sees everybody. I'm still doing my duty, but I'm doing it the way I want it, with no dictation from anybody else.

ANDREA: A happy ending! That's what we like to hear!

SHERRIE: Yes, because in the past it was very stressful, with argument after argument. So now I won't allow anybody to pollute my house in that way. If anybody starts an argument, or if there's an atmosphere, I'll say, 'Can you please leave?'

I don't care who it is, whether it's a member of my family or anybody else. If you cause tension, you have to leave my house, because I will not have it polluted. I had enough of that for twenty-five years, and I won't put up with it any more.

During the worst time in my marriage, I seemed to spend my life treading on eggshells, constantly being careful about what I said, always worrying: Is he upset? Is he in a bad mood?

I remember Keeley saying, 'Mummy, can we go out? I think Daddy is in a bad mood.'

So I'd take her out all day and we wouldn't return until the evening. We spent hours and hours in the car, going round and round, even when she was little. We went to parks and cafes; we walked around shopping centres; we did anything to avoid going home, so that she didn't have to put up with that atmosphere. That's why I won't have it any more in my house. I can't bear that horrible ache in your heart when it starts. It used to destroy me. It did me a lot of harm. It took me a long time to get over it. I can still feel it now.

It still affects me to this day to be honest. I'll be at a party and I'll see a girl on the other side of the room and think, 'Oh yes, Ken will be after her.' Then I pull myself up and think, God what am I doing? Stop it. I'm still doing it after all this time.

Nothing leaves you – particularly at Christmas time. It's a very hard emotional time. We see family we don't see for the rest of the year and sometimes people don't get on. People in families often don't get on. When you know they're not going to get on, you can always get sozzled and think, 'I don't care,' I suppose, but I'm not that kind of person.

I'm always the person in the middle, saying, 'She didn't mean that! She didn't say that.'

These days I say, 'You know what? Deal with it, because it's not my problem any more.'

I make it clear before people come on Christmas Day. If you start a row on Christmas Day, you do not deserve to have Christmas Day and you go. Go and have a row some-where else. If you come to my house, you can do anything you like as long as you're happy, jolly and have fun. But you do not create an atmosphere, cause an argument or have a go at anybody; otherwise you leave through that door, straight-away. Everybody knows that about me now. They come and have a good time and the music goes on, no upset. I had that for years, so I don't want it again.

JANE: It's good to make a stand! You'll be so much happier in the long run.

COLEEN: What about you, Andrea?

ANDREA: Well, my worst Christmas was the first year after I got divorced, because Finlay went to his dad's and I was on my own. It was beyond hideous. Anyone who has ever been divorced knows that when you do the year-on, year-off thing with your kids at Christmas, it's absolutely awful on your year off. It's actual physical pain not having your child with you at Christmas.

I just went to bed and pretended it wasn't happening until he got back and then we had our Christmas. My poor sister was staying with me and she had a really miserable time, because I wouldn't indulge in anything. It's got easier now that he's got a bit older, because we all know now that we hold off Christmas until Boxing Day and do it a day later.

LISA: It's all about family, isn't it? My mum and my ninety-five-year-old nan come to me at Christmas every year and it's very much a family thing. But one year I wasn't talking to my mum and so neither of them came. That was a really unhappy Christmas for me. I was so sad.

SHERRIE: What happened?

LISA: It's a long story! Mum and I are quite explosive: she was a single parent and I was an only child. I was brought up by my mother, my grandmother and my grandfather, so I had three parents who all had very strong personalities.

LYNDA: That all sounds rather complicated.

LISA: Believe me, it was. You see, in the early 1960s, my mum fell madly in love with this guy; the week she found out she was pregnant, she also found out that he was married and his wife was expecting a baby too. In those days, it was a really shameful thing to have a child out of wedlock. The fact you were having sex with somebody wasn't that bad, but only as long as you didn't get pregnant. If you got pregnant you got called all the names under the sun and my mum had a really tough time.

My grandparents were quite tough on her too, to the point where she was going to be sent off to a mother-and-baby home. Her case was packed by the door and she was about to leave when she said, 'I don't want to do this. I don't want to go.'

'I'll have a word with your dad and see what I can do,' my nan said. Apparently, my granddad was adamant that we didn't want to bring shame on the family.

Finally, they decided that mum didn't have to go and she could keep me. I didn't have a cot or anything, though. I slept in a drawer, because I wasn't really supposed to be around. Then, as time went on, I became the apple of my granddad's eye and my nan came to worship me – and still does to this day. But I think my mum had a very difficult time shaking off the shame that she felt. A lot of the problems I've had with my mum are born out of that very difficult time. I think Mum handled the situation as best she could, but it's had a profound psychological effect on me in so many ways that I didn't even fathom until I had a child of my own and began making decisions about parenting. There I was, thinking, What would my mum do?, and then I thought, Oh my God, I remember what she did. How odd! I would never do that.

But I think my mum would be the first to admit that she has struggled to shake off the shame she felt at the time surrounding my birth. We can trace many of our problems back to this. I felt her shame and it put a lot of responsibility on me. As a result, although she loved me and told me she loved me, I grew up finding it hard to believe people when they told me that they loved me, which is fundamental in life.

We've addressed this, talked about it and come out the other side, so I'm not saying anything against her. An example would be that there were times when my mum made me feel guilty about not making her feel special in a room full of people, because she felt so insecure. She would say things that would make me feel very small in front of others, to 'put me in my place'. I was confident and popular and all the things she wanted me to be, but often she wanted me to be that way because it validated her. 'Look at this wonderful child!'

'Isn't it great? You've done such a great job with her.'

When it stopped being about my mum she no longer felt validated through me; she felt left out.

She used to lie about things. My poor mum felt so much shame and insecurity that she didn't tell me that she hadn't married my father, because she thought that I'd be in some way disappointed in her. But I have no issue with any of that and never would. Finally, I don't think she does any more, but for forty-odd years she did.

So that was the kind of thing we fell out about. But although it was sad, the fact that we stopped speaking and spent that Christmas apart was in retrospect actually a positive thing, because it got so bad that we both had to do something about it and sort it out. It made us address everything and we've now come out the other side. We're incredibly close, actually; we get on fantastically well. We know each other better than anybody else knows either one of us.

ANDREA: Is there much of an age difference?

LISA: No, I'm forty la-la and she's sixty-seven now. But it was hard for her, because she was never able to be a mum in her own right, either. As she wanted to validate herself through me, in some ways she couldn't, because my nan and grand-dad were like my mum and dad and her role was a bit like my sister. So the roles were confused and my mum's identity was eroding. Fortunately, now she's finding out exactly who she is, which I'm really chuffed to bits about, because I've always been comfortable with the way I came onto this planet and I'm actually really proud of how courageous my mum has had to be.

Sorry Jane, you're a bit too big to sit on top of the tree

Curly always knew how to pull a Christmas cracker

Coleen gets into the Christmas spirit

Carol as an elf on Ant and Dec's *Saturday Night Takeaway*

Is it a bird?
is it a plane?
No, it's Coleen!

Denise brings
out the big guns
in her bid to
become Mrs
Iglesias

Christmas comes early
for Coleen as she gets
up close and personal
with Paddy McGuinness.
At least we think it's him!

Denise and Zoe fight it out over Santa

A special Christmas package for Coleen

Ooh err missus! Jane braves the elephant's trunk

From top right:
Carol gets a helping hand
from Leigh Francis;
Andrea perfects her
passport photo pose;
Carol tells it like it is;
Coleen gets a little more
than she bargained for!

From top left:
Carol gets a special Valentine's delivery; I'm a Loose Women get me out of here; the amazing Bette Midler joins the girls for a sing-along; Carol prepares for the holiday hangover; Nil Point. Lisa and Denise take on Eurovision!

Lynda, Lesley, Sherrie and Andrea get glammed up for a night on the tiles

Lisa and Sherrie show us
their catwalk moves . . .

Denise and Lynda work the cameras – watch out for the hand, Lynda!

Carol, Coleen and Jane stir up a scandal on Jonathon Ross

Carol and Andrea on *The Justin Lee Collins Show*

Watch out, here we come!

SHERRIE: Oh, that's so good, love. What a story! I remember the 1960s well and some of the social attitudes were still very rigid, despite what they say about it being a swinging, anything-goes era. But you both got there in the end, that's the main thing.

ANDREA: What about you, Carol? Have you ever had a miserable Christmas?

CAROL: The Christmas after my mum died was very sad. She died at the end of September in 2003 and I was in a pretty bad place for a while, so I just went away, on my own to Thailand. I wanted to be on my own because I didn't want to be with a lot of people, partying. That would have felt a little bit forced and contrived, I think. When I'm feeling low, I don't particularly feel like partying or drinking, because it just makes me feel worse. Then halfway through the holiday, some friends said, 'Come over to Australia!' and for some reason I did. I didn't have that good a time, though, because it was for a wedding and they were all very happy and I wasn't feeling particularly happy. I had an all-right time, but it wasn't great.

LINDA: It takes a long time to get over the death of a parent, doesn't it?

CAROL: Yes, I didn't realise it would take so long to get over my mum's death. You just have to let it work itself through and, for me, it took about three years until I started to feel normal again.

LYNDA: I had a very bad time over the Christmas after my parents died. They died within a month of each other in 2005 and so Christmas 2006 was the first Christmas without them. I'd never had Christmas without my family, never in my life, and it was very sad without them. The first Christmas after my sister died was also terrifically sad. So Christmas was a very specific time of year for me and it will always be tinged with sadness. But again, there will always be people to do it for, which makes it all worth it.

JANE: That's what keeps you going, isn't it?

SHERRIE: Were you sad the Christmas after your divorce, Carol?

CAROL: Actually, I wasn't miserable at all after my first marriage ended. It was weird because it was a bit of a relief and I felt quite liberated and free. I can't remember what I did that Christmas but I know I wasn't miserable. In fact, I was quite happy to be on my own because the whole marriage was just wrong.

ANDREA: Have you ever had an unhappy time at Christmas, Lesley?

LESLEY: Yes, my worst Christmas was when I lost my voice. I'm afraid it's another long story, like Lisa's!

ANDREA: Take your time; we're all ears.

LESLEY: I got married when I was a student to a really lovely man. He was the son of the organist and choirmaster at the church where I was the soprano in the choir. We were very happy while I was a student, but things changed when I became a professional singer and was suddenly offered a lot of work. Of course, I wanted to accept it all, because I'd been training for six years for this eventuality at the Royal Academy and at the National Opera Studio, so I said to my husband, 'I'm sorry, but I must go and do this work. I just have to; it's my destiny.' I knew I had to do it. I was twenty-six and had been married for three years by then.

Neither of us had expected that I would get so much work so soon. We tried to keep the relationship going, but I just went into another world completely. He was a school music teacher and we lived in a sweet little house in Tring; I quite literally just left it behind. I still feel guilty about it to this day. I just didn't have the wisdom and the skill to manage my relationship and my career. I worked and worked. I did every job I was offered, and I was offered a lot of work. In the meantime, I didn't look after myself: I lived out of a suitcase on girlfriends' floors and in cheap hotels.

I'd been touring with Opera North singing the role of Susanna in *The Marriage of Figaro* when I started to get really bad abdominal pains. I was in a lot of pain all of the time and struggled to get to the end of the run. Afterwards, I went home to my parents and it became clear that their relationship was breaking down.

JANE: That sounds like a lot to cope with all at once, love.

LESLEY: It was! But there's more. I went to see my parents' doctor and he said, 'I think you've got appendicitis. You need

to go into hospital straight away.' So my father took me to hospital and they admitted me. They were very close to ripping out my appendix and then they thought, Hang on, these test results don't really add up! They did an IVP X-ray, where they inject you with a dye to show up your kidneys and bladder. It was then they discovered I have a pelvic kidney. In other words, my right kidney is tiny and very shrivelled and in the completely wrong place, squashed between my appendix and my uterus, about nine inches too low and in the front of my body. Apparently it was very badly infected, so I was in hospital for some time while they dealt with the infection. It took a lot of sorting out.

I went to see surgeons who wanted to remove it. I was also told that it would be very difficult for me to have children, because the kidney was very close to my uterus and in the way of the birth canal. The combination of the breakdown of my first marriage and the various factors of this quite serious illness meant that I totally lost my voice. I couldn't sing; I didn't know how to sing; I couldn't remember how to sing. I just lost the will to do it.

So that was the worst Christmas ever: I was at home with my parents, who were going through a very bad time in their relationship; I couldn't speak; I just didn't think I'd ever sing again; and I'd lost my husband. I'd lost my way in life, in fact, and I was really sad. I cried a lot; I was really low. Thank goodness that my two younger sisters were there, because they are great and I'm very close to them.

My singing teacher, Joy Mammen, saved my life. She's still my singing teacher and my dear friend to this day. I cleaned her house and in return she gave me singing lessons for free. Over the next nine months, we very gradually found my voice again, although it was never the same. I never again had the confidence that I'd had before just to sing anything. I used to be able to throw my voice at anything and it would respond, but now my voice became very careful. It became like a third child. I often think of my voice as a third child.

I always wanted three children but I wasn't able to do it. My two children were actually my two last eggs. I didn't have a period after Chloe, my second, and nine months after she was born I started having hot flushes. That was it! I went into a very early menopause, just like my mum had, only she forgot to tell me. Apparently, it runs in families.

It was funny, because when I was carrying Jeremy, my first, they did the blood test that determines whether you need to have an amniocentesis test for Down's syndrome. I was thirty-seven, so they thought that it would be unlikely I'd need the amnio, but the blood test results came back saying that there was a one-in-sixty chance that I'd have a child with Down's syndrome, which was more likely for somebody in her mid-forties. We couldn't understand it. It wasn't until after I had Chloe that I realised that my ovaries were saying, 'It's later than you think, honey!'

Strangely, when I had Jeremy, I had an overwhelming urge to be pregnant immediately. I just had to be pregnant again. It was almost like a bereavement that I was no longer pregnant, that I no longer had a child inside me. What's more, I had a Caesarean with Jeremy and it took a little while to get over that, physically and psychologically. Then I got pregnant as soon as I could, without telling my husband. There's only fifteen months between my children!

JANE: That's another nice happy ending! How about you, Denise? What's yours?

DENISE: My worst Christmas was the first Christmas that I didn't go home; I was in my twenties and appearing in my first pantomime. I was in digs in Bury St Edmunds, and it was too far to go home on Christmas Day, because I had two shows on Boxing Day. I was staying in a family house and the people sort of invited me to join their family Christmas, which was really nice of them. But I didn't know them and I felt so lonely, so when my gay friends Lester and Paul said, 'Why don't you come and spend Christmas Day with us in Brighton?' I said, 'OK!' It was still a journey, but not as far as going home.

On Christmas Eve, I started feeling really fluey, but I thought, I've got to go to Brighton! I've got to drive there! So I got up on Christmas morning and it was absolutely terrible weather. I had an old Hillman Avenger, which cost me about two hundred and fifty pounds – Tim always says it was two-tone blue and rust – and I started on my way to Brighton, freezing cold, because the car didn't have a heater.

I was halfway there when a stone landed on my windscreen and smashed it. Suddenly, I couldn't see anything. I swerved off the road onto the hard shoulder; fortunately, I didn't hit anything.

In the freezing-cold rain, shaking like a leaf, I tried to punch out the broken glass. But I couldn't dislodge it. It was in the days before mobile phones, so I trudged off to one of those yellow phone boxes to call for help. A call-out on Christmas Day! For the next two and a half hours, I sat in the back of the car, shivering in my coat, waiting for someone to come.

When he did eventually arrive, he charged me a hundred and ten pounds to fit a new windscreen. I remember it so well, because it was my entire wages! I had to hand him my little brown wages envelope.

I carried on to Brighton, arrived at Paul and Lester's house and burst into tears, because it was the worst Christmas ever. Nothing they could say or do made me feel better, so it completely ruined their Christmas, too. I felt incredibly poorly by this time. I felt so dreadful that I couldn't even enjoy my dinner. The next day, despite still feeling very poorly, I got up early to drive back for my matinee, because you don't have an understudy when you're in a local pantomime, of course.

On the way back, the brakes went and I had to pull over. Since I had no money to call anyone out, I had to drive the rest of the way at about one mile an hour, pumping the brake. I just about got to the theatre in time. Well, during the matinee, I was halfway up the beanstalk when I fainted and fell to the floor. Curtain down! I ended up in the hospital with pleurisy, desperately moaning, 'I have to get back to the beanstalk!' It was definitely my worst Christmas ever!

ANDREA: Oh dear, that sounds horrendous! What about you, Lynda? Have you got a sad yuletide tale?

LYNDA: Well, I had several miserable Christmases when I was married to my second husband. It was all about control – letting your family know that you're in a bad mood and you're not speaking to them, so that the umbrella of darkness descends upon the house in the run-up to Christmas, which gives you pleasure, because you know your wife loves Christmas. You deliberately ruin it. Where before there was an air of anticipation, now there's a threatening air and it feels like everything is all going to go wrong.

There was a year when I knew he was not speaking to me. I also that knew his temper could turn on a sixpence and a row could erupt. So on Christmas Eve, as I was wrapping everything up, I was listening for the footsteps, the key in the door and the door opening with a terrible sense of foreboding. There I was doing all those things that in my psyche have always meant happiness to me, like wrapping the presents, listening to carols and having a glass of champagne, but there was no joy in it at all. In fact, I was thinking, I'd better not have any more champagne, because if I'm a bit drunk, it will make things worse.

I'd be hoping that nothing got broken, that the tree didn't get knocked over. Then I'd go to bed and lie there and wait until I heard the key in the door; it would be a huge relief if nothing happened. But he still wouldn't be talking to me when I got up to cook in the morning, so it felt like I was playing this game of pretend. It felt like I was walking on eggshells. 'Right, we're all going to open our presents now!'

I'd do the turkey, the gamut, with all the trimmings, and then the Christmas pudding, the Stilton; every single course was perfect, but one year he took his plate of food into the other room and watched television. Meanwhile I went through all four courses, on my own, in the kitchen, with the candles going. It was grim. The boys were running around and I didn't want them to notice that there was anything amiss, so I just said, 'Go on then, as it's Christmas . . .' and I left them to play. It was very difficult. I cried a lot that year.

ANDREA: How awful for you! Christmas can be a very unhappy time, as these stories show.

LYNDA: But I always think that it can also be a time of renewal and hope, so it's important not to dread it, because you never know what it may bring this year.

ANDREA: Wise words!

Chapter 6

Happy New Year!

Party like it's 1999

New Year's Eve should be the best night of the year. But how many of us have spent weeks planning it, bought a shiny new outfit and shoes we can't walk in, and then on the actual night, drunk so much you've fallen asleep by quarter past ten, had a row with your other half and then spent the first four hours of the new year trying to get a taxi home.

Yep, we've had a few of those . . .

But New Year is also an opportunity to start afresh – to leave behind the disappointments of the year before and emerge like a butterfly gliding into the new one. Well, that's the plan anyway!

Every year on 1st January we write a list of resolutions – usually exactly the same ones as last year – and fully intend to ban all bad habits, lose a stone and always be nice to everyone.

But then we realise it's January. And January really is the most depressing month. It's blooming freezing, there are no parties to look forward to, it gets dark just after lunch and we're feeling fat after Christmas.

It's enough to drive anyone to the biscuit barrel . . .

New Year's Eve: party like it's 1999 or stay at home and see it in with Terry Wogan on the telly?

JANE: I've had some belting New Year's Eves. The only thing is that, being an entertainer, I'm usually working on New Year's Eve. Still, that can be great, because you're creating the atmosphere, whipping everybody up into a frenzy. I think my best New Year's Eve was some years ago, back when I didn't live with my mum, but I was only down the road. I'd done this club in Wakefield and all the family and all my mates had come. Then everybody came back to my house for a party. It was great! I love parties and I like having people round.

ANDREA: Have you ever had a New Year's Eve that you didn't remember?

JANE: Fortunately not! I never get that drunk. I like a drink, but I'm never out of control. I get very merry and then I stop. I've got a cut-off button, which a lot of people are not blessed with.

COLEEN: New Year's Eve is an absolutely mammoth excuse to get trashed, but I'm not a drinker or, at least, I don't get smashed. So I wouldn't care if there wasn't a party on New Year's Eve because it's all about people getting horribly drunk. I used to get smashed in my youth. I had my head down the toilet enough times to think, 'I can't do this any more.' I reached that point very early on, while I was young. I didn't like that feeling and so I'll have a drink now, but I don't get drunk. I might get a bit tipsy, but that's the point at which I stop drinking and put the kettle on.

I hate feeling drunk and I hate feeling sick, headachy and knackered all day the next day. It just doesn't seem worth it. I'd never stop anyone else getting smashed, though, and we usually have a party that goes on until about eight the next morning, or we'll go to one.

I love watching everyone having a good time, but of course the next day they're all like zombies. Meanwhile someone has to clean up and make breakfast. Ciara is seven, so she still wants you to play with her Christmas toys and I'm the only one capable of doing it, so I get a bit annoyed. Ray loves New Year's Eve, but if he genuinely said to me, 'You don't have to come if you don't want to', I'd be quite happy to stay at home. The only time I want to be there is at midnight, to say Happy New Year to him and the kids and give them a hug and a kiss. But then I'd be quite happy to say, 'Night, then!' or, 'I'm putting the telly back on now.'

CAROL: New Year's Eve is always good for me. I quite often don't make it to midnight because I'm a lightweight and can't take my booze, but I still have a good time. We usually have a few beers on the beach during the day and go out in the evening, so I'm probably fast asleep by eleven p.m. Last year I was awake, though.

ANDREA: Yes, and we all know why!

LYNDA: In the old days, I hated New Year's Eve, so I didn't party as much as you'd think. I went to bed a lot. New Year's Day was often the one day of the year that I didn't have a hangover.

I hate that false happiness. To me that is real pretending.

 New Year's Eve is a classic example of going out with false expectations: you always think you're going to have a wonderful time, but you very rarely do. I hate the idea of standing in a room full of strangers who then stick their tongues down your throat or hug you at midnight! You're thinking, Who are you? The next day I invariably rang my parents in tears from wherever I was. I wonder, did I ever really believe that all the tragic things in my life would transform overnight, just because it was a new year?

I've had lovely New Year's Eves in the last three or four years, though. We've been all over the place and had jolly times and quiet times. A couple of years ago, we spent New Year's Eve having an amazing meal in a restaurant in Valencia. We saw in the New Year in Valencian style, with grapes; as the clock strikes, you eat a grape, for some reason!

In Naples, they all make their own fireworks, which would horrify Health and Safety here. You're in the high rises, on your balcony, and it's like being in war-torn Beirut. It's so exciting. I remember being in my sister-in-law's flat in the foothills of Vesuvius one year and looking at Vesuvius, while all these home-made explosions went on all around me, thinking, That's a big bloody firework!

ANDREA: I like Christmas, but I don't really like New Year's Eve. I don't like the enforced feeling that it's supposed to be amazing. My idea of a nice New Year's Eve would be to go to the local pub, count in the New Year and then come home. I wouldn't want to go to a great big organised party, because it's just hellish and you can't get home.

LESLEY: A local party is infinitely better! We always go to my dearest friend Mandy's New Year's party, if we can possibly make it.

ANDREA: So do you like New Year's Eve?

LESLEY: Yes, New Year's Eve is a time of great excitement for me. It has an incredible significance, because my first child Jeremy was born two weeks early one New Year's Day. And every year we relive the memory of his birth, because Chloe and Jeremy always want us to tell the story again.

ANDREA: I've got a feeling this is going to be good!

LESLEY: The story begins with the most wonderful New Year's Eve party at Mandy's house. This particular year, I very naughtily consumed rather a lot of Mandy's extraordinary sherry trifle, so when I woke up with an awful pain in my stomach at three a.m. on New Year's Day, an hour after I'd got to bed, I immediately thought, Oh my God, I shouldn't have had all that sherry trifle! Then, after a couple of hours, when the pain began to come every three minutes, I thought, Oh no! This is not sherry trifle. This is a baby!

I got out of bed, packed a bag and started cleaning the house. I decided that there was no point in waking up Peter, because he was just going to have the mother and father of all hangovers, so he wouldn't be any use to me anyway. When he finally woke up, I was in the back bedroom of the flat where we lived at the time, huffing and puffing on all fours. 'What are you doing, love?' he asked. 'Are you moving furniture?'

'No-ah-I'm-ha-having your baby!' I yelled.

I heard a thud as he fell out of bed. Then he rushed through into the bedroom and it was like something out of *Dad's Army*: 'Don't panic, Mr Mainwaring! Don't panic!' Peter's a GP-obstetrician, but all he could say was, 'We've got to get you to hospital!'

'You may have forgotten sweetheart, but this is my first baby,' I reminded him. 'It's going to take a lot longer than this, you know it is.'

'But your contractions are coming every three minutes!' he said.

'You don't need to tell me!'

It was about midday by the time he got me into hospital, where they couple you up to a machine that confirms you are in labour and you think, Oh get lost! I know I'm in labour! I've been having contractions for nine hours!

Coincidentally, in the early evening, BBC2 was televising an opera that I had recorded nine months before, called *Street Scene* by Kurt Weill. It was on in the common room of the labour ward. By this time, I had discovered that the best way to have a baby is to sing, and so I was singing through my contractions, because operatic breathing is the same as the breathing for giving birth. Not a lot of people realise this, but I did!

Every contraction had a massive arpeggio and a top C, so everyone knew where I was. All these nurses kept poking their heads round the door and saying to each other, 'You know that woman in Room Two? She's on the telly in the common room, quick!' So I was in two places on the labour ward.

After eighteen hours in labour, I simply wasn't dilating; I'd got to two centimetres and stuck. I did the maths and worked out that at this rate I'd have to be in labour for the rest of the week if I were going to get to ten centimetres dilated!

DENISE: That sounds bad! Were you OK?

LESLEY: Finally, they gave me an epidural and it all calmed down, so I sent Peter off to get some food, because he'd had nothing to eat all day. He went off to find a sandwich, which on New Year's Day was quite an undertaking, and just after he left, my waters broke! A load of meconium came out too, which meant that Jeremy was in distress. So the registrar said that I had to have an immediate Caesarean.

Just after that, the most gorgeous Hawaiian anaesthetist turned up and said, 'I think you need some opiates.'

'You're damn right, honey,' I said.

He gave me this stuff that made me very happy indeed and they wheeled me into the operating theatre. Then, just as Jeremy was being delivered, Peter burst through the door in floods of tears. It was just like *Casualty*! Poor thing, he'd got back to where I'd been in labour, discovered I wasn't there and thought I'd died. It took a while for him to find out where I was and he rushed in just as Jeremy was being lifted out.

He was in tears; I was in tears: it was so romantic! He came over and gave me a big kiss and I said, 'Never mind about me, sweetheart. Go and look at the baby.' Jeremy wasn't crying at that point and they had to work on him to get him going. Soon Peter came back holding him and we cried again.

Just at that point – it was eight thirty by then – *Street Scene* came to an end in the common room. 'Oh darling,' Peter quipped, 'trust you to be making curtain calls in two theatres at the same time!'

ANDREA: That's a brilliant story. What a drama! So you like New Year, then?

LESLEY: Yes! It's one of my favourite times of the year!

It's New Year's Day!
Do you detox or retox?

LYNDA: Never mind the detox, just get though New Year's Day!

ANDREA: There's absolutely no point trying to be good on New Year's Day, because you feel so awful. So I think New Year's Day is a day for hoovering up all the leftover chocolates and half-drunk bottles. You might as well clear everything out, because the detox starts a few days later. I try and recover gently from the excesses of December in January. I don't do a massive detox, because I think it's a bit pointless really, but I do try and calm down a little bit.

SHERRIE: New Year's Day is a funny day. I've always thought that it would be far better to have a party on New Year's Day, because everybody's always depressed. It's definitely one of the most depressing days of the year. Christmas is over, there aren't any more presents, the run-up to New Year's Eve is in the past. It's a case of, 'Bloody hell, it's January now!' I hate January. So I think you should start January with a big party at lunchtime on New Year's Day, with lots of lovely food and champagne, or sparkling wine.

JANE: I'm with you there! I say: keep eating, especially if you've still got a load of stuff in. You've still got that fantastic pork pie and there's all that lovely trifle stuff left. I really let myself go at Christmas and New Year.

I don't diet: I just cut down if I want to lose a pound or two. That's because I'm a rebel, so if you tell me that I can't have something, I'll have twice as much of it! I can't diet for the life of me. Instead, I think, well I'll have that sandwich, but I'll only have half of it. I tend to cut down later in January and February.

CAROL: I just carry on and re-tox usually, because it's a holiday. You don't have to go to work the next day.

COLEEN: I always start the New Year with a new fitness regime and these days I manage to stick to it! And I get through the grey winter months by telling myself that it'll be spring soon.

ANDREA: I understand why divorces and suicides peak in January, because you put yourself and others under so much pressure at that time of year. I don't know why you expect people to behave differently at Christmas than they do the rest of the time, but you do. You hope that people will put petty things to one side; you know, peace and goodwill to all men? So when they don't, it's really disappointing.

I know it's unrealistic and perhaps you shouldn't expect it of people, which means that you have no right to be upset about it afterwards, but that's what happens, in a lot of cases. I think that's why there are a lot of problems in January, because we hope things will be better and – to be honest – human beings are fairly weak creatures and it's normally not better.

CAROL: Yes, it's probably because people build the Christmas season up into something that it's not. It doesn't help that it starts at the beginning of November now, so people are working up to this massive event that is just not particularly exciting. Then, when it's all over, you realise you've spent all that money, you've eaten all that food and you've drunk all that booze, and now what? It's a total anticlimax.

Actually, Christmas is probably a bit like booze, in that it's an enhancer. So if people are feeling happy, Christmas is great, but if they're lonely and they don't spend Christmas with anyone, it highlights their loneliness and causes sadness and depression.

JANE: It's such an anticlimax, isn't it? It's another New Year, you've got all the debts from Christmas, everybody's been and gone and you just think, I've got three months of grey, cold debt ahead of me. Oh, let's all just shoot ourselves now!

CAROL: I'd rather go on holiday and just miss Christmas and New Year altogether!

SHERRIE: Well, I think that New Year should be a time of hope and anticipation. My advice would be to wear bright colours and focus on the fact that spring is on the way!

As the memories from the night before flooded back to haunt her,
Judy spent the 1st January writing her new year resoltions.
Top of the list: Thou shalt not drink

New Year's Resolutions – does anyone ever keep them?

COLEEN: I used to make them, but I don't any more, because I've totally forgotten them by the second of January.

SHERRIE: I make the same resolutions as everyone else – I always say that I'll lose weight, I'll do this and that – and within two days I've broken them. But then I make New Year's resolutions every week and nothing changes. Every week I say the same thing: I must lose weight, I must join a gym; but I never do it. I'd probably go once and it would be a huge waste of money.

CAROL: I've had the same New Year's resolutions for about the last twenty years and I never follow any of them through, so I don't even bother thinking about it any more. I can't remember all of them, but two were to write a book and learn to speak French.

ANDREA: I can never decide which one to make. Then New Year passes and by the time I've decided on my resolution, I realise I've already failed and it's February!

JANE: I've made loads of New Year's resolutions and I've never kept any. They include: I'll get thin; I'll go to the gym; I'll learn a new language; I'll be nicer to people. All the things you say in a drunken moment, and then think Ah, sod that – life's too short!

Chapter 7

Winter Dressing
Work your wardrobe

As the nights draw in and we reach for the comfort food, we can feel very different about our bodies. In summer we tend to show off a bit more flesh, but the wonderful thing about winter dressing is that you can keep everything under wraps for a while.

But however cold it gets, it's still important to look good.

If you care enough about yourself to make a bit of effort then others see that and take notice. At the same time though, one of the things we really love about winter is the opportunity to curl up on the sofa with a mug of hot chocolate, ideally in front of a roaring fire and wearing our cosiest pyjamas and big furry slippers.

It's just that every now and then you have to pull out all the stops and in this chapter we'll share our secrets for looking hot even when the weather's definitely not!

Would you freeze for fashion?

COLEEN: I hate to say it, but yes. I remember going out many a time in my youth and my mother saying, 'You'll catch your death of cold! Put a coat on.' I'd look at her with horror.

Q: Why is winter better than summer dressing?
A: Layers, layers and more layers!

You just don't take a coat when you're young, do you? Not only was it uncool, but I couldn't be bothered queuing up for the cloakroom. I'm better now, in that at least I bring a coat occasionally. But if I'm going out in a lovely evening dress, I don't want to ruin it by putting a Parker over it, so I say to myself, 'Oh well, I'll just be straight out of the car into the venue.' Being a smoker, though, I spend half the night outside smoking, so I freeze, unless I nick my husband's jacket, which I normally do.

DENISE: I should say yes, because I'm a Geordie and in Newcastle it's illegal to wear a coat. I'm sure that you actually get arrested if you walk along the quayside in Newcastle wearing a coat. It happens in every major city, but in Newcastle it's legendary. It appears that the colder the weather gets, the skimpier the costumes get. I've seen girls standing at the bus stop on New Year's Eve in the middle of a blizzard wearing sleeveless tops, with corned-beef legs and a fag out. They will not wear a coat! I can understand it if you're going from bar to bar; but they're not just going from bar to bar, they're walking the full length of the town and then standing at a bus stop for half an hour at the end of the night.

SHERRIE: Brrr, it makes me cold just thinking about it! Two young girls stopped me the other night for an autograph. It was very, very cold and they were both wearing tiny little miniskirts and tiny tops. There was nothing covering their arms or legs.

'Aren't you freezing?' I asked one of them.

'Absolutely frozen to death,' she replied.

'It doesn't make sense,' I said.

'I know,' she said listlessly. And off she went to the next bar, chilled to the bone.

Maybe it's something you do when you are young, because looking good is more important than feeling good. But these days, I won't go through that. I'll slam the heating on whenever I want, without hesitation. I have to be warm.

DENISE: I've never been as bad as that and I would no longer freeze for fashion, not in a million years. I have to be warm now; the cold actually makes me cry, so I would definitely have to take my coat, even though I wouldn't be planning on standing at a bus stop, I'm not quite as nesh – or delicate, as you say down South – as my mum and sister Debbie, though. I don't know how Dad has managed to live in that house with Mum all those years: you could literally grow tomatoes down the side of the settee. She takes her electric blanket to Spain and puts it on at night when it's thirty-five degrees! So I'm not quite as bad as them, but that's the kind of house that I come from, so it's not surprising that I can't bear being cold. I even wear thermal underwear for work, although I don't think I'd wear it on a night out.

LISA: Oh God, I used to freeze for fashion, but not any more. I used to go out in some ridiculous clothes in my twenties. I went to Stringfellows every night when it first opened...

JANE: Stringfellows?

LISA: It was *the* club in those days, don't you remember? It was where everybody went; it wasn't a lap-dancing club back then.

I'd just left Italia Conti and I used to go star-spotting there, every single night. I didn't have any money, but blokes used to buy me drinks and dinner. It was a really fun time.

One night I went out in a pink and white 1950s gingham swimsuit; it had a white ribbon halter neck and was all ruched across the front. It was cute rather than sexy, but it's still hard to believe that I went out in it. I wore flat silver pixie boots with it. I never wore high heels with an outfit like that because I didn't want to look too rude.

My granddad was alive then and he just couldn't understand it. I remember him saying, 'Go and put some clothes on! You can't go out like that.'

'All right,' I'd say, and I'd pretend to run back upstairs and put something on. Then, when he wasn't looking, I'd dash past the living room and out the front door. I used to freeze coming home at night, wandering the streets in a 1950s swimsuit, freezing me legs off, although I didn't actually feel the cold, probably because I was under the influence of alcohol.

These days, I wear thermals. I never used to go on cold holidays, because I didn't want to wear cover-up clothes, but now my favourite thing is to go to Cornwall in the winter and walk on the beach or in the hills. I love wrapping up warm and putting on as many layers as possible. But in my twenties and thirties, the idea of doing that was just torture. I hated putting on really unattractive clothes and having to brave the cold.

SHERRIE: We all suffer for fashion, don't we? But if I'm going to a do and I'm wearing a pretty dress, I will always have a coat with me. I take it off for photographs, but I'm never without it. I won't suffer in the freezing cold.

CAROL: I couldn't care less if I turned up at a premiere in a parka or an anorak, because I can't bear being cold. It's more miserable than being hungry or tired for me. So I won't freeze for fashion, absolutely not!

JANE: I absolutely would not freeze for anything, because I'm miserable when I'm cold. Once again, cashmere is good for keeping warm. Oh, what am I like? I would always take a shawl out; I also have a lot of shrugs that I just throw over. They look very stylish. Someone crocheted me a gold-threaded shrug and it's absolutely fantastic; I've worn it so much. I was wearing it the other day and Carol said: 'Who have you come as? You're a bit overdressed for the daytime.'

I said, 'Darling, you can never be overdressed!'

SHERRIE: Jane, you always manage to arrive in style in winter. You have a coat on in the car, don't you? But it will be gone before she gets out. You always wear the most beautiful long dresses, too.

JANE: You are kind, Sherrie! Thank you for saying that.

LESLEY: I couldn't go out if it didn't look right, so I think I would suffer. Otherwise, I'd just feel uncomfortable. I'd still find a way of making sure I was warm, though. I have many memories of singing oratorios in freezing cold churches wearing fabulous damask dresses, with Damart thermal underwear and lots of pairs of tights underneath. You find ways. You have to. I'd wear a wrap of some kind, but I baulk at the term 'shawl'!

JANE: Well that's the word we use where I come from!

LESLEY: Still, there are some really fabulous fake-fur stoles and stone-encrusted wraps.

ANDREA: But didn't you once take all your clothes off on stage, Lesley?

LESLEY: More than once, actually! Yes, about fifteen years ago, I appeared in an opera called *Die Fledermaus* at the English National Opera, in which I had to take my kit off.

JANE: Completely?

LESLEY: Completely! I've never had a problem with naked-ness, to be honest. I basically paid my way through the Royal Academy of Music by posing as a nude model twice a week. That's how I lived. So I wasn't bothered about appearing naked on stage.

JANE: Rather you than me, love!

LESLEY: The costume I took off to reveal my nakedness was fabulous. It was at the time Madonna was wearing the Gaultier brassiere and I had this fantastic corselet with a wonderful great pointed conical brassiere top, which I then whipped off. It was the best fun. People often said to me, 'But what did your husband think?' Well, he didn't think anything of it at all. My husband is a GP and sees naked women all day, every day!

SHERRIE: What about your parents?

LESLEY: My dad didn't come, but my mum came and laughed. The furore that bit of nakedness engendered was just a mystery to me. It was perfectly clear in the script that was what the character needed to do.

Actually, it was a godsend for me, because I'd had a bad car accident the week before we were meant to start rehearsals, about six weeks before we opened. I broke my breastbone and some ribs down my right-hand side, which made singing top notes very difficult. You have to brace for a top note, which involves a connection between the back and the chest, and that was really painful. Well, I was supposed to sing a top C the moment that I ripped my kit off and I was able to avoid it because I facing upstage. I turned and threw my corset into the wings in place of singing this big crescendo with a top C. Getting out of singing that note was all I cared about, and so I was more than happy to take my clothes off on stage! I was hoping that at least the public would feel they got their money's worth.

COLEEN: I'm sure they did, after that!

LESLEY: Actually, the reaction was just bizarre. In those days I was just starting out, so I wasn't aware of the effects of public- ity. I'd just put my first album out and sales just rocketed when I did this naked stunt

for the English National Opera. I hadn't planned it at all – I'd accepted to do *Die Fledermaus* a year before, because opera is booked well in advance. So it was a complete coincidence and it hadn't occurred to me that it would affect my album sales, because I was only just getting into that whole world. But it was a lesson I learnt very quickly: if you have an album out, everything you do will affect the sales of that album.

ANDREA: A little nakedness goes a long way – or in your case, Lesley, a lot of nakedness! I admire your courage, and your resistance to the cold!

LESLEY: Thank you!

JANE: What about you, Andrea? Do you suffer for fashion?

ANDREA: Never! If I'm going on the train or tube, I wear something that's comfortable and practical and carry a brolly. I once turned up at my friend Penny Smith's book launch in my comfy clothes, thinking I was early enough to nip inside and get changed. But the paparazzi caught me on the way in! 'Please don't take my picture now, I look like a wreck!' I pleaded jokily. They laughed and took them anyway. Then I got changed inside and went back out again: 'Ta-dah! I'm ready now!' One magazine printed a before and after picture, which was really embarrassing.

Kim and the girls didn't care if their lips turned blue. At least they looked good, and they wouldn't have to pay for the cloakroom...

Can you ever look sexy in a woolly jumper?

LESLEY: Woolly jumpers are phenomenally sexy, particularly the bobbly Aran knits. I love those. My grandmother, my father's mother, used to knit the whole family these incredibly complicated Aran sweaters and I used to wear them off the shoulder, with leggings and flat boots and a hat. Now my daughter's doing exactly the same thing.

My husband is never happier than if I'm in a little cardigan. He finds very unusual things attractive. He loves little woolly cardis and he loves flannelette and winceyette. Whereas some men prefer silk, my husband prefers flannelette. He likes me to wear it anytime, but particularly in bed. He's in heaven with flannelette sheets!

JANE: That's unusual! But I also like being cosy, so I love woolly jumpers. I have two favourite cashmere jumpers that I wear at home a lot, usually with leggings. Someone bought them for me, because cashmere is an extravagance I would never indulge in for myself. It feels very luxurious sitting at home in them. I can't wear itchy wool.

CAROL: I find cashmere itchy, though. I just gave a load away because I never really wore it. I love cashmere shawls and blankets, but I wouldn't want to wear anything really close to my skin, because it always itches slightly. Cardigans are OK, but then I'm not really a cardigan person either.

ANDREA: Really, Carol? You must have very sensitive skin.

CAROL: I think I have, actually. When I'm drying my hair in

the gym, if there's a hair on my back, I can feel it. I've got friends who've left the plastic tags on the back of their jeans for three years, ever since they've owned them, yet I have to cut the labels out of everything because they itch and irritate me. Some people just don't have any feeling do they?

ANDREA: Like Jane, I've discovered the joys of cashmere and, once that happens, it's really difficult to go back. Cashmere is lovely because it's warm without being big and bulky. I don't slob around the house in it, though: I wear things that I don't mind getting covered in paint or Weetabix. The last thing I want to do is say, 'Urgh, no, stay away from me!' when Amy runs towards me to give me a massive hug, covered in yoghurt, or paint.

So, I live in yoga trousers, fleeces and jumpers at home. My wardrobe mainly consists of jumpers; I don't care if they're sexy or not. My main concern is to be warm. Steve's a builder and comes home covered in soot and dust and bits of wood, so between the two of us, we look like a train wreck. We are Mr and Mrs Worzel Gummidge, but that's why it works. When we go out, we both like to spruce up. I'll put on some heels and he'll put on a pair of nice smart clean shiny shoes, trousers and a shirt. It makes a nice change. We'll look at one another and say, 'Oh, I forgot you can look like that!'

DENISE: I really like woolly jumpers, especially hand-knitted woolly jumpers. My mum always used to knit for us when we were kids: always plain and pearl, nothing elaborate. I also like wearing big men's jumpers in the winter.

CAROL: Well, I'm not really a woolly jumper person. I don't think they can ever really be sexy unless you're Julia Roberts in front of a fire in a movie, with nothing else on. Most people don't look sexy in knitwear.

LISA: Really? I think knitwear can be very sexy. I've done photo shoots where I've worn a loose baggy jumper that's a little oversized and it's just slipped off one shoulder. It can look quite cheeky and sexy with nothing on underneath. And I've got a lovely black-and-white knitted dress, which is a really thin knit. It's one of my favourites because it's a one-piece, the kind of thing you just bung on and look great in. It's very figure hugging and simple.

SHERRIE: I'm with you, Lisa. Most things can be sexy, even woolly jumpers. I'm sure you could make a woolly jumper with ripped jeans and Ugg boots work. However, generally I'd say I'm not a woolly jumper person. I'm into ripped jeans at the moment. I steal my fashion ideas from you, Carol, as I'm sure you know! Carol always looks amazing. She often wears ripped jeans, so I thought, I wonder if I should buy myself some? I don't know if I should. She is only nine years younger than I am, after all . . . OK, I will! I quite like it as a look now, although obviously you're paying for the holes, but I would never wear them with a woolly jumper.

CAROL: Because you're not Julia Roberts!

SHERRIE: No, unfortunately!

Do you wear sexy winter nightwear or are you a Rip Van Winkle?

JANE: Rip Van Winkle! It's a bit of a shame, seeing as I've just got engaged, isn't it? But thankfully he's older. He's not like Carol's; he's not twenty-seven. He's fifty-five, mine, so he gets as cold as I do and he's in his long johns as well.

LESLEY: I tread the path between sexy and Rip Van Winkle, because my husband has this thing about brushed cotton, which is quite a challenge to find. I'm a sucker for cashmere bed socks, because I get cold feet; my husband loves them, too. Silk is very warm, so I tend to wear a lot of silk pyjamas in the winter. I have to have something across my shoulders. I don't mind the rest of me naked, but even in the summer I have to wear a little vest.

COLEEN: I don't wear satin negligees or little baby dolls, but you wouldn't see me in a long winceyette nightie, either! I've got little lace-trimmed pyjamas that are three-quarter length on the leg that I wear with a little vest top. It looks nice but it's comfortable and I'm not worrying about showing anything off if I'm hanging around in it.

CAROL: I don't really do nightwear. I wear a T-shirt or something, but that's the same all year round. It'll probably just be the T-shirt I was wearing that day: I just wear it to bed and put it in the wash the next day, so it doubles up and saves on laundry. My house is really hot, anyway. There's glass all the way around one side, so if there's sunshine, it heats the whole place up, even in the winter.

DENISE: My fluffy pyjamas are my favourites. I don't put them away until it's really hot. I'm very much a snuggly pyjama-wearer, not a nightie person. People can't buy me enough pyjamas; they're always a great Christmas present for me.

LISA: I'm a bit Rip Van Winkle, these days. Actually, I've never been into sexy nightwear. If it looks contrived, then it's not sexy, in my opinion. We live in England: it's cold. Paul would think I was on drugs if I came down in a long silky number and started swanning around my old Victorian house. 'Where are you going?' he'd say. 'Put some clothes on. It's freezing.'

He's a very hot person, whereas it has to be really warm for me to feel warm. I'll have the fires on with the doors open in the summer, just because I like it to be really warm, whereas Paul will wear a T-shirt in the winter. Trying to find the right balance between the two of us is almost impossible. So I have to wear significant clothing in order for me to feel warm in my house at night. A little silky negligee is just not going to happen. Instead I'll wear a T-shirt and a pair of white cotton trousers, something like that.

LYNDA: I've got really into nightwear since I discovered the White Company. I like their silky pyjama trousers, because they're a bit like very thin tracksuit bottoms and they have pretty tops to go with them. I've got lots now, because I love not wearing clothes at home. The first thing I do when I get home is put on a pair of these pretty, thin, baggy pyjamas. Actually, they make your bum look nice, so they're quite sexy, and you can always put an actual shirt on the top.

ANDREA: They sound lovely. I love wearing pyjamas.

LYNDA: I was brought up to wear nighties, but Mr Spain is naked in bed, so I look a bit silly if I go to bed with my nightie on. However, I have got some sexy satin nighties, which I'll suddenly put on because I don't want to be boring.

We were watching television in bed one night just before our last anniversary and I said, 'Do you think we should go out more?' I had a hell of a schedule at the time.

'When?' he said, laughing.

'I know, but I don't want you to think that I'm taking you for granted.'

When I have those thoughts, I rush to put on one of my glamorous nighties. And he'll either say, 'Wow!' and ravish me, or he'll say, 'Very nice, that's lovely. But it's all right, you're not taking me for granted. Now can you just relax, sip your hot chocolate and watch television?'

I'm really getting into 'about-the-house' wear in Spain and I've got some amazing, see-through creations. Rigby and Peller do some fantastic beachwear that you can float about the house and pool in.

SHERRIE: That sounds lovely, Lynda.

I didn't like living in Spain. Perhaps that's because I was with the wrong person, though. With the wrong person, you could be in a penthouse in the middle of Monte Carlo and it would still be the unhappiest, darkest period of your life. But with the right person, you could be in a tent in a field and it would be glorious.

Anyway, back to nightwear: I've been menopausal for a very long time, since 1992, in fact. So I boil in the night. If I'm in a hotel, I have to have the air conditioning on full blast all night, so that the room is freezing. At home, I have my windows open and a huge fan by my bed, which always has to be on, even in the winter. It's a total nightmare.

JANE: That sounds awful.

SHERRIE: It is! Sometimes I wake up in the middle of the night, absolutely frozen. But I don't do anything about it, because within fifteen minutes, I'll be boiling again! I could never live with a man again, because he would die of pneumonia. That's why I have to live on my own now.

I can't take HRT because I'm allergic to it, so I've had to live with boiling hot water dripping down my body for all those years. It used to be twenty-four hours a day, but now it's mainly at night. It's really annoying. I can be frozen as I get into bed and I think, This is awful, I can't live like this! Then, within fifteen minutes, I will boil into a real heat, to the point of rivers of sweat. I have to get up and go to the bathroom and splash freezing cold water all over me and then stand in front of the fan. The fan then freezes the water that's on me, so my body temperature drops dramatically and I can get to sleep.

JANE: That's horrific! Have you been to the doctor?

SHERRIE: The doctor says it's just one of those things. My body's thermostat has gone, so it can't control itself at all. I'm assuming it won't

come back. It just makes sleeping impossible. It's horrible. I can't imagine what it
must be like to sleep a whole night: to go to
bed at night and wake up in the morning. It
must be fantastic. Instead, I sleep for about
two and a half hours, and then wake up, and
then probably sleep another two hours, but
that's it really. I have to live with it, which is
really hard.

JANE: You must be knackered, love!

SHERRIE: Sometimes in the afternoon I'll have a sleep for an
hour and a half. I have to! I worry that will stop me sleeping
at night, but I need to charge those batteries. I always think
sleep is the one thing that will cure everything.

ANDREA: You poor thing! Perhaps you should get a nightie
like mine, Sherrie, because if you get hot, you can roll it up a
bit and if you get cold, you roll it down. It's my favourite thing
to wear in bed – it's a long nightie with long sleeves. It sounds
hideous, but it's really very pretty: white and quite clingy, to
the floor, with a deep V-neck of lace and long sleeves trimmed
with lace. I honestly don't look like the grandma from *Little
Red Riding Hood*! It's a mixture of cotton and Lycra, so it's
really comfortable.

SHERRIE: OK, I'll try anything!

Marcus couldn't help feeling that Deborah might not be in the mood…

Do you have a summer/winter system for your clothes?

DENISE: I would love to say that I have a system, but at the moment my bedroom resembles a charity shop before they've sorted it out. It's in such a mess! My selfish nanny/housekeeper has gone off to have a baby and I'm not coping very well without her. I realised this week that I've got a complete mixture of winter and summer clothes in my wardrobe, all of which I hate! I'm sure I remember going in to shops that weren't charity shops and choosing some nice clothes over the years, but I don't know where they are. It's just full of stuff that I hate. I want that woman who used to do *The Life Laundry* to come round to my house and de-clutter my life. I need de-cluttering.

COLEEN: I sorted out my wardrobe recently, because it was so stuffed and disorganised that I couldn't find anything in there. I came across things from years ago and got rid of about seven bin bags. I sent them to my sister Linda and she took loads; then she gave the rest to a charity shop. It was really satisfying. I'd definitely recommend it.

DENISE: I bet! I must do it! And I want to be one of those people who has a capsule wardrobe, with just a few items that you mix and match. I'd like to have all my winter stuff folded away in the summer and then put all my summer clothes away in the winter. Of course, it's all very difficult in our ridiculous climate. One day last summer, I was sat outside a restaurant in Alderley Edge in a sleeveless top – and then a day later I had hypothermia in Rochdale. It's very difficult to divide your wardrobe into seasons here, because you'd spend your life scrabbling around trying to get out your summer or winter clothes again every time the weather changed!

Will I ever be organised? Probably not, as I'm fifty-one now and that's been my ambition ever since I was twenty-one. But I'm going to strive for it in my fifties, because my untidiness and my lack of domestic ability are starting to really grate on me. It's a time thing, I suppose. My days are so long when I'm filming *Waterloo Road* that by the time I get in at night and put Louis to bed, I just can't be bothered even to put a load of washing in. And when I'm doing *Loose Women*, I'm up and down to London all the time.

I get a bit frustrated that people are having to live my life for me while I'm away – as in, do all my housework – but when my home is tidy, then I'm much calmer as a person. It's so cluttered at the moment that it's making me feel a bit claustrophobic.

I don't like doing housework, but at least I would be more in control of it if I spent more time at home. When somebody else is doing it for me, I can't find anything when I get home, whereas if I'm there, even if somebody's doing things for me, or with me, at least I know where things are.

LESLEY: I have a fantastic personal assistant who is also my wardrobe mistress; she's everything, really!

DENISE: Oh, send her to my house, please!

LESLEY: She helps me to coordinate my wardrobe and we put the winter stuff away in the summer and vice versa. Of course, there's an autumn and spring patch, where they merge. I have one room to myself in my house and that's my office, which also contains two long wardrobes. All my evening dresses and the clothes I'm not currently wearing are in those wardrobes; the clothes I'm wearing are in the dressing room in my bedroom.

A lot needs throwing out, but I've got some very lovely concert dresses. I've given some to charity, but I've saved a lot, too. Some fantastic designers have designed dresses for me.

LISA: I've got a few fairly posh frocks in my wardrobe too, but I find that the more you're on the telly, the fewer clothes you have to buy, because you can borrow stuff. You get stylists saying you can have that for nothing if you're going to a do where you'll be photographed.

LESLEY: Wonderful, isn't it? We're very lucky. I was a bit alarmed when my daughter turned out to be a tomboy and wasn't interested at all in any of it, but last year she turned the corner. Her style is very different to mine, though. She has a much simpler way of dressing, which I admire very much. I tend to over-accessorise and I love colour. I use colour possibly too chaotically, whereas she likes grey and earthy colours.

SHERRIE: It's so funny with daughters, isn't it?

LESLEY: Yes, it has been strange watching her grow up and become this wonderful young woman who is actually quite different from me.

COLEEN: Well, if she's not going to wear them, you should do a big clear-out like I have.

LESLEY: I'm not good at throwing things away, though. I'm a natural recycler. I think anybody who has parents who were children in the Second World War is automatically brought up like that. I'll make or mend, and I can't throw things away; I have to pass them on or find useful homes for them. I also find hand-sewing very satisfying. I keep thinking of all these things I'd quite like to do when I retire, except I'm never going to retire, so I'm not sure when I'm going to do them. I'd very much like to do tapestry. I find stitching incredibly therapeutic, especially while sitting in the garden listening to the radio.

LISA: Like you, Lesley, I'm not very good at throwing things away. I've still got all my daughter Beau's old clothes vacuum-packed up in the loft. Everything she's ever worn, I've still got it all.

DENISE: Did I hear you say vacuum-packed?

LISA: Yes! One thing my house lacks is storage; I've got a dreadful storage situation going on. Coats are very bulky, so I tend to put them in the loft in proper storage boxes in the summer and then get them back out when it's winter again. I vacuum-pack them in those bags that you heat-seal using a hairdryer. It protects them from everything, from the damp to moths.

DENISE: Well I never!

SHERRIE: Stop doing spring, summer and winter clothes. That's what I say. Mix it all up! In the past, I've noticed that I live in black in this country, perhaps because it's grey a lot of the time. When I go abroad I call it, 'getting out of your blacks'. It takes me three days to get out of my blacks and turn into a sunshine person. Well, it's a waste. So over the last six months, I've made a concerted effort to get out of black. When I go shopping now, I absolutely refuse to try anything black on, no matter how beautiful it looks. I'm really trying to go to colour. It's made a real difference to me psychologically.

If we wore more colour in this country, I think it would make a big difference to our outlook. It changes your attitude to life if you're wearing bright blue. When you're abroad and you wear yellows, pinks and reds, you smile more, don't you? Then you get back home and it's all grey, taupe, brown and black, and the smile disappears. Well, no wonder! We should buy colour instead: I don't care if it's winter!

I now have colour-themed rails in my wardrobes: one rail is totally black and the rest go from creams and whites to colours. But I plan to shove all the black clothes to the back of the wardrobe, so that they're out of sight and I'm not tempted to wear them.

It's very hard for me to do this, as I'm a very taupe, grey and black person. But I think it's good for me. It may not feel totally natural to wear white with a bit of sparkle, but I'm going to do it from now on. It doesn't matter if it is winter. Look at Su Pollard. How outrageous is she? But at least she brings a smile to your face when you look at her. And that's my point: we need to smile more.

CAROL: I don't really have a summer and winter wardrobe, but I do make a conscious decision at some point in the year to stop wearing socks and start wearing sandals, and I do put my boots away and hide away the few woollies I've got.

LYNDA: I had a friend who started a business where she'd come and get your furs and put them in refrigerators. I was terribly impressed with the thought of anyone doing that.

CAROL: That sounds pretty over the top! Since I live in London and it's never really that cold, I've probably worn my winter coat about three times in the last two or three years. Last year when we had the snow it was really cold, but I don't have to walk to school any more so I'm never freezing. I just get in the car or on a train.

ANDREA: And when is your favourite time, summer or winter?

CAROL: I don't prefer summer or winter. I like the seasons changing, although they seem to be changing less as I get older. But at least we do get a winter and a summer. Autumn is lovely as well, with the leaves falling off the trees, and spring's lovely with the blossom. I certainly don't mind the winter. People are always saying, 'I hate being cold', but I don't mind it. I quite like getting snugly.

So I like living in the UK, because you get the choice. I wouldn't want to be where my friends live in LA or where my brother lived in Singapore, where every day you wear the same thing, because it's always hot. By the end of the summer here, I start to look forward to wearing more clothes: thick black tights and boots, heavy jackets and hats. Equally, at the end of the winter, I really look forward to wearing jeans and sandals and T-shirts. So I prefer both. What I don't like is the interim periods where you don't really know what to wear because it's not hot and it's not cold. It's too cold to wear just a T-shirt, but it's too hot to wear your jacket, or it's hot in the morning and cold in the afternoon. The answer to all those problems is usually a pashmina.

LYNDA: I now have a dressing room, which I've always wanted, so there's room for me to have a wardrobe of winter clothes and a wardrobe of summer clothes. I seem to spend less money on summer clothes. They're kind of more disposable, aren't they? I've got a lot of stuff that I've taken to Spain, where I just wear wraps and loose clothing most of the time.

In the UK, every time I think it's summer, I whip out the white linen jacket, only to get halfway through the day and realise that I've made a terrible fashion faux pas! And I've either got to walk around like a complete idiot in this very summery outfit, go home and change, freeze to death or carry a coat round. It requires much cleverer fashion sense to live in England, if you haven't got loads of dosh. You have to think, can you use that autumn jacket on a chilly English summer's day? You can never shut the old winter wardrobe down completely.

I find the winter wardrobe so much easier, because I can cover everything up. I have to be much more ingenious with my summer wardrobe: it's harder to make it look interesting without looking as though I'm covering up. I love wearing baggy cotton trousers, but there's a downside to them: they're baggy and floaty, which is great for the summer, or so I always think, but then I see a photograph of myself in them and in fact they haven't hidden anything – when I'm fat, I look fat, especially in floaty things.

In order to wear long floppy comfortable trousers, you've

either got to be six feet tall or wear very high heels, which defeats the object, because as you get older your feet hurt. So then you go and buy loads and loads of wedges, which I do, in a rush, and that isn't always very sensible.

Last spring I bought ten pairs while I was on tour, because they were in a sale in Norwich. Two pairs ended up fitting and the other eight pairs are agony, so I can only wear them when I haven't got to walk anywhere. Again, you think: It's a lovely sunny day and I'm going to saunter through the streets to work! But of course it's agony. And the only pair of shoes you can really wear is a flat pair, which means your trousers are dragging on the ground. I get quite frustrated.

JANE: And you don't like wearing uncomfortable shoes either!

LYNDA: Now, now! Not everything is about sex!

ANDREA: Moving swiftly on, I'm a summer person without a doubt. The moment the weather starts to turn, I get really excited and dig out all my three-quarter-length trousers and summery shirts. Then, of course, there's the crushing disappointment when the weather turns and it's back to fleeces again. I keep my out-of-season clothes in the spare room and swap them over when need be. It means that our poor guests don't have any room at all, I'm afraid!

JANE: Like you, Andrea, I'm a summer girl. But I prefer winter fashion. I'm happier in the summer climate and I like wearing light colours, like white trousers, but I much prefer the cut of a good material, which you would usually wear in the winter. I like good coats, for instance, and dressing smartly in suits and

boots, so for me the winter wardrobe is actually a better one.

DENISE: I love winter clothes and I love hats. Now I've got my hair short I can wear more hats because I don't get terrible hat hair any more. I just scrunch it around and it's done.

LESLEY: And it looks great. However, I prefer summer clothes. I love flowing chiffon and floaty cotton and very light layering. Silk is the best. I've got a lot of silk in my summer wardrobe.

COLEEN: Well, I admire people who can be bothered to have a wardrobe system and have the time for it, because I don't. I find it easier to dress in the winter because I'm just concentrating on being warm. The summer is much harder: you have to expose bits of your body that you wouldn't usually.

LYNDA: That's exactly what I find!

COLEEN: The only drawback about showing my legs – well, about showing my whole body – is that I'm really pale, milky pale. So my legs look like milk bottles. It's not a winning look really! I feel a lot better now since I've lost weight, but I still can't get away from those milk bottles. Unfortunately for me, I'm allergic to all brands of fake tan: it brings me out in giant hives.

LISA: That's no bad thing, because it really smells, doesn't it? I was spray tanned for the BAFTAs, which was horrible. You have to stand up in a pair of paper knickers while this complete stranger looks at you stark naked, saying, 'OK, arms up for me,' and, 'Turn around.' It's just so undignified and it stinks. You suddenly start smelling like an old carrot. It may look nice, but it's only good as long as nobody comes anywhere near you. And it absolutely annihilated my white bed linen. My pillow had a little brown head imprint in the middle, showing where my face had been during the night.

COLEEN: That's very funny! But I still find it quite annoying that I can never get that tanned look. I can't sunbathe because I burn, I don't go on sun beds because they are dangerous and I'm allergic to fake tan, so I'm just destined to be very pale.

LYNDA: But you've got that wonderful alabaster skin!

COLEEN: Oh yes, all these tanned women say they love my pale complexion. In fact, they love it so much that they plaster themselves in fake tan! I went on a sun bed when I was about fifteen. It was one of the old-fashioned ones that you lie down on: I stayed on it too long and it burnt me. Afterwards, I had big red tube marks all the way down my back. You could kind of guess how I'd got my tan.

LISA: I used to love a sun bed, back in the day! I don't really go in the sun that much any more, because I'm too old and I find it a bit irritating just lying there doing nothing. But in the past I just used to concentrate on my tan and bake. It was all part of my big vain thing for exposing bits of my body. My reasoning was that, if you're going to do it, those bits have got to be tanned. It's all so different now.

JANE: I look shocking when I'm really pasty, which is why I wear a lot of makeup. So that slight sunny glow is essential for me; I look a lot better with a bit of a tan. But, you've got this wonderful white porcelain skin, Coleen, so you look great pale.

COLEEN: There you go again, see?

Would you wear fur?

SHERRIE: Never. It's cruelty, plain and simple. I would never, *ever* wear fur. Why would you wear an animal fur on your back when it should be on the animal?

ANDREA: I wouldn't, either. It's very hypocritical of me, because I wear leather and sheepskin and some people might say, what's the difference? You can't be kind to one animal and unkind to another. But I do think there's a difference, because it's part of the food chain: we eat the meat, use the skin for warmth and protection against the elements and turn the rest into things like soap and candles. I feel as though it's the order of things. On the other hand, I wouldn't feel comfortable wearing the fur of an animal that's kept in a tiny cage just so that you can wear its skin.

JANE: I know I should say that I absolutely wouldn't wear fur, but maybe I would wear it, because I'm a big meat eater. I wear leather shoes, after all, so I think it really would be hypo-critical to say I wouldn't wear fur.

SHERRIE: Do you wear much leather, though?

JANE: Well, I love my boots, Sherrie, as you know.

SHERRIE: I don't wear a lot of leather, but I know it's a dilemma for people, because we buy handbags, shoes and gloves. The practicality of life doesn't lend itself to finding things that aren't leather, shoes in particular.

I'd never buy a leather coat, though. It's a problem for every-one, I think: we don't like the thought of an animal dying and would never wear fur, yet we have leather in our lives everyday. Still, if you can make a stand, at least make it with fur.

DENISE: I'm a bit on the fence about all of this after watching a documentary about the fur industry. The journalist present-ing it was totally against it, but he came to realise that it was quite humane when done properly. Still, you can't really justify animals being farmed just for their fur.

CAROL: There are always two sides to a story, aren't there? The animal activists will tell you that the animals suffer and it's all hideous, but the people who actually run these farms tell you that when they kill the animals it's completely painless. Who do you believe? It's who you want to believe, really. I don't really listen to the arguments. I just think it goes on, like everything else. People don't like stuff, but it just goes on.

DENISE: So would you wear it, Carol?

CAROL: I might, just because I don't want to be told what I can and can't do by extreme people. But I certainly wouldn't go into Harrods and buy a fur coat. However, if – say – my grandmother had a lovely fur coat that she'd bought years ago, I wouldn't throw it away or be scared to wear it, because if I didn't wear it or make the most of it, then the poor animal died in vain anyway. So I might as well just make the most of it.

LISA: That's exactly my dilemma, because I have a very beautiful mink double-breasted fitted jacket that I inherited from my nan. It's a beautiful coat and it looks fab on me. I wish it was fake! It's the perfect size for me – and, being small, it's very difficult to get anything tailored to fit me, let alone a tailored mink.

JANE: That's a tough one.

LISA: I want to wear it because it belonged to my nan more than anything. I've put it on a few times, but then my partner Paul and daughter Beau have said, 'You're not going out in that, are you?' Beau says, 'You can't, Mummy. First you'll get attacked and then we'll all get attacked if we're walking along with you.' She's a bit of a drama queen, my daughter. Everybody reacts negatively to it, so it just doesn't get worn.

JANE: See, I think that's a bit of a shame.

LISA: Well yes – and I always think, well, I didn't kill it and you can't bring it back to life. If anyone's to blame, have a pop at my nan! She was the one who made the judgement call about whether to buy it or not. Of course, I definitely wouldn't go and buy fur now: I tend to think that fur looks better on animals. I wonder how much of a fashion victim would you have to be to want to buy a new fur coat, even though it causes offence to just about everybody?

CAROL: If someone shouted abuse at me, I'd probably tell them to get lost, basically, because no one has any right to tell anybody what they can wear. It doesn't matter if it's fur, a burkha or a tracksuit and trainers. Who is to judge people for what they wear? I find it really bizarre.

I really hate the way people tell other people how to be, because they're different to how they are. Women with kids, for instance, always say, 'Why haven't you got any children?' Like I'm the weirdo! No, *you're* the weirdo! It's often a topic of conversation in the newspapers. Earlier in the year, I remember a piece in the *Daily Mail* in which a journalist said something like, 'I'm not surprised bosses don't trust women without children, because they lack a certain humanity.' Get lost! I can't stand it. Why do women without children always have to justify their decision? Yet women with children never do. It does my head in, it really does. I think of myself as child-free and not childless.

Not having children has become more of a lifestyle choice. Generations ago, that's just what you did: you left school, had a job for a few years, got married and had kids. That was it. But it never occurred to me: it just wasn't on my list of things to do. Ever. I didn't want to go down that road. I saw

 my mum struggle with four children as a single mum and it must have put me off, I suppose.

But back to fur, if I lived in Russia I'd be wearing fur every day, and in places like New York, people wear fur and nobody cares, so it just seems to depend on where you live.

LYNDA: I can understand someone giving me a hard time if I was wearing a fur. I can understand them saying, 'How can you wear that?' What I can't understand is people bombing people and throwing paint over them. I don't think it's worth that kind of abuse.

COLEEN: I used to have fur when I was younger. One Christmas, when I was about sixteen or seventeen, my mum and dad bought us all fox-fur jackets. Linda and Bernie had red fox fur and I had a silver fox. I liked it at the time because it was stylish. It was back when everyone wore fur, whereas nowadays you just don't. We didn't think twice about it, whereas now we're all so much more aware.

SHERRIE: My grandmother used to have a fox fur. Do you remember the foxes people used to hang around their necks and the heads used to go round the waist? How awful is that? A dead fox hanging round your waist! I can remember them well: she had a silver fox and a red fox. It's a disgusting thought now, but back then it was the height of glamour. It's weird how things change, and we change, isn't it?

COLEEN: Oh God. I couldn't do that now!

LYNDA: It's true what you say though, Sherrie. Attitudes change. In the early 1970s, we all had fox-fur coats and I was terribly proud of my three-quarter-length, red fox-fur jacket. The thing back then was to wear it with your jeans and sling it casually over the back of the chair. The idea was that you didn't treat it like a fur coat – you treated it like you'd got hundreds and it didn't matter if somebody trampled all over it! Awful, isn't it?

ANDREA: Yes, times have definitely changed. It wasn't an issue when we were young. I used to watch all the Doris Day and Rock Hudson films, thinking that the women looked so elegant in their wraps: it never occurred to me what they were actually wearing. I just didn't twig.

JANE: It's true. Once upon a time, you saw Elizabeth Taylor, Joan Crawford and Bette Davis in beautiful mink coats and you just thought it was the ultimate in glamour. There was always a sense that you'd made it if you had a mink coat.

LESLEY: Yes, when I was little, fur was synonymous with wealth and status and glamour. It went with diamonds and champagne. Well, diamonds and champagne I do, darling, but I'd rather wear feathers than fur. Feathers just scream 'old-fashioned glamour', I think. When I think of Fred Astaire and Ginger Rogers, when I think of Marlene Dietrich and when I think of Busby Berkeley, I think of feathers, not fur. So I wear a lot of ostrich feathers.

SHERRIE: What about the poor ostriches, though?

LESLEY: They don't kill them for their feathers!

SHERRIE: I've heard you can get coats made out of cobra skin. Well, how dreadful! It's disgusting. I love snakes. They're among my favourite creatures in this world. I would keep a snake, if I didn't have the lifestyle I have, because I think they are incredibly gorgeous. They are magical creatures. I don't understand people who don't like snakes. The touch of them alone is absolutely wonderful. Whenever I'm near a snake, I feel compelled to hold it or put it round my neck.

JANE: Yuk!

SHERRIE: No really, I think it's one of the most calming, therapeutic things you can do, because there is a coolness and a calmness about the quality of a live snake's skin. To think that people turn them into handbags or coats! I wouldn't even go near something like that. I'd hate it.

COLEEN: I wouldn't consider wearing real fur now, but I'd like a fake mink coat or jacket, I think. I haven't bought one yet, because every time I see a fake fur coat that I like, it's on someone else. It would be good to have something to keep me warm during my train journey to London to film *Loose Women*. The train is at six in the morning, when it's still pitch black and freezing on the platform.

DENISE: I know what you mean. I film half the year in Rochdale and there are times when I would kill for a fur coat, because it's so bloody cold!

LISA: Real fur definitely keeps you warm. When I went to Lapland, we didn't freeze because they put reindeer skins over us in the sledges. An old woolly blanket isn't going to cut it in the middle of Santa's grotto, let me tell you.

DENISE: I wouldn't wear fur. I just wouldn't want to have paint thrown at me in the street. I don't know how people have the brass neck to do it. Anyway, there are so many fake furs now that look pretty fantastic that I don't think you really have to resort to real fur.

It's amazing, though, how people like Naomi Campbell put their necks out on those PETA campaigns and then, two years later, you see them wearing fur on the catwalk. That's just ridiculous after she was the blood-splattered face of the anti-fur brigade!

LESLEY: Strange, isn't it? I probably wouldn't wear fur because I am a great animal lover and there are perfectly acceptable substitutes. We don't need to wear it. I probably would have worn it if I'd been born in the 1930s or 40s, though, when that's all there was, but I don't think it's necessary any more. We've got such interesting, glamorous fabrics now.

LYNDA: Well, I probably would wear fur. It's very hard for me, this thing about animal rights and vegetarianism, because I'm a farmer's daughter, so I view life from a completely different standpoint to people who haven't been brought up in the country. I do maintain that all children should spend time on a farm to understand the cycle of life.

I've probably reached a point where I wouldn't

condone fox hunting, but I wouldn't necessarily stop other people from doing it. I think
people should be allowed to do it if they want
to. I'm in favour of a free country and I just
think there are many more important issues
to worry about.

I agree that it's a bit grim for animals to
be bred for their coats, but let's not forget
that the natural order of things used to be that we skinned
something in order to live under it, sleep under it and wear it.
We can certainly do without fur these days, but I don't have
a horror of the idea of wearing an animal on me, especially
when it comes to leather.

If Mr Spain bought me a mink jacket, I probably wouldn't
wear it in England. I suppose I'm a bit of a coward – and
I hate confrontation. But if you went to Canada or Italy or
France, say, you could wear it to your heart's content. So you
just have to be careful where you wear it. Still, you know, I'm
not that desperate for a fur coat. I'm quite happy without one.

Of course I'm sad the little fox had to die.
But darling, don't I just look divine?

Chapter 8

Dear Loose Women

The Loose Women agony aunts answer some of your most difficult dilemmas

We get tons of letters at *Loose Women* and we love to hear from people that watch and enjoy the show. They often ask us for advice when they've found themselves in a bit of a quandary, and ask us what we would do in their situation.

It always makes us chuckle to be honest that they think we're in any position to dish out advice when we're just muddling through like everyone, but we thought it might be good to select some of our favourite, juiciest dilemmas from over the years and to describe how we would cope with them.

We've tried to cover a whole range of problems you can be confronted with in life – ranging from how to react if your best friend's partner makes a pass at you, whether it is ever OK to tell an overweight friend she needs to go on a diet; to how to cope and get through some of the really tough times life can throw at you – like a break-up or a bereavement.

We're not claiming to be know-it-all experts or anything, but we have made all sorts of tricky decisions and been through some very tough times ourselves and we've always come out the other side, so we hope you find some comfort and a few giggles in what we have to say.

Does my bum look big in this?

If your friend says, 'Does my bum look big in this' and it does, what would say?

JANE: I'd get round it by saying, 'I prefer you in that other outfit; I think you look fabulous in the other one.' I'd never say, 'Oh, you look atrocious in that!'

DENISE: I would say, 'It doesn't look big, but I think you should wear something else, because it's not doing you any favours.'

ANDREA: Always be honest. Tell her that it does. Be nice about it, but say something like, 'Maybe that's not the best I've ever seen you look. Have you got something else?' She'll know what you mean.

CAROL: It depends on who it is, I suppose. I might just say, 'It doesn't look big "in that", because it's just big, so it's going to look big in anything!' If it were a really good friend, I'm sure she could handle it. But with anyone else, I would just say, 'No, it looks fine.'

This is another weird women thing. Women don't want the real answer. It doesn't matter if they're asking you, or the boyfriend or the husband, they want you to say, 'No you look fine! If you say, 'Actually, it looks massive,' it would start an argument. People can't handle the truth, so they just shouldn't ask. They're making you lie, and if you don't, it's going to start a row. This is why poor men always slip up, because they just don't know the right answer, and women aren't ever going to listen to their advice anyway. If you say to a bloke, 'What do you think?' and he says, 'Hmmm . . .' you say, 'Well, I'm wearing it anyway!' So what's the point in asking?

JANE: Yes, sometimes I feel quite sorry for the poor blokes! They can't get it right.

COLEEN: Ah, the poor things. It must be hell to have their women parading around half-clothed in front of them. They should thank their lucky stars!

Can you ever tell a best friend or partner to stop stuffing their face and get down the gym?

JANE: No, I'd always wait for her to say that she wanted to lose weight first. Then I'd say, 'Do whatever you feel. To me you're always lovely. But if you do feel that you need to lose weight, then off you go and I'll help you.'

LISA: If I knew someone who was unhappy because they felt they were overweight, I would probably come up with some suggestions to try to help them find a way of losing weight. It wouldn't necessarily be by saying, 'Stop stuffing your face and get down the gym.' It would be more like, 'Look if it's really getting you down, then I can find out about some classes you can do and a really good way of helping you lose the weight.' I wouldn't have a problem being honest with somebody.

ANDREA: You can tell a close friend or partner to stop

 overeating and go to the gym, but it doesn't make you very popular. I did it with Steve. When I was pregnant with Amy, I put on four stone and he put on three – out of sympathy, I think. It was fine for ages, because I was too wrapped up in the new baby to mind. Then I gradually started losing my weight and I noticed that he wasn't losing his. I felt really awful about admitting it to myself, but I didn't like it. He'd gone from just being large to being fat and I found that I didn't like looking at him.

I kept thinking. How do I broach this? First, I was really enthusiastic about my own weight loss and said, 'Come on, we can do this together!' But he didn't get the hint at all, so one day I just had to say, 'I don't really like the way you look.'

It was hideous, because I really hurt his feelings. But it worked and he's done really well – bless him, he looks gorgeous now. I still feel bad about it, though, because I basically said, 'I don't find you as attractive as I used to now you're this big.'

Part of me was thinking: If this was a man saying this to a woman, I'd be up in arms! 'You can't say that to a woman!' The difference was that I couldn't help getting big, because I was pregnant, whereas he could, as he was just eating pies. Still, I only had to say it once.

It was a really hideous few weeks. Afterwards I felt awful, and he was obviously really hurt. I wished I could have taken it back. But now I am constantly praising him and saying, 'Wow, you look so great! Look at you!' And if I go a bit quiet, he knows that maybe he should back off the beer a little bit for a while. So I try and do it that way, with mostly positive reinforcement.

A friend asks you to an Ann Summers party – do you go?

ANDREA: I've been to a few Ann Summers parties and they've always been a good laugh.

LESLEY: Yes, I'd go in a second! I've never been to one and I long to go. So, if any of you are having one, ask me!

JANE: Yeah! Book us in! I've been to one or two, and they've been a right giggle. I've never won a prize though, thankfully. It's like, 'What do you do with it? Really???' I'm a bit naive, so it's an education for me.

DENISE: Yes, it's a great girlie night. I had one last year, for the *Waterloo Road* girls. It was a hoot! Our party organiser was called Maria. We first heard about her through one of the girls at work, a really vivacious, booby, red-haired, sexy bird who wears loads of makeup. This girl kept telling us about her flat-mate Maria, who did Ann Summers parties. Well, naturally our mental image of Maria was very similar to the buxom redhead, so we nearly died when she walked in, because she was about the size of Janette Krankie. She was wearing a little cloche hat and she looked about fourteen. She was twenty-eight, apparently, but she certainly didn't look it.

I thought: You cannot possibly talk to us all about vibrators! But she did, and she was very good.

The best party like this that I've had was at my house, with forty girls and my gay friend Nick, who kept going upstairs to model some of the gear for us. One great thing about having it at your house is that the hostess gets a goodie bag. Maria presided over the party again and it was really fun. It's not so much about what you buy — it's about having a laugh — but I bought lots of lipstick vibrators for presents. They're my favourite, because if one drops out of your bag, it just looks like a lipstick — unless it starts going 'drrrrrrr', of course! I'm not a fan of the rabbit, though. There are too many unnecessary bits to it, if you know what I mean.

JANE: I don't! Let me make that very clear right now!

LESLEY: Denise Welch, make sure I'm on your party list in future!

DENISE: OK! My hairdresser had a stripper at her Ann Summers party. I couldn't go, unfortunately, but he was apparently fantastic fun. So I'm going to have him at my next one. I'm about due another party; I want to restock a bit!

SHERRIE: Oh no, male strippers wouldn't interest me. I suppose some girls would think it was fun to go to see the Chippendales or some such show, but I'd find it very boring, I think. Once one of them has come out all sweaty and taken things off, it would be a case of, And? Next? What else is there to see and do? I'd sooner have a good meal. Give me asparagus spears any day.

LISA: Asparagus spears? Well, I've never been to an Ann Summers party, but I think it would be a giggle. Whether or not it's an Ann Summers party, girls getting together with products is quite a giggle. I'd go. I think it would be a good laugh. I wouldn't necessarily want to find out about the vibrators and bits and bobs, though. Actually, maybe I would, because until recently I didn't even know what a Rampant Rabbit was.

A guy at work was talking about them and he couldn't believe that a broad-minded woman in her forties who has lived a diverse life and travelled a lot didn't know what a Rampant Rabbit was. I never watched *Sex and the City*, you see.

'Stop it!' he said. 'Don't do that whole naïve, innocent little girl thing with me.'

'I don't know what you're talking about,' I said. 'What's a Rampant Rabbit?'

'How come someone like you doesn't know?'

I was really quite offended when I found out what it was. 'What do you mean, "someone like you"? Do I strike you as the kind of person who is sat at home with their Rampant Rabbit twenty-four/seven?'

Maybe I should know more about things like that, but when you've been in a relationship for a long time – thirteen years in my case – if you fancy a bunk-up, you have a bunk-up, don't you? And if I want a quiet moment to myself, it's usually because I want to sleep.

SHERRIE: I've never been to one. That sort of thing has never interested me, mainly because I'm not that kind of underwear person. Underwear doesn't interest me in that way. It's functional. I'm not really bothered as long as it's white, crisp and clean. I never wear black underwear. If I've got something colourful on, I will try and wear a nice coloured bra.

Carol is much more into underwear than I am; Carol has to have matching underwear and she can't actually function without it. If she's not wearing matching underwear, she has to go home and change. That's insanity. I'm not that person.

CAROL: Yes, Sherrie, I may like my matching underwear, and yes it does also have to match what I'm wearing that day. But I wouldn't go to an Ann Summers party, because I don't like all that contrived messing about with stupid toys. It's not really my scene. I'd rather just go down the pub!

SHERRIE: I don't suppose it's really me, either. I come from a time and a background where even to say the word 'vibrator' would make you feel quite sick. You couldn't even say it, let alone think that somebody actually used one. Denise is about six years younger than I am and she's at the other end of the scale from me. She is wild and I'm not. If all the *Loose* girls went, perhaps I'd think it was funny (and quite shocking and hysterical), but it's not somewhere I'd naturally go.

DENISE: Go on, Sherrie. You might find it liberating!

SHERRIE: Disgusting, more like! I wouldn't know where to look if someone started showing me a whole load of vibrators.

DENISE: Well, try looking at crucial things like size and speed-control adjusters, for a start!

SHERRIE: Denise, I have no idea what you're talking about.

JANE: And believe me, you don't want to know, either!

The hen party really perked up when Stavros arrived.

A friend gets in a strip-o-gram for your birthday – do you laugh or cry?

CAROL: Hmmm, I think my friends know me well enough not to do something like that! They wouldn't dare. They know it's not really me. But if they did, I would take it in good humour.

JANE: I would die. It would be the worst thing for me, especially publicly. No, I don't do that! I'm a bit of a Mary Whitehouse, don't forget.

LISA: I couldn't bear it. It undermines the people that are doing it and the people that are on the receiving end of it. I was at a party once where someone sent a really overweight woman strip-o-gram to this guy. I just couldn't understand why she was doing that to herself, because people were reacting to her size and saying, 'Oh, that's gross!' I'm not saying that if you are a large girl then you shouldn't be a strip-o-gram, but inevitably people are going to judge you and it's not necessarily going to be a good reaction. If you have enough nerve to do that, then all credit to you, but I know I would just flee.

ANDREA: What, even from your own party?

LISA: Look, anyone who knows me would never send me a strip-o-gram, even if it was a gorgeous bloke. I don't think there is anything sexy about a bloke taking his clothes off in a room full of people and being pointed at and humiliated in that way. Maybe I'm too anal and I sound like Jean Brodie or something. But it would ruin the whole party for me, especially if I'd gone to a lot of trouble and organised a bloody good birthday party and then somebody killed it by sending in a nude person. That would just be awful.

ANDREA: I would absolutely hate it, too! I got a bit worried before my hen weekend last summer, as I would rather die than have a man strip in front of me! Luckily, it didn't happen. I'd happily go to somebody else's party where there's a stripper, but personally I'd rather go for a nice spa break! I'd prefer a pedicure to a stripper.

DENISE: I would hate it as well. I love organising surprises for people, but I hate getting them. Tim was in a play in Newcastle for my last birthday and I said, 'I'll come up and see the show on Saturday. Then we'll go out with some friends and have some dinner.'

'Oh, I'm sort of planning something for you,' he said.

'Nooo, please don't!'

It reminds me of when I was on *This Is Your Life*. That was such a pressured gig for me. I was thinking, Oh dear, has Tim organised this himself? If so, it will be rubbish! There'll be nobody I know well there, just all the people I hate: Der-dum-dum-daaar! 'Whose voice is this?'

'Errrr . . . oh no, not him!'

Luckily my dad had had a lot of input into it, so it was good. But it's quite a tense experience, because you're looking around and thinking, I hope he hasn't forgotten so-and-so. I hope they're going to come.

It was a strange day generally. It was a shame, because I wasn't very well. Everything seemed a bit weird, but I just put it down to my depression. I was supposed to be opening a motor trade show in London; it was back when I was in *Coronation Street* and I was being offered a lot of personal appearances. I remember my agent asked Tim to come with me, and I thought, Why is he coming with me? Well, it was to stop me drinking, apparently, because they knew I wasn't very well.

So I went down to London, opened the show and got on the train straight back. I really wasn't well at all and I just wanted to do the next thing and get home. Then, to my surprise, my agent Barry was on the train! He said he was going to Manchester to see somebody.

'Are you all right?' Tim asked.

'No, I'm not very well,' I told him. Next I was supposed to be opening a garden centre in Bolton and I wasn't sure if I felt up to it.

'Well, why don't you put some makeup on?' Tim said.

'Hmm, no, I just can't be bothered.'

'Go on, put some makeup on!' he insisted.

'But why? I'm only going to a blooming garden centre in Bolton!'

When I got off the train, I spotted a man with a video camera. What's going on here? I wondered. I didn't suspect anything, but there was something weird about it. Then Barry and Tim said that the car was at another exit to the one we usually used. So I followed them there and then bloody Michael Aspel got out of a white limousine! Aaargh! It was just a bit too much; I really wasn't well.

Worst of all, I then had four hours to wait before I went on and I spent them on my own with the makeup girl. I was really quite panicky. So it wasn't the experience it could have been, because of my illness.

There's a nice ending to the story, though, because some time after that, they had a massive party for a thousand people who had been on *This Is Your Life*. I was number one thousand, so that was really cool, and it was a great party. I felt really quite proud looking around at all the other people who were there.

JANE: Just remind me how we got from strip-o-grams to *This Is Your Life*, again?

DENISE: Sorry, that one went all round the 'houses! I just wanted to say that I hate surprises, really.

JANE: OK, I'll bear that in mind when your next birthday comes around!

You suspect your friend's partner is cheating. What do you do?

JANE: I'd keep my mouth shut. I think it's their business. The messenger is usually the one that's shot. Then, if they get back together and get over it, you're the enemy.

CAROL: Too right, so I would do absolutely nothing. Women are very perceptive and intuitive and I think that if their partner is cheating, they probably already know but don't want to accept it. So I reckon that if you're the one who gives them that news, they're just going to fall out with you. They need to find out for themselves. I don't know any woman who's ever thanked another woman for telling her that her partner's cheating on her, ever. On the other hand, I know quite a few women who have fallen out with women for bringing them that news.

It's another story if she asks you. First I would say, 'Are you sure you'd want to know, if the answer was yes? You need to be prepared for that news.' I wouldn't give anything away, but I would ask her to think about whether or not she really wanted me to answer the question honestly.

SHERRIE: Well, I had a friend who knew my husband was cheating, but she didn't tell me, so I fell out with her over it later. 'You watched me go through hell because I didn't know where he was,' I said, when I found out. 'Why didn't you tell me? I was absolutely sure he was cheating, but I couldn't prove it.'

I could have left him, but I could never be sure that I was right. When I confronted him, he always said to me, 'You're mad. Of course I'm not doing anything.' He said he had never even looked at another woman, when in fact he was having a big affair and going off to all sorts of places.

Later on, I found out from him that my friend had known all along. She'd not been his confidante, but she'd known what was going on and hadn't said anything. My husband said, 'Well, I'll tell you who did know.' It was a real stab in the back. Awful.

I was so angry with her. 'If you had told me, I could have left him, made a new start and a new life,' I told her.

'But you wouldn't have believed me,' she said. 'And it wasn't my place to tell you.'

She was so wrong! 'You saw what I was going through and you knew that he was cheating,' I said to her. If she'd said to me, 'Actually, Sherrie, he is,' then I'd have said to him, 'You are cheating, and you can get out of this house now.' But all along I thought it was my problem. I thought, I'm going absolutely mad! He's not cheating. It destroyed my life. In the end, I thought, It's so terrible that I keep persecuting this man when he's not doing anything. I thought, I'm really bad. I'm a bad person.

My friend used to say, 'Maybe he's not really cheating.' How could she say that? You can't do that when you see somebody suffering like that. In my book, she was a liar and she had a responsibility to tell me.

I would have much preferred her to say, 'Actually, I do know he is having an affair.' Then I would have been angry. I would have gone crazy, but I would have dealt with it. However, as it was, I had nothing to deal with, so I believed I was mad.

If I were in her shoes, I wouldn't mind losing her as a friend as long as she found out about the lie she was living and had the choice to get out of it. It turned out that she'd seen him in a park kissing another woman. 'Why didn't you tell me you saw him snogging another girl?' I asked her.

'How can you tell somebody that?' she said.

Well, I damn well would tell someone. Absolutely I would. And if they didn't talk to me again, at least they'd know the bloody truth about the person they were living with. I wouldn't do it for myself. I wouldn't do it to keep my friend. I'd do it because I wouldn't want her partner to get away with it.

'You knew!' I said to her. 'How could you not have told

me?' I didn't speak to her again for a long time. We have spoken since, but I can't forgive that. I suppose that one day we might be friends again, though.

But I can't help thinking that if she'd told me, I would have chucked him out instead of letting him leave me. I might have got married again and had more children. Keeley could have had siblings; she might not have been an only child. I would have had a whole new world, had I known.

CAROL: You wouldn't have chucked him out! You knew what he was up to for ages. The fact is that women always blame other women for everything. You're blaming your friend for not telling you because you feel bad that you wasted so much time and didn't get out when you knew you should have done. That's just what people do. Women are weird. It's never the guy who gets all the crap in this situation. It's always the other woman. I just find that strange.

LYNDA: Well, that's not always true, Carol, but I know what you mean. It's a problem, isn't it? I think I'd have a conversation with her and see if she knew or had any idea. If he was a serial philanderer, I might say something like, 'Aren't you ever worried that he'll go back to his old ways?' I'd do it in a roundabout way and see what her response was. If I knew for sure, I think I'd have to tell her, at the risk of losing her friendship.

My first husband was a serial philanderer and nobody ever told me. I had an inkling that he was and I wanted somebody to tell me absolutely positively, but nobody would. Now, would that have helped me in the end? Probably not, because maybe I would still have make excuses for him. But the not-knowing is agonising and I've been there – before we were married, I once sat outside my first husband's house all night. He was cleverer than I was, though, and I didn't catch him out.

After we got married, I sat outside another person's house, but still I couldn't catch him out, or not until much later. So I absolutely understand the agony. It builds and builds until it is absolute torture. In retrospect, I would try to avoid letting it get that far. I would confront him, although that's not going to get you anywhere if he's a seasoned liar, of course. What's more, you believe what you want to believe. Would I hire a detective? If I had the money to pay someone else to sit outside someone's apartment all night, I probably would! Certainly now, yes, because I wouldn't waste my time with that person if they were cheating and I would want to know if they were. Life is too short. That would be the end of it.

I used to do interviews when I was married to the serial philanderer and when journalists asked questions about marriage and fidelity, I'd think, Do they know something that I don't know? Even now, I'm hesitant, because it's like tempting fate. But I can honestly say, with my hand on my heart, that I don't think Mr Spain would do that to me and I certainly wouldn't do it to him. If it's got to that point where you feel the need to be unfaithful, then you'd better split up first and then be unfaithful.

But there's nothing worse than everybody else knowing and you not knowing. That's the main reason I think I'd tell my friend. If she didn't speak to me as a result, I'd wait for her to get over it. People do get over things and they do talk to you again, especially as you get older.

ANDREA: Would you consider going one step further on from a detective and setting up a honeytrap for someone you suspected of cheating?

LYNDA: I would never consider that, because there are a lot of layers of attraction. A honeytrap is not the way to do it. It's just too obvious. If I went out and found a girl who was physically my husband's ideal woman and put them together, he might well be flattered and they might well flirt. But what is your idea of 'giving in'? She might well try to kiss him, he might well respond; but that doesn't mean he's any intention of going to bed with her, or has been unfaithful in his head to me. People are human; I understand that.

If he went on to be unfaithful – well, that's a much more complex area. You'd have to look at what state your relationship is in. You could be really big about it and think, Oh, there is a problem in my relationship that I didn't know about. But, equally, it's really difficult to step outside your own jealousies, insecurities and wounded pride. And yet, people aren't unfaithful because somebody's good-looking. Look at life! Why is she with him? Why is he with her? You see all sorts of apparently mismatched couples.

ANDREA: That's so true. You're very wise, Lynda! Back to the original question: would you tell your friend if you suspected her partner was cheating, Denise?

DENISE: I wouldn't tell her, because people shoot the messenger. Like Jane, I've seen instances where someone has

 told her friend and then become *persona non grata* when the couple got back together and resolved their problems.

God it's always such a difficult one, isn't it? If she asked me outright, I think I would alert the partner that she might be aware of it. Hopefully, that would either make him end the affair, or be more careful. Morally, I wouldn't judge anybody, even my best friends, because I don't know what the dynamic is in their house. It would just be a case of telling him that I know, and that maybe other people know, so maybe he should get his house in order.

If I were her, I wouldn't want to know if it was a one-night stand. I really wouldn't. But if it was an affair, I suppose I would be angry if she'd known and not told me. It's a really tricky one, a real dilemma. I'm fortunate in that I've not really been in that situation. In this business you tend to turn a blind eye, because everything goes on. I'm not condoning it, but it happens and seeing it is just a part of my life. What about you, Andrea? What would you do?

ANDREA: I'd do nothing, I think. I'd just be there for them when they found out. Maybe I'd drop little hints, something like, 'Are you sure he's being as nice to you as you deserve? Because you're lovely.'

It's quite complicated, because sometimes they might know, but are pretending that they don't and they don't want it pointed out to them. So it's probably more important to let them know that you're there if things do fall apart.

If she asked me directly, I would tell her what I knew as nicely and as gently as I could. I wouldn't embellish or make a drama out of it. I wouldn't say, 'Thank God you asked, because I've been desperate to tell you!' I would just tell her straight. Even if the friendship was very strong, some people shoot the messenger and the last thing I would want is not to be able to help her. I've been in situations with lovely girl-friends who are seeing people that just aren't right for them. They know it and you know it and they know that you know, but all you can do is be there and wait.

LISA: Oh god. My personal experience of situations like this tells me that I would have to stay out of it. I would probably back off and withdraw from them both. I don't think there is any merit in being the one who points the finger, because you don't know how she is going to react. She might say, 'Well actually, I don't have a problem with it.'

By taking it on, you have to follow through. By that I mean that if you think what he is doing is wrong and you say that what he is doing is wrong, you are in some way forcing her to make a decision, when in fact some people just don't want to know.

But if she said, 'I think my husband or boyfriend is having an affair. Do you know anything about it?' I'd tell her the truth. I wouldn't lie.

'Yes, I think he is,' I'd say, 'because I've seen this, that or the other.' But if she wasn't aware of it, if it wasn't something she'd discovered or it wasn't worrying her, I wouldn't necessarily want to bring it to her attention.

I've been in the reverse situation actually, where my friend was cheating on her partner. When the partner asked me where she was and what she was up to, I lied for her because she'd asked me to. I got on really well with the partner, so I did feel for him, but by the same token I had made a decision about who I was closest too. I have to say that I didn't like being put in that situation in the first place; a friend that puts you on the spot like that is a bit naughty, really.

My past experience tells me if nobody asks the question or is aware of the problem, then I don't want to be the one that brings the problem to the door, because with that comes a whole bunch of responsibility that would only ever come back and bite you in the bottom. Whatever they decide to do, whether they perhaps make it up or split, you're getting far too involved.

COLEEN: I think I'd have a word with him first. I'd say, 'Look, I know what you're doing. Either stop it right now or tell her yourself and sort your relationship out. Otherwise, I'll tell her.' That's what I would want my friends to do with me.

The problem with telling your friend is that you have to remember that she loves him and she will probably forgive him. But neither of them will ever forgive you. So you could lose a friend. On the other hand, if you know for definite and don't do anything, and your friend finds out, she'll probably never forgive you anyway. I would never do it just on a suspicion, though, in case I was wrong.

LESLEY: Like you, Coleen, I'd probably encourage the partner to stop cheating. I certainly wouldn't tell my friend. If she asked me, I'd say, 'I think you must talk to your husband about that.'

A friend's partner makes a pass at you. What do you do?

LESLEY: I'd slap him down firmly and, when he'd sobered up – assuming that this was a drunken moment – I'd say, 'You must never do that again. That's completely out of order and I won't have it.' I'd make my boundaries very clear. I wouldn't tell my friend as I think that would be overstepping the mark, but I'd want to try to do something to stop it happening, for my friend's sake.

SHERRIE: I'd probably get a knife and stab him! But actually, it has happened a couple of times and I didn't stab them. One time, the guy was married to a girl I didn't know well, but I'd met her. He made a real thing of it, a big pass. 'You know I've always been mad about you,' he said.

When I said that I'd tell her, he said, 'What?'

I said, 'Well, why wouldn't I tell her?'

'Oh my god,' he exclaimed, going into shock. 'Please don't tell her! Please don't tell her!'

'Why? Didn't you mean it?' I asked.

'Yes, but oh my God, please don't tell her.'

I really made him suffer. I said, 'I'm sorry, but I'm going to have to.' I just wanted to see him squirm and get out of it – and he began more or less breaking down in front of me. In reality, I would never have told her. But he went green and he left. He was just trying it on. You little creep, I thought.

DENISE: It's happened loads of times to me. It's nearly always been drink-related, so I've just said, 'Oh, don't be so ridiculous! For goodness' sake, you've had a drink, etc, etc.'

I'm very flirtatious, and I remember one time when I was having a flirt with a friend at a party Tim and I went to. I assumed that this friend and his wife were happy together. They were both good friends of ours.

But a few days later I got this call from him. 'Do you feel the same way as I do?' he asked.

I thought, God, No! It was just a flirty-dancing-with-man-at-wedding scenario! Well, I'm not very good in that kind of situation. I hate hurting anybody's feelings. So I said, 'Oh, I'm really sorry if I gave you that impression, but she's my friend and I could never do that to her.'

'I'm really embarrassed!' he said.

'Don't be embarrassed, please don't be embarrassed!' I said.

'Well, we've just been having problems, you see . . .' he said. It was so awful!

LYNDA: Fortunately, my antennae are very quick to pick up those kinds of men. So I wouldn't allow myself to be in a position where he could embarrass himself or compromise my friendship with somebody else. It happened once, at a party. I basically told him to get lost. I tried to make it jokey and I think he understood I was saying no, but then he pushed it a little bit further and I had to say, 'I mean it. Don't even go there.' I just left it at that.

The kind of people who look outside their relationship for excitement, who flirt all the time and go round to each other's houses for dinner, aren't the kind of people I'm friendly with. I find it all very odd.

Despite the fact that I flirt with men and women, I'm very tactile and I'll hug everybody, very few people make passes at me. The husband I was married to for sixteen years accused me of sleeping with all and sundry, which was totally in his head and bore no relationship to reality. It was a classic case of not understanding the person he was married to. I would rather stand in a room of twenty men and make them laugh than try to go to bed with any of them. That's much more my thing. I'd like to be noticed, but that's as far as it goes.

COLEEN: I'm with you there, Lynda. I'd much rather see a man laugh than drool with lust.

SHERRIE: And that's much more likely to happen when you get to my age!

LYNDA: Seriously, it can be an insult in my profession if someone makes a pass. You think, Does that mean they don't think I'm talented? Why don't they just want to talk to me? Why don't they just want my talent? It's like the casting couch – why would they want to sleep with me? Why aren't I a good enough actress that they just want me for what I am? It's a very weird feeling.

COLEEN: Have you ever considered that they might want to cast you *and* sleep with you?

LYNDA: Well, that may be, but I'm talking about when they're just taking advantage!

LISA: For me, a dilemma like this depends on the circumstances. If it's at a party and everybody's having a drink and he's put his arm around me or put his hand in the wrong place, I would laugh it off and excuse it. But it would be different if somebody

lurched at me and tried to stick their tongue down my throat, although I still don't think I would tell my friend.

A couple of times a friend's partner has been just a little bit too fresh or tactile with me, or they've said something like, 'You know, I've always really liked you.'

In response, I've said, 'You don't really mean that, do you? Because if you say something like that, you're going to get into really big trouble, because I'm going to go and tell her.' I would always deal with it then and there. I wouldn't take the problem and then multiply it by a million by going to her and saying, 'Do you know what he did?' I'm a big girl and I can handle it myself. If he is out of order, I'll tell him that he is out of order and that if he ever does it again, I will tell her.

COLEEN: I'm quite offended because it's never happened to me. I must ask them all why! If someone did, oh my God, I'd be horrified. I'd hate it, I'd hate him and I'd just think he was a sleaze-bag. Plus, I don't fancy any of my friend's partners!

But if a man makes a pass at me in general, that's marvellous. Actually, it depends what kind of pass it is. If he's just flirting, that's fine, but if he tried to kiss me, I'd probably give him a good smack across the face and tell him to wait until we are in private.

JANE: Ooh, you minx!

ANDREA: What would you do if your friend's partner made a pass, Carol?

CAROL: I would make sure they knew that they were messing with the wrong person. I wouldn't say anything to my friend, though. I don't think that would be particularly helpful.

JANE: I would say, 'Don't be stupid!' and keep my mouth shut. I'm an outrageous flirt – I flirt with anything that moves – but I'd run a mile if anybody tried anything.

It's safe flirting though. I'm not implying, I want you in bed. It's just saying, You look good. It's about making people feel better about themselves. I get picked up on that all the time on *Loose Women*, but I wouldn't be the one to have the affair.

ANDREA: Like you, Jane, I'd tell him not to be so stupid. It happened once and I didn't tell Steve until months later. He was moaning about my friend not trusting her partner and I said, 'Actually she's right, he is a bit of a bounder, because he made a pass at me.'

'Why didn't you tell me at the time?' he asked.

'Because it wasn't a problem and I dealt with it and it's over.' I wouldn't have told him if he didn't need to know, but since it came up, I did.

JANE: That's him told, isn't it, love?

ANDREA: Well, you know how it is! Sometimes there just isn't time to beat around the bush.

DENISE: I'm not sure I agree!

You don't like your partner's best friend. Do you put up with them or try and edge them out?

CAROL: I wouldn't try and edge him out, but I wouldn't pretend I liked them. He hasn't got any friends that I don't like, by the way, but if he did, I would probably tolerate them for a while and then choose not to be around when they were around. I don't need to like all his friends and he doesn't need to like all of mine. After all, they're his friends, not mine. I didn't choose them. You do inherit certain friends and family when you hook up with somebody, but I wouldn't make a secret of not liking someone. I'd just say, 'I don't really like so-and-so. Do you mind if I don't come out?' I think if someone was grown-up they wouldn't mind that too much.

ANDREA: That's right. Just because I don't necessarily like someone, it doesn't mean they're not nice. So if they're perfectly nice, but I just find them a bit annoying and they're not my cup of tea, then I wouldn't do anything. I would just put up with them and hope that they grew on me. But if it was someone I didn't like because I didn't trust them – or I thought maybe they were taking advantage of Steve, or weren't honest – then I would say so. I'm very protective.

A really gorgeous man makes a pass at you. Would you be tempted, even if you were in a relationship?

JANE: No, I'd be such a letdown. I'm just not made that way. I can't be bothered with single men, never mind with ones who are attached. When I was single, the girls used to make me laugh by urging me to go on a second date with someone. But I couldn't be bothered with the hassle – and an affair would be all hassle. The only reason I'm with this one now is because we had a history before.

CAROL: Well, I'd be flattered but not tempted.

ANDREA: Come on, even with Russell Brand?

CAROL: Even with Russell Brand. They all had their chance and they blew it! No, I'm a proper one-man woman and I would never jeopardise what I've got, just by being an idiot for a night.

LYNDA: I'm a very loyal person, so I could fall out of love with my husband and not fancy him any more, but I still wouldn't be unfaithful to him. I wouldn't put myself in a position where I could be tempted. I would just end the relationship.

COLEEN: I suppose it depends what state your marriage is in. I'm very happy in my marriage at the moment – and, God willing, I will be forever more – so absolutely not. So I wouldn't jeopardise my happiness, no matter how good-looking he was. If you didn't really fancy your husband any more, or if you're not sure if you're happy, then I can understand the temptation. But then I think you have to sort it out really.

Years ago, I had an affair when I was with Shane. It was during a very unhappy time in my marriage, but it was still a mistake and it's still something I'm ashamed of. I should have gone to Shane first and said, 'I'm really unhappy. If we don't sort this out, I'm vulnerable to somebody else coming along and paying me attention.'

If he still hadn't made an effort to change and I went ahead and had an affair, then I wouldn't have felt as guilty, because I'd have thought, Well, I did warn him this was going to happen.

But I didn't warn him. He knew we weren't right at that point, but he still didn't deserve what I did. People have said, 'Yes he did deserve it, because he was ignoring you and making you feel crap.' It's true, he was, but I should have talked to him about that. I learned from that mistake and I wouldn't do it again. If I ever felt that I wasn't happy with Ray, God forbid, or that our marriage wasn't right, then I would have to sit down with him and tell him.

ANDREA: When in the marriage did you have the affair?

COLEEN: It was after my second son Jake was born and Shane had just got the part of Nicky in *Grease*. He was wrapped up in his own world, while I was stuck at home with the new baby and a three-year-old, feeling very overweight and unloved. In fact, I felt very much like a single parent. Knowing that he was surrounded by beautiful dancers didn't help – it made me feel incredibly insecure.

Then I went off and did a summer season with my sisters, because I was still performing with my sisters back then. During the eight weeks I was away, I met somebody who gave me all the attention I had been craving. I fell for it hook, line and sinker. Suddenly I felt so much better, because this man made me feel attractive and funny again. It was so good to know that there was somebody out there who did find me attractive; it did a lot for my ego and my pride.

It was over as soon as Shane got an inkling that it was happening and asked me about it. It was over before then, actually, but it was definitely over then. I couldn't stand the pain in his face and I can't lie about things like that. It made me feel horrendous and I realised that I didn't want to lose what I had. It was a big wake-up call for both of us. For the next two years, our marriage was probably the best it had ever been, because we both made a real effort. I think that's why I was so shocked when he ended up having an affair – because we were so happy at the time. If I'd been a bit of a bitch or we'd stopped having sex, then it would be easier to understand why he did it. But we were dead happy and our sex life was great.

I suppose he just wanted the best of both worlds – the girl he had an affair with was around eighteen, so his ego was being massively fed; but at the same time, he loved having the family to go home to. It started just after he moved to Manchester to do *Grease*. I stayed in London to look after the boys, which meant that we were only seeing each other two Sundays in a month. We were living separate lives, really.

LESLEY: That is always tough – you need to make time for each other to keep the spark alive.

COLEEN: Yes, and when we did have time together, it wasn't quality time. He'd drive back to London from Manchester after the show on a Saturday night and be absolutely knackered by the time he arrived. So he would sleep most of the day Sunday and leave very early on the Monday morning to go back to the show. I said to him, 'Maybe I could move to Manchester?'

'No, no, no,' he'd say. 'It would be silly to move the boys.' Of course, the affair had already started by then. And it started pretty quickly, that was the thing. It wasn't like we did four months of it, and then he had an affair. It started almost on day one of him going away. It just shows: you have to take extra care to think of each other when children come along, because you get so wrapped up in the kids.

Now I hate the saying, 'What happens on set, stays on set.' Not for me, it doesn't. I've made that mistake once in my life and I would never, ever make it again. It was horrific. I see it go on a lot, though.

Apart from loving Ray, I like him too much to make a fool of him. You know the kind of situation: where everybody knows except him, where he comes onto set one day and I'm pretending everything is fine, while everybody on set knows. I couldn't do that to him. It's just awful. In a way, I suppose it proves that my first marriage wasn't right, because I just can't imagine doing that now.

ANDREA: There's not a lot of point in going through bad experiences if you don't learn from them, is there? It's great that you're so happy now, Coleen.

LYNDA: Hear, hear!

ANDREA: What about you, Sherrie? Can you imagine ever being unfaithful?

SHERRIE: Well, there was one particular person who will be absolutely nameless. I suppose you could call it an emotional affair, but I don't consider it to be real infidelity. Things were bad for me at home and things were bad for him at his home. It wasn't like we were happy and just playing around. We came together because of unhappiness.

I don't want to sound as if I'm frivolous or that I was being unfaithful emotionally, because I wasn't. I was very true and loyal. It was a bit like the affair Wendy Craig had on *Butterflies* – she wasn't actually unfaithful, but she had clandestine meetings. It was the same for us. 'Where can we meet?' he'd ask. One of us would pick a road in the A to Z and we'd agree to meet there. It was exciting. 'Here's the postcode, see you there.'

So I'd find this road and his car would be there. I'd get out of my car into his car and we'd just drive around. Sometimes we'd just go for lunch, but it was truly exciting.

DENISE: That's really no different to actually sleeping with somebody, though, is it? You were still being unfaithful.

SHERRIE: I don't agree. I would never, ever have let it go that far! Whatever happened, I was still married.

DENISE: It's still a betrayal, though.

SHERRIE: No, it wasn't betrayal, because I wouldn't consider anything to have been a betrayal in that marriage. It wasn't like I had a husband who was totally loved-up and loyal. If I had, I wouldn't have done it. I'm a truly loyal person right to the end.

This man used to ring me and say, 'I'm in London today. Meet me in such-and-such street. I'll be wearing a white carnation.'

'You don't need a white carnation! I know what you look like!'

'I know, but I just like to wear one.' We got a bit silly, really.

We really did like being in each other's company. You know when you meet somebody and the day goes too fast? You meet at ten a.m. and suddenly it's ten at night, but it feels like it's been just an hour.

It was wrong, but not in my particular marriage, it wasn't. I wasn't really interested in the other guy's relationship problems. I just assumed that he was as unhappy as I was. But I was quite young and, when I look back, it was just magical. It ended, of course, for no particular reason other than we were both married, and it was awfully sad when it ended, but it was a magical time in my life.

I was married and there was never a possibility of it going further – I had a child; he had two children. In the end, he left his wife and married somebody else; he's very happily married now. I occasionally bump into him and we are great friends when we do, but we don't really talk about it. Perhaps we look at each other and smile in remembrance, but nothing more.

It was a long time ago, but I remember. I think it saved me in many ways. In the deepest, blackest moment, when I found out all the things that my ex-husband had done, I was able to think about the joy of our meetings and cherish the fact that I'd experienced it with him. It would make me smile and helped me get through the disaster I was living in.

ANDREA: I wouldn't be at all tempted – unless it was George Clooney, and then that's allowed. But when I met David Hasselhoff, I didn't even flicker across his radar, which was devastating, because he has a bit of a reputation for being a twinkly ladies' man. Even a little bit of flickering is quite nice – you want to register!

COLEEN: As everyone can see on *Loose Women*, I'm a big flirt. But I know exactly the kind of flirting that Ray is cool with and exactly the kind that he wouldn't stand for. It's totally tongue-in-cheek and if I meant it I wouldn't be doing it in front of a million people; that would just be ridiculous.

I've always said to him, 'You'd have to let me with George Clooney, though.'

'OK, but then you'd have to let me with Angelina Jolie,' he says.

You say yes to people you assume they will never meet, but the funny thing is that there's every chance I'll meet these people, being in this business. When Enrique Iglesias came on the show, I proved that I'm a bigger flirt than he is, although he's quite good at it. In reality, I'm a cowardly flirt, the biggest wuss you've ever met in your life. I can flirt in front of a million people and my best friends on *Loose Women*, but if I met Enrique backstage, I would run a mile. I'm shocking. I'd say something like, 'I was only joking,' and then leg it. I can't bear it if they think I'm serious. Not that Enrique would, but there have been times in the past where I've flirted with blokes in general and then all of a sudden you're left on your own with them and you think, Oh my God, I was only joking. It's horrible if they think you're serious, so I start to get pictures of my kids out.

Do you have an obligation to behave yourself when you represent one half of a couple?

CAROL: Don't look at me! I don't get drunk so often now I'm with Mark.

DENISE: Really?

CAROL: The problem with Mark and myself is that I always end up getting drunker than him. It's because there's an age difference of twenty years between us – when I was twenty-seven I could drink all night and I still wouldn't fall over, whereas it's different now.

DENISE: I know, but you only let him have alcopops!

CAROL: Don't start! The thing is that I'm a lightweight, although I try to pace myself. I do try not to make a fool of myself when I'm with Mark, or when I'm anywhere, in fact!

LESLEY: Do you succeed?

CAROL: Well, he had to carry me out of the taxi the other night, but it was my birthday.

LESLEY: That's OK then!

CAROL: When I'm in a situation with a lot of people I don't know, I'm well behaved and I know when I have to go to bed, but when I'm with Mark and my friends it's completely different.

DENISE: We always say that Carol is like the rabbit with the battery. Wait! I didn't mean *that* rabbit with the battery! No!

LESLEY: Yes you did!

DENISE: No, I mean the little pink toy rabbit that jumps around. She goes on jumping until she suddenly just keels over. She doesn't get that battery flash warning that the energy's running out.

CAROL: He doesn't seem to mind, actually.

LESLEY: I have to say that I've never, ever seen my husband paralytic. He gets very giggly and like a girl when he's had a bit of a drink. Me, on the other hand . . . Well, I actually blame my dad for this, because when we were young, my dad used to make home-brew out of anything organic, from old tyres to the chair leg. He mixed it with lemonade and you wouldn't know what it was. So we always had family round, drank my dad's home-brew and then had a singsong. That's my big problem – I sing when I get drunk!

CAROL: Well, that's natural. You're a singer!

LESLEY: But I got into a terrible trouble with Michael Ball at a wrap party once. You know what wrap parties are like – you're all tense and you've done your series; it's been really hard and then you let it all go and get drunk. In that situation, drink is three times as potent, it seems to me, and Michael led me astray. We ended up singing 'Nessun Dorma', I think!

The next day the family was going to Thailand on holiday and I threw up at every stage of the journey, even in the bins at Heathrow! That was the last time I was ever that naughty.

DENISE: I love that image! Oh, Lesley! I'm much less tolerant of Tim when he's drunk than he is of me when I'm drunk. What I can't bear is when he becomes like the pub drunk and does that sideways walking thing. Whisky turns him into the biggest know-all in the world, so if someone has run a cats' home successfully for twenty years, Tim will say, 'You know where you're going wrong with your cats? You don't want to be feeding them that! They want the dried food.'

'Darling,' I say, 'I think you'll find that they've been doing fine for twenty years and since you've never even had a cat in your entire life, would you just shut up?'

When it comes to me, when I have been carried out of the taxi by the taxi driver, who once had to imagine where I lived because I couldn't even talk, Tim's much more tolerant, unless I come in cruising for a bruising.

CAROL: Poor Tim!

DENISE: What do you mean, poor Tim?

CAROL: It's sweet that he tells everyone how to run their business!

Should you give something up if your partner wants you to?

LYNDA: I have a very poignant story about this. When I met Mr Spain, we both drank too much or, at least, sometimes we had too much to drink. He gave up drinking for medical reasons and I continued on my own, because why shouldn't I have a good time? My friends and I liked to go out for one of those long Sunday lunches that would last all day and long into the night, but it's quite boring when you don't drink; I now find them quite dull.

Michael didn't try to stop me drinking, but he said, 'Now I don't drink, it's boring, so I'm not going to come over from Spain and spend all Sunday with you when you're inebriated. Let me know, if you're going out to lunch, that's fine, and I'll come the weekends that you're not.'

It was very clever really, and it lasted two weeks, because I thought, I'm not having such a good time now! He meant more to me than anything, so I gave up drinking. I realised that it had become a huge divide between us, and there comes a point when you do start to drift apart, for all sorts of different reasons. With us, it could have been much worse. If it had ended up with me continuing to drink and him not drinking, I don't think we'd have a relationship.

SHERRIE: You've got to drink together to have a good time, haven't you?

LYNDA: Well, it doesn't often work if one of you doesn't, let's say.

LESLEY: It's so easy to start to lose your partner without realising it, isn't it?

SHERRIE: Oh, I'm glad I lost mine!

LESLEY: Yes, you realised it! No, but I felt a little bit vulnerable in that way myself by the time I was in my eighth month of doing eight shows a week of *Carousel*. Peter, my husband, is a doctor, so he was at work all day doing the day shift; I was doing the night shift and we hardly ever saw each other. I found that incredibly hard. He managed to crawl into the theatre once a week to fall asleep on my settee, just so that we could get to see each other.

I partly gave up international work because I didn't want this to happen; I wanted us to be together. Having been a straightforward opera singer for fifteen years – at the English National Opera, predominantly – I began to expand my career and started to sing internationally, which is the next stage after a domestic career. But it got to the point when I didn't want to travel any more. The worst moment was when I missed my daughter's first birthday. I was performing in St Louis and I sang Tchaikovsky's 'None But the Lonely Heart', and burst into tears in front of fifteen hundred people. 'I'm really sorry,' I said to the audience. 'You're really lovely, but I just shouldn't be here. It's my daughter's first birthday and I should be at home.' They thought it was wonderful and gave me a standing ovation. That gave me the impetus to sing the rest of the concert and then I immediately came home. I didn't do that again; well, not without my son and daughter, anyway.

SHERRIE: You have to make these choices in life.

LESLEY: Exactly, and so I mainly took on work that kept me in this country, particularly in London. But, during *Carousel*, even though I was in London, I wasn't seeing him. The last few weeks were very difficult. I didn't realise it could happen. It crept up on me unawares.

ANDREA: Yes, you really need to see each other more than once a week to keep the spark in a marriage.

LESLEY: I originally said I was going to do it for six months. Then I was persuaded to do it for longer and Peter found that very hard. I felt very torn, because I was very committed to the show, but obviously my first and most important commitment is always to him and to the family. Still, he was very generous in allowing me to continue with it, because we were trying very hard to keep the show going. I'm blessed with a very understanding partner. It was tough on us and we got quite tetchy with one another, which isn't something we do. Selfishly, I'm glad that the show ended when it did.

SHERRIE: I would have been so thrilled in your situation, Lesley! I didn't want to be in my marriage and didn't know how to get out, so I would have thought: Yes, I don't have to go home! I'm not going to see him for eight days!

LYNDA: No, but when you were still involved emotionally with him and you saw that coming, there must have been a moment when you thought, This can go one way or the other. That's when it's time to confront it and do something about it, because if you do let it go, then the distance between you just grows wider.

LESLEY: Yes, fortunately I saw what was happening and I had a chance to do something about it. It was hard, because I did love being in *Carousel*! It's that kind of pull that's really difficult to deal with.

SHERRIE: You need to be a stay-at-home girl now.

LESLEY: Yes, Sherrie, I'll try and stay at home and be good.

SHERRIE: That'll probably last about five minutes!

LISA: I know exactly what it's like to feel that pull between work and home life. I partly left *The Bill* after seven years because I wasn't seeing enough of my family. The other reason was that I had two miscarriages last year, one in January and one in July.

COLEEN: That must have been awful for you. Did you have to go on working?

LISA: Well, I worked through the first one and I didn't think twice about it, because I'd got so used to working through everything. When you have a schedule like that you don't have sick days. I'm a pro and I always turn up and try to deliver. So the first time I thought, OK fine. Just carry on. I didn't want to let anybody down. I wasn't very far gone – just five and a half weeks pregnant – and since you can't tell anyone about it for the first three months, no one was any the wiser. Obviously I was very sad about it, though. Being forty la-la, you think it's your last chance – or one of the last chances – to have a child and I never really addressed it. I just worked through it.

I couldn't believe my luck when I got pregnant again. This time, I came very close to the time when you can tell people. Then I noticed some spotting and called my partner Paul. 'Come home now,' he said.

At first I was going to work through it. 'Oh, it's not going to make any difference,' I said. 'Whatever will be, will be. It's nature's way and all of that.' But then I thought, What the bloody hell am I talking about? I had really wanted the pregnancy to work.

COLEEN: Did you tell anyone at *The Bill*?

LISA: I felt very strongly that I didn't want to share my miscarriage experiences or my feelings of hurt with the guys at work, because most of the cast were men and it's quite a male-dominated scenario. I'm sure they would have been fine about it, but I was thinking, I can't talk about it because then they will think I'm vulnerable, weak and not able to cope with being a woman and all the pressure that goes with this job. It was a case of life imitating art.

It had got to the stage where I found it easier to be Sam Nixon, my character in *The Bill*, than to be Lisa and face up to real-life stuff that was going on. There weren't enough hours in the day to deal with my real life and get the job done. Working women nowadays are expected to be bloody invincible and I don't think we should be expected to be invincible.

ANDREA: No, that's right. Everyone has a breaking point. So what did you do?

LISA: I'd just rehearsed a scene and they'd given us a ten-minute break while they lit it before we went back to shoot it. It was a really light-hearted scene, the kind of scene that only really worked if you have a twinkle. It's hard to manufacture those twinkles. You have to convince yourself that you are in a really happy place.

Well, I was working with Patrick Robinson, a really fantastic actor, and he and I got on incredibly well. We were about to film a really charming scene and we were both on the verge of giggling, which gave it a lovely dimension. So when I had the spotting during the lighting break, my first thought was, I'm not going to be able to twinkle when I go back! I can't be on the verge of giggling any more, which means that the scene is going to lose a really important dimension. How unhealthy is that? I should have thought, I'm losing this baby and I need to go home and look after myself.

I confided in my friend Roberta Taylor, another actor on the show, and she said, 'You just cannot work through this, Lisa. I'm going to talk to the bosses right now because you are going to kill yourself if you don't go home.'

'Oh, all right then,' I said. It seemed easier to make a decision once somebody else was taking care of it, especially as she too was a consummate pro. I thought: Well, if she thinks that's the right thing to do, then I'll go with it.

But by now, Paul, bless him, had already rung my agent and said, 'Tell the producers that she won't be coming in tomorrow.'

It's good that everybody around me took care of it for me, because I would have just carried on and I think I would have suffered as a result of that. There are some things that you do have to address; you can't just ignore them. The deep psychological pain doesn't just go away.

ANDREA: It's better to face it, isn't it? No matter how hard that is.

LISA: Miscarriages are often hushed up and I think the secrecy perpetuates the kind of unhealthy attitude that I had – which is not to tell anybody, because you should be able to get on with it and deal with it, without it affecting your schedule or anybody else's life. Admittedly, that's a really big chunk of my personality anyway. I've been working in this industry since I was a child, so I have a ridiculously strong work ethic.

COLEEN: Join the club, love! So did you manage to have a proper break?

LISA: They were very sweet at *The Bill* and gave me a month off immediately, but it took me a while to stop feeling guilty about taking the time off. I knew that it meant that certain other actors would be called in on their days off to do my dialogue, so I felt like I was letting people down. As an actor

I'm very much a team player, so for the first week I kept thinking, Maybe I shouldn't have a whole month off. Maybe I should have taken a little less because it's going to screw up everybody else's time off.

I got it all wrong. What I really should have been thinking about was that Paul was equally sad about what had happened and this was something that we needed to go through together. Paul is always the voice of reason and he said, 'Stop worrying about all the other stuff. You need to spend some time with your family.' He was right. After the first feelings of guilt went away, it was heaven just being a mum and a partner, doing normal stuff like the school run, cooking dinner for Beau and having her mates over.

COLEEN: Did it change your perspective on work?

LISA: Absolutely. I told *The Bill* that my new contract would be my last contract. It felt like completely the right decision. It was so liberating to know that I was going to be free. I wasn't even worried about whether I'd work again.

ANDREA: And you were right not to worry, because we were just desperate to have you on the show!

LISA: That's so sweet of you! Yes, the very day that it was reported in the *Sun* that I was leaving the show, the *Loose Women* people rang up and said, 'Can we get you to come in regularly?'

I thought, Cor blimey, why not? It's a totally different vibe for me and the hours are amazing compared to *The Bill*, where I was working fourteen-hour days, six days a week. Beau's nine years old and I've not seen her very much over the last seven years, although one thing I've always done, no matter what, is read her a bedtime story. But it's great to be spending time with her again, and with Paul. I feel very lucky.

ANDREA: And how are you finding being a Loose Woman?

LISA: Being a Loose Woman is a much easier gig. I mean, you do a little bit of work and then you go down the pub. That's my kind of job. So I'm loving it!

ANDREA: You're definitely one of the girls!

After a relationship split, do you move on quickly or wallow in misery?

JANE: I like a wallow. One particular break-up was like a bereavement for me; it took me a long time to get over it. I was devastated; it was a massive thing. So I took the bottle of vodka and retired to the bathroom, many a night! And the pain went. It was marvellous. I'm not very good at crying in public, so I like to hole myself away and have a good cry. I spent about nine months drinking vodka in the bathroom! The crying wasn't like a sob or two, it was that howling type of crying, 'Aaaeerrrgh!' It was like a primal sound.

COLEEN: Who was outside that bathroom door? What on earth would they think you were doing in there?

JANE: The upside was that when I did finally think I was over the grief and I looked at myself in the mirror, I had long hair and I'd lost two stone!

COLEEN: Like a butterfly, being reborn!

LYNDA: I'm always very suspicious of people who get over these things really quickly. If you've been emotionally involved with somebody, just to stop feeling involved and carry on with life is a bit hard, I think. Still, I'm a bit more that way than some people are. I tend to dust myself down and start all over again. The trouble with me is that I'm so busy trying to start again and forget it that I don't learn any lessons from it. You also need to look at the mistakes you've made. Turning to the bottle is a bit of a danger, though. You might have left the bathroom eventually, Jane, but some people don't.

COLEEN: People tend to drink, thinking that it's going to help, when it can actually make things worse.

LYNDA: It's fine if it kick-starts a good cry, but you do have to leave it behind. The tendency to wallow is a bit irritating, I find. We've all got friends who've done that. After a while you think, Shut up!

 JANE: Also, having children means that you have to carry on, whereas I didn't have anybody. I didn't even have a dog!

JANE: No comment!

ANDREA: I do think you have to acknowledge the pain. You can't ignore it.

COLEEN: Yes, it's definitely healthy. Then one day you wake up and it doesn't hurt so much, and that's a great feeling. I went through it, but unfortunately for me, I went through it with that person in the same house for two years, which is really difficult to do.

JANE: Two years?

COLEEN: Yes, yes, oh dear. It was really difficult and I had wallowing days when I phoned up my friends and said, 'Don't come round, because I'm wallowing today.' I'd get all the sad records out: 'Separate Lives' by Phil Collins; 'All By Myself'; and 'Why' by Annie Lennox. It's good to have those days, but I'd only let myself have a day like that once or twice a week. The next time I wanted to stay in bed, I'd think, No, I have to get up and start trying to get happy again and get over it. Then, all of a sudden, you wake up and think, It doesn't hurt today. And he walks in and you think, I don't love you any more. Off you pop!

JANE: Yes, see ya! What a great feeling that is.

Do you keep reminders of loved ones who have gone or do you throw everything away?

COLEEN: I've got a lovely picture in my bedroom of my mum with Ciara. Looking at pictures is the way I remember people, along with the memories that I'll always have in my heart, which will always be with me. I haven't actually got any of my mum's jewellery or stuff like that, but Ray's got his dad's gold wedding band and all his war medals. He keeps them in a little box and he likes to get them out and it brings back memories.

JANE: Aaah!

COLEEN: I know it's lovely, but I've been hearing it for nine years! If I hear one more story about the war medals . . . I sometimes feel like I've been in the war. Still, it is lovely.

CAROL: I keep little things; I've got my grandma's wedding ring, which I wore when I was married the first time, because my grandma had a sixty-year marriage and I was hoping that mine would last as long. But my marriage only lasted two years! The other reason I wore it was because Chris didn't believe in jewellery, so he wouldn't buy me one, but I think it's important to have that symbol of being married.

When my mum died, we went through all of her stuff. I got a little display case to put on the wall and inside it I put all the funny little things that remind me of my mum. There's a metal claw-like implement to pull pickled onions out of the jar, which I've never seen anywhere else, ever! There's also her little clock that she was given when she became the *Daily Mirror* 'Barmaid of the Year' in 1973. She also had this cross-word-puzzle solver: you type in a word and it comes up with the word that the crossword is probably asking for. There are some other things in there as well and they all really remind me of my mum and how sweet she was.

JANE: That's really lovely, Carol. Mine's a plant. My gran had this lovely big plant that always looked very healthy. Well, I remember going to her flat once and saying, 'I just love your plant!'

'I'll give you a couple of cuttings,' she said.

At the time I thought, What are you giving me cuttings for? I don't know what to do with them!

But now I've got these two massive plants in my house that were the cuttings from my gran's plant and I get so much joy from seeing them all lovely and big and green now. I always look at them and think, That's my gran!

My brother Tony, my sister Janet and I pass round my dad's key ring, which is a jack-o'-lantern. So if one of us is going through a bad time, the other one will say, 'Right, you need our dad's jack-o'-lantern.' It's just a little bit of comfort, really.

COLEEN: That's lovely!

CAROL: Really nice. The other thing I kept was when Chris left. He left all his stuff and I went through it and thought, I might keep something if I think it's of value. But you know what I kept? Well, he forgot to take his toothbrush! I thought, If I keep his toothbrush and the toothpaste he was using at the time, when he's not around any more, that might be worth a few quid! I've still got it in a box somewhere.

COLEEN: That's an unusual memento of love, to say the least! As for me, I didn't keep anything from The Nolans' days.

JANE: Nothing?

COLEEN: Nothing. But since I've met Ray, he's collected all of it, even stuff from things we did years and years ago that I'd totally forgotten.

JANE: Oh no, Coleen, he's a stalker!

COLEEN: Well, he is my biggest fan! But I like it. He does it for me. It's nice to look back and remember.

Should you embrace the future with technology or is it okay to miss the old days before the internet?

JANE: In the old days, you all went into the family room to watch the telly, but nowadays, everybody has their dinner and makes a mass exodus to go on the computer. So I miss that family time of watching TV. Speaking of TVs, men have got this thing about upgrading televisions, haven't they?

CAROL: The bigger the better. With everything else, they say,

'Size doesn't matter.' But size really matters when it comes to TVs.

JANE: I went to get a new telly and I was talking to my two friends behind the counter, Alex and Nick, and this little old lady comes in and says, 'I'd like a new wireless.'

How sweet! I thought.

She said, 'I want it to be as good as the one I've got.'

'What have you got now?' Nick asked.

'I've got a very old Bush,' she said. The silence in the shop was deafening! You can't beat it, can you?

ANDREA: Did she upgrade her Bush?

JANE: I think she did.

ANDREA: And did you get what you wanted as well?

JANE: Yes, thank you, I did!

CAROL: I'm a little suspicious about the government being so obsessed with getting high-speed broadband into every home. I'm a bit of a conspiracy theorist and I don't like the State monitoring me with CCTV and telling me what to do. In the novel 1984, which I often quote from, there's a telly screen in every home, which means that Big Brother is watching you, because it's a two-way telly. The way the government is so obsessed with getting this internet broadband into people's homes worries me a little bit. Why do we all have to have it? If people don't want it, why should they have it?

ANDREA: They're just giving them the option. They're not forcing them.

CAROL: They're saying that they want it in every single home. What they're going to start doing is taxing people on their landlines in order to pay for it to go into everybody's home. But not everybody needs it and not everybody wants it. What's the agenda here? I'm not sure.

SHERRIE: I'm not sure what high-speed broadband is.

CAROL: You do know what it is, Sherrie, because you've got a dongle.

JANE: I bet she hasn't! What is it?

CAROL: It's a mobile broadband wireless adaptor.

SHERRIE: Is that what I've got?

CAROL: Yes, you plug it into your computer and you can use the internet everywhere.

SHERRIE: Oh, I didn't realise!

ANDREA: Going back to the whole conspiracy theory thing. Does that mean that you think they'd be able to look back at you through the screen?

CAROL: Yes.

ANDREA: That would be really boring viewing, though. Ours is in the spare room. All they're going to see is some ironing.

CAROL: It'll come through your TV, I reckon.

SHERRIE: You mean they'll be watching you day and night?

CAROL: Yeah, it could happen! Beware!

SHERRIE: Fifteen months ago, I couldn't even open a laptop. Now, as well as doing 'Save' and 'Save As', I can do folders. Did you know that you can put one folder into another folder?

CAROL: Amazing! And you've got a dongle.

SHERRIE: And I've got a dongle, even though I didn't know it!

JANE: As the bishop said to the actress . . .

SHERRIE: Yes, it's not particularly scientific sounding, is it?

JANE: It doesn't matter, just as long as you know where to put it, love!

SHERRIE: Well, I do love my dongle.

CAROL: And I love the internet! I don't know what I'd do all day without it. It's important to me, but I do think it's beginning to take over people's lives. When you think about it, we still managed when we didn't have any of that stuff. We still managed with one phone on a little table in the hall, next to the phone book.

There's a fly or bug in the room.
Should you kill it?

CAROL: No, not always, but I wouldn't mind if every single fly, mosquito and cockroach in the whole wide world was swatted out of existence, because they're all hideous, disgusting and annoying and they shouldn't be here, really. I used to have the most awful spider phobia. It was seriously bad. I couldn't go in the room if there was one in the room, even a relatively small one. But for some reason, it's just gone away. Now I can't kill them!

SHERRIE: You know why, don't you?

CAROL: Why?

SHERRIE: Because they're my dog! My dog went into the spirit of spiders!

CAROL: But what would your dog be doing in my flat?

SHERRIE: He's now looking after it.

CAROL: Really, Sherrie? You do surprise me. The other night there was a spider on the bath mat. I saw it, but I was late and I couldn't be bothered to do anything with it, so I picked up the mat and shook it into the bath.

ANDREA: So you didn't say, 'Here, dog!'

CAROL: No! Perhaps I should have. Well, spiders can't climb out of the bath, so I knew it would be there in the morning. When I got up, I went upstairs, got an envelope and a cup and slid the envelope under the cup to trap it. The little thing was panicking away, but I managed to take it up onto the balcony and throw it away. There's no way I would have done that in the past.

ANDREA: How many floors up do you live?

CAROL: Two floors.

ANDREA: So it died a really horrible death . . .

CAROL: I didn't throw it *over* the balcony. I put it *on* the balcony! It probably stepped outside and thought, I'm getting straight back inside in the warm!

ANDREA: I would have done roughly the same thing, but it would have involved a vacuum cleaner or a shoe!

SHERRIE: Don't say things like that! You mustn't hurt a spider. It's bad luck. It's my dog!

CAROL: They get the other critters as well, don't they?

JANE: Critters? Do you come from Texas now?

CAROL: A little critter is a little bug, isn't it?

SHERRIE: Yes, spiders keep your house clean from other bugs. What I can't bear is ants; I can't bear them at any cost. Now, never mind what's going on in the world, I'm going to give you a big tip. When you've got ants in your house, feed them on white sugar. They think, This looks nice! I'll have a bit of this! Off they go with the sugar on their backs and when they get home the kids say, 'This looks nice, Mum. Where did you get this?' About twenty minutes later, they all keel over. It kills them all, because white sugar has poison in it!

CAROL: How come they can go all over my jam without dying? Jam's full of sugar.

SHERRIE: It takes more than jam. It has to be pure white sugar.

CAROL: I don't know about that.

JANE: I think flies understand us a little bit. When I've got a fly buzzing around and trying to get out of the window, smashing against the glass like a kamikaze pilot, I always say, 'Right, I'm going to open the window for you and if you don't go outside, I'm going to swat you.'

It works a treat, because I open the window and the fly obeys, 'OK, I'm off!'

CAROL: The best invention in the world are those tennis racquet things with the little buzzer on them. When the fly hits the little tennis racquet bit, it goes Bzzzzzz! That reminds me – you know there's an enormous fly that lives in the *Loose Women* studio?

SHERRIE: It's a bluebottle, isn't it?

CAROL: It's a bit dozy and sometimes it lands on your face or on a guest's hair or something! One time Jayne Middlemiss was here and we were doing an interview with Nick Bailey, who played Dr Trueman on *Eastenders*. We were talking about something quite serious and suddenly the bluebottle landed on Jane's nose. She started laughing and I saw it and I couldn't speak for laughing. Sherrie was getting really cross and kicking me under the desk to say, 'Stop it!' The more she did that, the more we laughed. Meanwhile, the fly kept going round and round Nick in the middle! It was so annoying!

Chapter 9

Be Our Guest

The handbags and the ratbags

One of the things that makes *Loose Women* the show it is are all the fantastic guests we have on the show. It's been wonderful to have the opportunity to meet people we're huge fans of and really admire. There have been some classic moments, like when Russell Brand snogged Carol, and when we were all star-struck when Bette Midler flew in from America to be a Loose Woman!

Here we'll share our favourite guests and reflect on one or two that we were less keen on!

A guest comes on the show and you find yourself really disliking him or her. Has it ever happened? What do you do?

SHERRIE: I remember one guest who was very obnoxious. This is going back a long time to the days when we used to film in Norwich. This guest was there to talk about her book, but she didn't seem happy and wasn't at all nice. In fact, she was quite rude. Most of the time when we asked her something, she answered with a straight 'yes' or 'no'. She was almost completely monosyllabic.

It was awful. We all sat there looking at each other, thinking, What are we going to do? The conversation went like this:

'So did you enjoy writing your book?'

'No.'

'Why didn't you enjoy writing it?'

'I just didn't.'

'Would you write another book?'

'No.'

Well, each reply was a complete conversation stopper. There was nothing we could add on to keep it all flowing. I kept thinking, Why have you come on? Fortunately, it was a recorded show, so it was edited quite heavily afterwards.

We were coming up to a break and one of us said, 'So, are you off back to London now?'

'No,' the guest said.

'Where are you off to next, then?'

Well, to everyone's horror, she said, 'I'm staying on for the second half.'

We came off air for the break and she turned to me and said, 'I want to talk about my book.'

It was terrible! None of us knew how to handle it and she wouldn't go. In my eight years on the show, it was the only time that I've squirmed and thought, I don't know what to do, help! In the end she stormed off saying that she'd had the worst interview of her life and she'd hated it. Meanwhile, the producers didn't know how to edit the show. So we went on talking about the topics of the day after she'd left, so that the producers could cut the extra footage into the existing footage. It was a very difficult situation.

JANE: You can't like everybody and not everybody's going to like you. So as long as you remember that, it's fine. It might be their personality that's the problem, or there's a personality clash; they might just be having a bad day, or I might be. Whatever it is, I try to be as courteous and polite as I can, because I hate bad manners.

Whether you can or can't stand someone who comes on the show – and there have been a few I haven't liked – that person is your guest, *guest* being the operative word. You have to be polite. So I would never show it if I didn't like them and I'd probably let the others take over. The great thing about *Loose Women* is that you're not alone.

I really enjoyed having Whoopi Goldberg on the show. My God, she's been through a lot in her life, yet she's the most grounded, personable lady I've ever met – and I use the word *lady* advisedly. She just was a joy to interview the day she came on the show. She's so intelligent and interesting and she's done it all; she's been a producer, a director, a writer and an actor. She doesn't have to try to be anything; she just is. She really blew me away and I admire her hugely.

SHERRIE: I loved Diana Rigg. I thought she was so funny. David Essex is always one of my favourites and Kelvin Fletcher is always lovely, as is Sally Whittaker, who is also one of my friends. I could go on and on!

JANE: You definitely could! I love it when other performers come on. I'm always interested in what they're promoting and I ask questions like, 'How's the touring going?' 'How are you coping being away from the kids?' because I understand what they're going through.

DENISE: Enrique Iglesias was my favourite guest, without a shadow of a doubt. I've convinced myself that I'm engaged to him. You girls think I'm deluded, but if you watch the tape, which I have done about forty-eight times, you'll see that he clearly is flirting with me. He said that I was horny! What more proof do you need? I'm in love with him and he clearly is with me. Denise Iglesias . . . it definitely has a ring to it!

JANE: So does Jane Groban! I loved Josh Groban.

DENISE: I wasn't on the day Josh Groban was on, but my mum said to me the other day, 'Do you know who I loved?' 'Who?' 'That Rogan Josh!' she said!

ANDREA: Ah, that's a classic! We've had so many great guests on the show! Of course you don't gel with everybody who comes on, but I'm a professional, they're a professional, and I'd like to think that someone wouldn't even have a clue that I didn't like them. My job is to make everyone feel as relaxed and comfortable as possible, so that they want to chat, so it would be really unprofessional of me to make it obvious that I didn't like them.

Sometimes it's a gut feeling. Sometimes it strikes me that someone's being rude to one of the other Loose Women and I feel very defensive. We interview the guests jointly and sometimes a guest hasn't been as respectful as they should be in the way that they've spoken to someone. Hey, that's my friend! I think. In that case I would just very gently steer them off whatever it was that was causing the trouble and move onto something else. But afterwards or at home I'd think, Hmm, I didn't really like them very much.

As for the guests I've enjoyed having on the show, I absolutely loved having the Spice Girls on; I loved it when Emma

Bunton was part of the panel. I thought she did a fantastic job, so it would be great to see more of her again. I'd love Victoria Beckham to come on, of course, because then we'd have had the full set. They've all been so fantastic – and they're such legends! After all, the Spice Girls were like girl Beatles for a short while. I like the fact that they've all grown up and they're doing their own thing and we're still interested in them. They're Spice Women now.

I'm curious about what the real Victoria is like. I think she's really misunderstood and probably far smilier than people give her credit for. I bet she's lovely when she's behind closed doors. I really liked her when I met her – she's very warm and very nice – and I would love to have her on *Loose Women*, so that people can see that.

LESLEY: Bette Midler was easily my favourite guest. She's a legend! I'm always full of admiration for women in particular who have got to the top and stayed there, because I think it's one thing to become successful and it's another thing to maintain and develop your success. She's very inspiring.

Another thing that impressed me about her was her inquiring mind, and she was incredibly generous towards me, which I was flabbergasted by. Her first words were: 'Now which one of you is the opera singer?' I introduced myself and she said, 'How do you do that? I want to know.'

I thought, My God! Bette Midler is asking me for singing tips!

When we got off set, she said, 'Come on, show me how you do it!' So I demonstrated a bit of opera singing for her. She's very curious about singing techniques, different voice categories and different styles of singing, so we had a very animated conversation about repertoire, technique and the places we've both sung, particularly in Australia.

I actually saw her live show in Australia, while I was performing at the Victoria Centre and she was in this great stadium. Coincidentally, her entrance – one of the greatest entrances of all time – was on the back of a carousel horse. I was performing in *Carousel* when she came on *Loose Women* and we had a real laugh about that. She was really interested in how I found singing musicals after singing opera.

She's a warm-hearted, awe-inspiring, lovely woman who happens to be someone I've admired all my life. She's also had a very varied career, which I identify with, obviously to a much lesser extent. She's done film, TV and stage work, as well as concert and recording work, and these are areas I've diversified into myself. So we seemed to have a lot in common when we met and she was generous enough to want to talk to me about it. We bonded on lots of levels and I loved her to bits.

On top of all of that, she was hysterically funny! So you can't get much better than Bette Midler, in my view, she's an amazingly talented performer and incredibly funny, warm-hearted, generous and inclusive. She lit up the set, included the audience and bonded with everyone in the room. Another thing I love about her is that she's outrageous and very comfortable with being outrageous. I'm occasionally outrageous, but then I feel I'm being very naughty, whereas she has no such qualms. There aren't many stars of her stature in the world, so I felt very privileged to meet her.

ANDREA: I'd love Will Smith to come on. He's a huge star. Earlier this year he was on *This Morning* and even though he was in a different studio, the excitement was at fever pitch, just because we knew he was vaguely around. So if we could ever get him on the show we would be very, very happy, but bagsy me to talk to him first!

CAROL: Yes, I'd love to see Will Smith on the show. The guests I didn't like were Harriet Harman, Jacqui Smith and John Prescott. Actually, to be fair, I came away liking John Prescott more than I thought I would, but I absolutely can't stand Harriet Harman or Jacqui Smith. They're both sneering, patronising women and I don't like their attitude. Tessa Jowell, she's another one, and Hazel Blears: they've all got that manner about them. I definitely wouldn't want to spend any time with them.

When they came on the show, they talked down to us and to the audience, especially Harriet Harman and Jacqui Smith. I started having a go at Jacqui Smith about her expenses and she just sort of smirked and said, 'Yes, well, they've been looked into . . .' Get lost!

I wasn't nasty or rude to any of them because I don't think there's any point inviting someone on a show and then being rude to them. But I might have pulled a face when I thought they weren't looking, and maybe the director just happened to have the camera on my face! A couple of people have said to me, 'Your face was a picture when you were sat next to Harriet Harman!' I didn't mean to express my dislike openly, but maybe I'm not very good at hiding what I'm thinking.

The problem with some politicians is that they go on *GMTV* and *Loose Women* instead of *The Today Programme*, because they don't want to be asked difficult questions. They think it's lightweight and so they're going to get an easy ride, spouting their propaganda and hyperbole to anybody who will listen. They think they can come on and say, 'We're doing this and we're doing that,' and they expect the audience to think, Ooh brilliant! That's why I tried to ask questions that I thought people at home might want to ask – the tricky question or two. They don't like it when you do that.

ANDREA: You're very knowledgeable about politics, Carol. Have you never been tempted to try becoming an MP?

CAROL: No, it's too much work if you do the job properly, and I'm too honest. It's just a bear pit these days. The House of Commons is full of people who only have their own interests at heart. They're not bothered about improving the lives of the people that they serve. Maybe they're not all like that, but in the main they are. For that reason, there's no way I'd want to get within a hundred miles of the job. It's too difficult.

LESLEY: No, it's much nicer being a Loose Woman! I love meeting all the guests, but the main reason I do *Loose Women* is because it's my girly social time. I don't have girlfriends like these outside of the programme and I need them! I love exchanging views with all of you and it's a wonderful privilege to be part of a group of women who are so happy to be candid about themselves and to share personal experiences. It's a very supportive group.

LISA: Isn't it? I haven't always been one for going out with the girls, because I've got a lot of male friends, so it's amazing to have a female support network all of a sudden. It's quite nerve-racking doing a live show, but you've all been so brilliant and supportive in helping me over the initial hurdles.

It's also really quite liberating. I keep thinking, 'Hey, I've never really spoken about that before!' I get so much validation from all of you, because you'll say, 'We've all been through that!' and I'll think, Well that's all right, then! Coming from a show like *The Bill* that has so much testosterone flying around

on set, it's great to be surrounded by birds. It's fantastic.

Have you ever had a bizarre dream about a celebrity/guest on the show?

SHERRIE: Yes, Alan Alda on from *M*A*S*H*! I've always thought he was truly wonderful. I read his book and dreamt about him two nights before he came on. In the dream, I was in *M*A*S*H* with him and then he turned into somebody else and then he turned back. You know, one of those dreams! He wasn't particularly nice in the dream and I woke up thinking, I wonder if that's some kind of omen to warn me that he's not going to be very nice on the show?

But he was so charming when he came on that I couldn't speak, because it was Alan Alda. He sat down and said, 'Hi,' and I melted. I could hear the producer saying in my ear, 'Sherrie, Sherrie, say something! Close your mouth!'

I wanted to say, 'I've read your first book. It was fabulous.' But I couldn't speak. It was like Cary Grant coming on! He was just wonderful, a real gentleman, sweet, kind, lovely, talented, with lots of great stories to tell. I was just so in awe of it that it was just ridiculous. I hated myself afterwards, because I'll never meet Alan Alda again in my life.

Afterwards, I thought, Sherrie, you'll never see him again and you've just completely messed up!

JANE: I've had lots of dreams about David Beckham! They're not sexual; usually, we're having a cup of coffee and a chat and I think, What a nice lad! In one dream we were having a real heart-to-heart and he was telling me all about Victoria. It was brilliant!

CAROL: Don't you fancy him, then?

JANE: Well, everybody's a fan of David Beckham, aren't they? For me, fantasy land is wonderful, but I'd never want to go there in reality.

I also once had a bizarre and incredibly vivid dream about Eric Morecambe in which we were laughing and telling jokes to each other. I have no idea where that came from, except that I love Morecambe and Wise.

COLEEN: I've had two or three very bizarre dreams about Simon Cowell. I don't fancy him at all, but after these dreams I woke up and said to Ray, 'I'm in love with Simon Cowell!' Even since then, I find myself blushing whenever he's on telly, because I know what we've been through. I get this little twinge – I won't tell you where – and I think, 'Oh!' It's weird, because I know I wouldn't fancy him if I met him. He's just not my type at all. I'm sure I'm not his either, but how strange to have dreams like that, out of the blue.

JANE: That's just what I'm saying. Where do they come from?

ANDREA: Have you had a dream about Enrique, Denise?

DENISE: Yes, several.

ANDREA: What happens in those dreams?

DENISE: What do you think happens?

ANDREA: Er . . . sorry, I shouldn't have asked!

the loose**women** script book

Excerpts from some of our
favourite celebrity interviews

We've had some wonderful guests on the show. Here are extracts of some of our best interviews in recent times.

Multi-award-winning star of stage and screen, whose roles have included the iconic part of Emma Peel in *The Avengers*, Dame Diana Rigg came on the show before she appeared at the Chichester Festival in Noel Coward's *Hay Fever*.

DIANA RIGG: I think that women are more candid than men. We've got the ability to be more truthful about ourselves and that's one of the reasons why we're probably rather better than men, aren't we?

SHERRIE: Ask a man a question and he won't tell you the answer. But ask a woman and she'll tell you the truth whether you want to hear it or not.

DIANA RIGG: Absolutely. There's also that thing about being able to talk about your emotions freely and openly and not be ashamed of them. I was listening to you girls – and you are girls compared with me – I was listening to you talk about how horrible old age is. Well, old age is no joke – and I'm an old-age pensioner – but how you approach it is really what matters. From time to time, I look at my arms and the way they hang down and I kiss myself anyway, because my body has served me really well. I say thank you to it from time to time. You must! I mean, what's the alternative? Hate yourself? Be ashamed of yourself? Why?

JANE: What is your secret for keeping young, though, Dame Diana? You're so vibrant. Look at you, you're fabulous!

DIANA RIGG: Well, I had an eye operation when I was forty-five; I had the eyes jacked up. But since then, I don't do Botox and I don't do exercise. I think the secret is being curious, in finding all sorts of things in life that are interesting, and pursuing them. The brain is the secret to keeping young and looking young.

DENISE: And red wine?

SHERRIE: And fly-fishing?

DIANA RIGG: Yes, although not at the same time!

DENISE: Have you found that you've got better roles as you've got older, or roles that you would consider to be better?

DIANA RIGG: Yes, because when I was young I was given all those glamorous parts and I was always two steps behind the leading man. It was so boring. Then, as I got older, I started playing really meaty parts and it's been wonderful. From fifty onwards, it's been absolutely wonderful.

DENISE: Really?

DIANA RIGG: Yes, keep on truckin'!

DENISE: I'm digressing here, but earlier we were talking about sex and babies and I wondered why you threw all your contraceptive pills out of the Hilton Hotel that time?

DIANA RIGG: Well, I was there making a film and I got bored, frankly, and I thought, How about getting pregnant instead?

DENISE: With any particular man?

DIANA RIGG: Yes, with the man I subsequently married. I didn't call room service!

SHERRIE: And you did get pregnant!

DIANA RIGG: I did get pregnant with my daughter Rachel, who is also on the stage. It was absolutely wonderful.

SHERRIE: Did you want to have a baby anyway, or did you want to have a baby there and then?

DIANA RIGG: Oh, it was the fact that I was passionately in love and I thought, There's got to be something better than turning up on a film set at six thirty in the morning. What I didn't know was that I'd have to turn up by the crib side at three thirty in the morning!

SHERRIE: And it's for life. It's not just a little baby . . .

DIANA RIGG: It's for life. I know.

SHERRIE: Now you seem to be really happy without a man in your life.

DIANA RIGG: I am. You have to be really careful not to sound defensive about it, because there are lots of women who have been married forever and are terribly happy. I did not succeed in marriage, but I really admire people who have done, because I know that somewhere along the line there's been compromise, sacrifice, sadness – all sorts of things. So I congratulate you, but I have been for a very long time incredibly happy by myself.

SHERRIE: And could you have a man in the house again? What about all the mess?

DIANA RIGG: No, no!

DENISE: Would you still be up for a bit of room service?

DIANA RIGG: No problem! As long as when I've given him the tip, he knows when to go.

SHERRIE, JANE AND DENISE: Wahay!

Writer, comedienne, actress and broadcaster Emma Kennedy came on the show to talk about her book, The Tent, the Bucket and Me, an account of her family's annual camping holidays.

EMMA KENNEDY: I've always maintained that you have not gone camping until absolutely everything you possess is ever so slightly damp and you've got an independent ecosystem going on in your clothes!

CAROL: How many times did you go camping?

EMMA KENNEDY: Every year, always with my mum and dad, from the age of three until I was thirteen, when my dad actually set fire to the tent because we'd had such an awful time. He'd had enough.

ANDREA: In the book you say that your tent was made of 'the crushed souls of holiday-makers.'

EMMA KENNEDY: It was!

ANDREA: Nice image!

EMMA KENNEDY: Part of it was that we were just really inept. We didn't know what we were doing.

CAROL: Well done for persevering, though!

EMMA KENNEDY: Thank you!

SHERRIE: You must have enjoyed those holidays. That's why you wrote the book, isn't it?

EMMA KENNEDY: No. It was breathtakingly disastrous.

LISA: The French camping holidays are a bit posher, aren't they? Did you go to France?

EMMA KENNEDY: They were, but my first trip to France was slightly marred by the fact that I fell into a toilet. You know, one of those holes in the ground. Well, the irony – the irony – of that was that I'd only been taken into the toilet because someone had been sick on my leg! I had someone else's sick on my left leg and then I fell into the toilet, so I had a whole host of other things on my right leg and I had to be taken to a garage and hosed down.

CAROL: Did this damage you in any way? Would you go camping again?

EMMA KENNEDY: No, don't be ridiculous, although having said that, someone does want to send me camping with my parents again.

CAROL: Will you do it?

EMMA KENNEDY: Well, I'm absolutely one hundred per cent positive that one of us will die. That's the only place we can go now.

ANDREA: Do your parents look back and laugh about it now?

EMMA KENNEDY: They absolutely love it. The whole idea for the book came about at a Sunday lunch with my mum and dad when we remembered our first holiday, the one where the caravan went off the edge of the cliff. That was our very first family holiday, so it set quite a high benchmark!

LISA: That should have told you something, shouldn't it?

EMMA KENNEDY: I know, I know!

SHERRIE: You were an only child, weren't you? Did you have any little friends you could have taken with you?

EMMA KENNEDY: No one wanted to come near us, Sherrie!

SHERRIE: So that wouldn't have helped, to have taken a little pal with you?

EMMA KENNEDY: Imagine if Stig of the Dump had gone on holiday. Well that's what we were like!

ANDREA: My family have never been camping, but my sister went when she was in her teens and we all happily waved her off. She came back with shingles, in such a mess. She had a rash, she'd stayed out in the sun too long and she hadn't eaten enough.

EMMA KENNEDY: Well, this is the thing. Sun cream hadn't been invented in the 1970s! I got the worst sunburn ever when I was thirteen in France and because it was a campsite in the 1970s and there was nothing to do, I became the entertainment for the entire campsite. I was laid out on this bed and a crowd gathered to see what was going on. Then the Dutch woman from the tent next door to us came over to my mother and said, 'I'm a nurse. Would you like me to take her temperature?'

My mum said, 'Oh thank you, would you?'

The woman came up to me, flipped me onto my front, pulled down my bikini bottoms and stuck the thermometer up my lady's excuse me! In front of a crowd! Someone at the back applauded.

Then she pulled it out, turned to my mother and said, 'Oh, she's hot.' Well I knew that! I could have told her that!

LISA: What's wrong with a bit of calamine lotion, eh?

CAROL: If you did it again, surely you wouldn't have to recreate the hideous conditions of camping in the 1970s?

EMMA KENNEDY: No, now there's glamping.

CAROL: What's glamping?

EMMA KENNEDY: Posh camping. They've got beds with linen, flushable toilets and showers!

SHERRIE: They've got *en suites,* haven't they? And an upstairs mezzanine.

EMMA KENNEDY: Well, not quite, but some of them come with butlers, honestly.

LISA: Really? So you just unzip the tent and there's a butler, tucked away in the side!

EMMA KENNEDY: Yes, and all the sleeping bags are covered in diamonds!

Former Spice Girl Mel B also came by ...

ANDREA: You look better than ever. Do you feel better now?

MEL B: I do feel better, actually. Older is good. I've grown into my own skin and I like it.

ANDREA: How does it feel looking back at the old clips of you when you were in the Spice Girls?

MEL B: It makes me laugh, a lot! I think, Did I really wear that and have my hair like that? It's good though. It brings back good memories.

ANDREA: How much control did you have? You all had your little names and looks. Who came up with your names?

MEL B: It was actually a teenybopper magazine that came up with all our names. I liked mine, because I began to frighten people without even having to say anything! It worked to my advantage, thank God!

ANDREA: Did you all play up on the labels?

MEL B: They did end up being quite fitting.

CAROL: It's a fantastic legacy, isn't it? We've had four of you on now and Emma was actually a Loose Woman for a while.

MEL B: She was! I heard that she was *Loose* for a whole week. I wanna be one!

CAROL: Come on then!

MEL B: I'd love to!

DENISE: You haven't gone all LA with your accent, have you?

MEL B: I can't get rid of my northern accent – and I don't want to get rid of it, either.

CAROL: Do you get sick of talking about the Spice Girls?

MEL B: No, I love it. That's where I come from. That's my everything.

CAROL: Would you change anything?

MEL B: No, I wouldn't change it for the world.

ANDREA: Can you believe that it's been fifteen years since you all got together?

MEL B: That *is* a long time, isn't it? God, I feel old now!

JANE: Are you loving LA, though? It must be fabulous.

MEL B: I love it and my kids love it and the sun shines every day. It's a really nice outdoor way of life.

JANE: Slightly different from Leeds, then, is it?

MEL B: Just a bit. But I'm back every month for work and to see the family, so I don't get to miss London or Leeds.

ANDREA: We were talking earlier in the show about finding Mr Right and obviously you have to kiss a few frogs before you find your prince.

MEL B: Tell me about it!

ANDREA: Is there any rhyme or reason to it? How would you say you've found your Mr Right?

MEL B: I think it was more of a gut feeling. Having said that, I met my husband eight years ago, so he was my friend first. My mum always used to say, 'Make sure they're your friend first,' and I never believed her, but now I do. He's my everything. We know each other inside out.

ANDREA: What would you say is the difference between him and other men you've dated?

MEL B: The other men are all horrible! Whereas he's lovely and he's the same age as me, so we have a lot in common.

CAROL: Did you ever have to search for anyone?

MEL B: Course I did, a little bit. I can't believe I'm even admitting that!

ANDREA: Did you make a list? Did you have a plan?

MEL B: I did have a little list, yes.

ANDREA: What was on that list?

MEL B: Do I have to tell you?

JANE: No!

MEL B: Good.

DENISE: Tell us a couple of the boxes that he did tick, then.

MEL B: I'm not going to tell you! It's too rude!

Jackie Collins, Hollywood author, popped in to talk about her twenty-sixth novel, *Married Lovers* . . .

CAROL: How long does it take you to write a book?

JACKIE COLLINS: It takes nine months to write it and I usually spend the other three months out promoting it. I've been away from LA now for a month. I've been in Moscow, where they love my books because they're all about hookers and gangsters. There are a lot of hookers and gangsters there, so that was fun! Then I've been in Ireland, in Dublin, which was great fun.

CAROL: How did you get around?

JACKIE COLLINS: I had a fantastic tour bus, a former Mariah Carey tour bus, with bedrooms, bathrooms and TVs; it was fantastic. I went to twenty-six cities in America and gave talks to four or five hundred women in every one. I loved it; they find me inspirational, because as I've told you before, I was thrown out of school at fifteen and I was a bit of a troublemaker. So when I speak to women, I always tell them how I followed my dream. Everybody said to me, 'You can't be a writer! You've got to go to school. You've got to go to college,' but I followed my dream. Anybody can do it.

CAROL: Talk about having the last laugh, because none of your books have ever gone out of print, have they?

JACKIE COLLINS: They haven't! I think it's because I write what people want to read. I write about all colours, all sizes, all ages, all sexual orientation. My characters speak like we all speak. They sound like real people. I also write strong women, and I know that all the ladies out there like strong women, right?

AUDIENCE: Yes!

JACKIE: People love as well to think they're getting that inside look at Hollywood, don't they?

JACKIE COLLINS: Yes, when they're reading one of my books, they're not getting the front page of a tabloid, they're getting the real deal, and they know that I'm at the parties I'm describing.

CAROL: There's a lot of guessing going on, isn't there?

JACKIE COLLINS: You like to play the guessing game, don't you?

CAROL: I love the guessing game!

JACKIE COLLINS: I wrote a book once called *The Stud*, and every guy in Hollywood thought it was about him! There's a good guessing game in *Married Lovers*. There's Cameron Paradise, who's a gorgeous personal fitness trainer. She has an abusive husband in Australia and she flees from him and comes to Los Angeles, where she meets Don Verona, a fantastic-looking talk-show host.

SHERRIE: Where do you come up with these great names?

JACKIE COLLINS: Don Verona can have any women he wants, except he can't have Cameron. So there's a nice little twist.

CAROL: Changing the subject, why don't most stars have long-lasting relationships?

JACKIE COLLINS: It's impossible! If you have two stars in a relation-ship and one career is up but the other isn't so up, and then one of them goes off on location with a fantastic-looking co-star . . . what are you going to do if they're irresistible? There's so much temptation.

SHERRIE: And it matters more in Hollywood about which level you're on, I assume, even in a marriage.

JACKIE COLLINS: If people are insecure, I think it does, and most people are insecure.

CAROL: Talking of marriage in Hollywood, do you know of any marriages that are a little bit fraudulent?

JACKIE COLLINS: Oh yes! I know exactly what you're saying. I wish I could name names. There are certain actors who are actually gay and were told that they'd better get married and have a couple of kids, so that they could give the impression of being straight. They make a bargain with the wife. There's a lot of bargaining that goes on.

CAROL: I want to take you out and get you really drunk so you'll tell me who they are.

JACKIE COLLINS: You should have seen me in Moscow! They couldn't understand me, so that was fortunate!

SHERRIE: Are you cynical about relationships in Hollywood?

JACKIE COLLINS: When I first moved there, my kids were eleven and twelve and I made sure that they stayed very English. I think that if you go to Hollywood and you've got that English humour and sense of the ridiculous, you'll do OK. I always felt like an anthropologist crawling through the jungles of Hollywood and being a very strict mother, too. My kids never had a Porsche at sixteen and a handful of credit cards. I took them to school and met them from school and made sure that they knew what life was all about.

CAROL AND SHERRIE: Well done!

JACKIE COLLINS: And they're great. They're my three best friends.

DJ and author Christian O'Connell came on to talk about his book The Men Commandments

CHRISTIAN O'CONNELL: I think men are quite confused. I was listening to what you said earlier on the show and I was quite reassured hearing that you don't want men spending too much time in front of the mirror or down the gym. Yet you don't want a man who has let himself go. I remember my wife said to me a couple of years ago, 'You've got to be careful doing the breakfast show, because you can become like Moyles.'

JANE: Awww!

CHRISTIAN O'CONNELL: I'm just saying that he's obviously big boned and it's OK to like a pie, but not too many pies.

JANE: You see, he'd be my ideal, because I like a pie.

CHRISTIAN O'CONNELL: But then he would have eaten all the pies and there would be none left for you!

JANE: We can't have that!

CHRISTIAN O'CONNELL: No, because then there would be a pie shortage.

CAROL: Your metabolism goes a bit weird when you get up early in the morning, doesn't it? It's like having jet lag all the time.

ANDREA: And you crave carbohydrates.

CHRISTIAN O'CONNELL: You do. Thank you, girls, for your understanding.

ANDREA: What would you say is the main difference between men and women?

CHRISTIAN O'CONNELL: Well, they reckon that there are seventy-eight genetic differences and I spent a chapter trying to list what all those seventy-eight are. A lot of people think that if you're a man writing a book about men, you're trying to have a go at women, but I think that men are just as odd, if not a bit odder than women, to be honest. People think we're quite simple, but men are complicated. They've got their weird rituals —

CAROL: You are quite simple, though. Men are, generally.

ANDREA: Straightforward is a better way of putting it, perhaps.

CHRISTIAN O'CONNELL: You wouldn't find a guy who would shave off his eyebrows and then ink them back in, so who's odder there?

CAROL: That's just ridiculous! But men are quite easy to please, aren't they?

CHRISTIAN O'CONNELL: Men are very easy to please, it's true. It starts in their pants and it goes no further.

ANDREA: You made a list of certain genes that women have. List-making is supposed to be in women's genes.

CHRISTIAN O'CONNELL: Yes, that's something that my wife does a lot. She will always be working from a list. I don't like preparing a shopping list, which is why I'm rarely allowed to go shopping. When I do go, I'll fill the trolley with stuff I'll never end up using: pancake mix; Doritos; stuff that you'd never use. Men just chuck loads of stuff in and they get easily swayed. Men are very easily distracted anyway, which is why they have affairs. They have quite simple brains.

JANE: Tell us about the 'I'll have one of yours' gene. What's that?

CHRISTIAN O'CONNELL: I think men can relate to this one, and women do this a lot. There's nothing more irritating than when you go for a meal with a lady and she will say, 'I'm not that hungry. You get what you want. I'll just have some of yours.'
You say, 'No, please, just order something for yourself.'
'I'll just have a salad,' she says.

Then the food comes and her fork comes over . . . But this is mine! I've ordered this for me, and she's coming at it. She's transferring all the guilt about having the big meal and all those calories onto the guy!

ANDREA: It's true! Somebody else's chips don't count.

CHRISTIAN O'CONNELL: Exactly.

ZOE: What's the 'nana knicker' gene?

CHRISTIAN O'CONNELL: Well, you've got your sexy knickers and then you've got your passion killers, those big things like parachutes from the First World War that are worn during the week. They're flame retardant and they will stop an erection at fifty paces.

CAROL: I don't have any of those!

CHRISTIAN O'CONNELL: You won't, because you want the fun all the time. You're a party girl.

CAROL: That's right. Also, you say that you've never ever met a woman who found farting funny. Well, I do!

CHRISTIAN O'CONNELL: Oh, Carol, nice to meet you! [Shake hands.]

JANE: Do you think Carol's more of a bloke, though?

CAROL: I'm quite blokey, I suppose.

CHRISTIAN O'CONNELL: No, I wouldn't say bloke. I think she's a real lady.

CAROL: A real lady?

JANE: Why is that?

CAROL: Oh, I can be. I'm getting more girly, but I still find farting funny.

CHRISTIAN O'CONNELL: You really find farting funny?

CAROL: Yes, I do.

CHRISTIAN O'CONNELL: So if we were on a first date and I let a little eggy puff-puff go, you'd find that funny and think: This is the one for me. I've met my true love! I find that hard to believe.

CAROL: I probably would, especially if it was a loud one!

JANE: Are you like us women, then? Do you try and hold it in? Because, for some reason, when you first start courting, you can't do it, can you?

CAROL: You can't; it's tricky.

JANE: Your stomach's going and you're thinking, Oh my God!

CHRISTIAN O'CONNELL: I think a man knows at what point in a relationship it's acceptable to break wind in bed.

ANDREA: Obviously, we're all pretty ladylike here, but is there anything you think isn't ladylike? Should a lady say 'Phwoarr!' for instance? Would that impress you?

CHRISTIAN O'CONNELL: If a lady said that to me, I'd be extremely flattered, but I'd probably think she had something wrong with her eyes, to be honest . . .

Hollywood star and diva Bette Midler also graced our presence and told us about her amazing retrospective album The Best Bette.

BETTE MIDLER: As a child I was very shy and retiring; I was a bit of a loner and a big reader, a bookworm. I loved to read, but in my little soul, I was a singer, in front of the mirror and in the shower, of course. People used to gather around outside my house, because I would sing in the shower around five o'clock in the afternoon. They didn't applaud; they would just listen to me making these raucous noises.

JANE: Could they actually see you?

BETTE MIDLER: No, they couldn't see me; it was on the second floor! But they could hear me, that's the point. I was really loud.

CAROL: So at that time, did you kind of know that you were going to make it big?

BETTE MIDLER: You know what? I sang in public for the first time in the first grade: 'Silent Night'. I stopped them cold. Ooh, there's something to this, I said.

LESLEY: How old woro you thcn?

BETTE MIDLER: I was about six and it was quite shocking, because I'd never had that kind of attention before.

LESLEY: So did the voice come first? Because you do so many different things, don't you?

BETTE MIDLER: I would say so. I found out that I could sing and people would listen to me. It was very exciting for me, because I didn't get much attention at home. 'Get outta here! Get outta here!' That was mostly what I got. So suddenly people were paying attention to me when I opened my mouth to sing.

In tho oixth grado I otartcd doing the talent shows, but I only knew one song and that was "The Lullaby of Broadway". I remember being in back of two girls in the eighth grade and they were talking about the next talent show. 'Do you think Bette Midler's going to sing again?' one of them said.

'Yeah, but she's probably going to sing that damn "Lullaby of Broadway" again!' said the other.

I thought, Oh God!

JACKIE: Fast-forward forty years and you have this amazing retrospective album, *The Best Bette* – good title. How do you go about choosing just nineteen songs from your repertoire?

BETTE MIDLER: I included all the hits because everybody loves the hits, but I also included the songs I really love to sing, like 'Spring Can Really Hang You Up the Most', which is not a terribly well-known song but it's a song I've always loved, and a couple of jazz ballads and a couple of songs that mean a lot to me personally.

LESLEY: It's so varied. That's the thing that amazes me about your singing. You have this sound that is so versatile. You can do boogie-woogie, you can do jazz, you can do pop and rock. How does that work for you?

BETTE MIDLER: Well, I love music and, to me, it doesn't really matter that it's not in my little niche. I sing it because I love to sing it, the song means something to me and I can be emotional.

I don't read much about myself. I'm like, 'Oh, don't make me read that!' I don't really look at much about myself either, but occasionally I happen upon something. One thing I read recently was, 'her emotional delivery . . .' I thought, 'Her emotional delivery'? Then I realised that what they really mean is that I'm so attached to these songs and to these lyrics that I make a big deal out of them and put my heart and soul into them.

LESLEY: But they must touch you.

BETTE MIDLER: They have to touch me and they do, because many things touch people.

JANE: Which is why you're such a great actress, of course.

BETTE MIDLER: Well, they are little playlets and you do act them. You put on the persona, you put on the character and you do act them out. I've been so lucky to be able to do practically anything I've wanted to do. Sometimes I think I'm just having this fantastic dream, and everyone's in my dream and it's great. Because how could I be so lucky?

I just can't understand why I got so lucky, because it's not the greatest voice. Really, let's call a dog a dog. It's OK, you know, but I'm lively and I'm amusing – I know I'm amusing; I wear clothes well and I have these little eccentricities that seem to make people say, 'Oh, she is so cute!' And that's great.

JACKIE: You're slaying them in Vegas right now.

BETTE MIDLER: They say I'm killing. It's true. We have a lot of Brits and I know this because I have a book signing every other month. I have this book that I ordered too many of, so of course I have to sign every one of them! People say that the Brits are the only ones who read any more and I'm always amazed at how many come from the UK. I'm really quite shocked.

JACKIE: How long is the show going on for?

BETTE MIDLER: Well, it's twenty weeks a year. I'm sharing the stage with Elton John – Sir Elton – and Madame Cher.

CAROL: Do you still borrow her clothes?

BETTE MIDLER: For her opening night, I gave her back a dress that I borrowed in 1978! I was playing at the Palladium here and I had nothing to wear for the opening night, so I called her and she sent me two dresses. I wore them both. I sent one back, but I kept one. So then she had the jitters on her opening night in Vegas and I thought, Oh Christ, what am I going to give her? So I wrapped this dress up that she had given me thirty years ago . . .

JACKIE: I hope you dry-cleaned it first!

BETTE MIDLER: Of course!

CAROL: And took it out.

BETTE MIDLER: She can still fit into the dress! I don't know if it helped her, actually. I really adore her, but she comes and goes in my life.

CAROL: For all the success that you've had – you're like a massive, mega, worldwide superstar – how do you keep your feet on the ground, because you are so down-to-earth?

BETTE MIDLER: Oh, it's just massive insecurity! It's so boring. Oh to be Christian Bale for just one day!

JACKIE: A few weeks ago, we talked about Radio Two presenter Steve Wright, who was pictured in a newspaper leaving work looking a bit heftier than usual. Today he said that, thanks to the *Daily Mirror* newspaper for printing the snap, he's motivated to take action and he's going to start a healthier eating and exercise regime. So good luck to him, but do you think it takes something shocking like that, whether it's seeing yourself in the mirror, or a picture?

BETTE MIDLER: Well, forgive me, but I do have a theory. There are not enough full-length mirrors, especially in my country. I think that people don't have full-length mirrors. They have the medicine chest that shows their head and shoulders, and that's all they see. But when you take your clothes off and actually look, it's a case of, 'Aaaahhh! Oh my God!' It really does take that.

CAROL: You do need to have a good look, don't you?

BETTE MIDLER: Yes you do. I was reading the *Enquirer* or the *Star* or one of those tabloids the other day and it said that Demi Moore takes her clothes off every day and checks herself out in the mirror. I thought, Every day? Of course you have to take your clothes off every day, but check yourself out, inch by inch? It seems a little extreme. Still, once a week, yes!

JANE: She's married to a much younger man, though. He's checking it out for her.

BETTE MIDLER: That's true. I don't check myself but once a year!

JACKIE: You look phenomenal. Do you work at it?

BETTE MIDLER: You absolutely have to work at it. It's terrible to admit, but it's true. People say, 'Oh, I eat anything! My metabolism is so high!' It's such a load of hooey.

JACKIE: What do you do, then?

BETTE MIDLER: I have to do the treadmill, or else I can't sing. The treadmill keeps the lungs flexible. You have to. Then I started doing yoga and I really like it, because it's all stretching. I used to think, I don't understand this! It took me years to understand that it's nothing but stretching. They stretch every single muscle and at the end you feel like a young person again. If you don't stretch, everything gets tighter and tighter.

JACKIE: We were talking earlier about women in film and the dumbing-down of roles for women nowadays.

BETTE MIDLER: How about Gwyneth Paltrow in *Iron Man*? I almost died! Gwyneth Paltrow? She won an Oscar! I was really shocked. All she does is come out and give him a cup of coffee on a tray. That was her job! That was her role. He didn't win anything. He's very nice, but he does mumble; let's call a dog a dog, he's a little bit of a mumbler. Of course, she can't get into the Iron Man suit, but still! That's why she's doing that website. Have you seen it? Too divine! Well, she's going to be the next Martha Stewart.

JACKIE: Really?

BETTE MIDLER: Well, she could be. It's called goop.com and it's adorably laid out with recipes and home tips. It's fantastic.

JACKIE: How about you? You've had some amazing roles. You've had your Oscar nomination and your —

BETTE MIDLER: But I never won!

JACKIE: I was going to say, does it irk?

BETTE MIDLER: It kind of irks. Most of the time it doesn't bother me, but occasionally I think I'd like to have won. I once had a producer who I loved with all my heart and he'd got to be a certain age and said, 'Just one more shot at the brass ring.' At the time I didn't really understand hanging on like that. Most religions say, 'Let go, let go, let go.' But he did take one more shot at the brass ring and he won all the things that he wanted to win and he was so happy.

JACKIE: Do you find that great roles come your way?

BETTE MIDLER: Not for me any more.

JACKIE: Why?

BETTE MIDLER: I don't want to say this because I don't want to offend anybody, but ultimately the public likes beautiful young flesh. They don't like to be reminded of their own mortality. I really do believe that. I'm sorry to say it, but I think it's the human condition.

JANE: You need to move here, then, because we love our older actresses, like Judi Dench.

BETTE MIDLER: Oh, she's divine.

CAROL: Helen Mirren.

JANE: You need to move here!

BETTE MIDLER: I do! Where all the good actresses go to die? Thanks a lot!

CAROL: I agree that we have a youth-obsessed society. Wherever you go it's like that. I equate it to looking at a fruit bowl and seeing the oldest apple in the fruit bowl that is slowly rotting and dying. You just throw it away, don't you? OK, that's extreme, but —

JACKIE: What about Katherine Hepburn in *On Golden Pond*?

BETTE MIDLER: This was thirty years ago and it was a very different world, before MTV, before video killed the radio star. All the values have changed.

LESLEY: One of your most successful films was *The First Wives Club* about three women who were taking control.

BETTE MIDLER: How fabulous did we look?

LESLEY: Amazing!

BETTE MIDLER: But we didn't get another shot at it. We didn't get to do the sequel. They said it was just a fluke. There are lots of very successful women on television, but not so many successful women in the film business. The men pretty much run the film business, but even they are very much cartoons. When you stop and think about it, the most successful films you see are not people who are playing parts of tremendous depth, they're men in iron suits! They're all fantasy, *Lord of the Rings* (which I loved); *Batman; Iron Man.*

JACKIE: Weren't you ever tempted to take the bull by the horns and say, 'Well if the roles aren't coming to me, I'm going to make it happen?'

BETTE MIDLER: I did that for ten years and the struggle that the production company and I went through was so painful. I remember submitting eighty scripts to my studio and they took one, and that was *Beaches.*

JANE: What a script, though!

BETTE MIDLER: I saw a piece of it the other day and I almost fainted. What the hell was I thinking with that red fright wig and those clothes? Oh my God, it was the 1980s, but even so!

JACKIE: That was such an incredible film, but I can totally understand why you didn't want to do the whole production thing. I did a little of it for a time in LA myself and it seemed that you either had to pick your career or you had to pick a family.

BETTE MIDLER: I did it for ten years and had my daughter about halfway through those ten years, so I managed both. I really tried very hard; we all tried really hard; but you just couldn't get them to understand what it was you were talking about. I remember having a meeting with a guy who said, 'We want to do musicals!'
'OK,' I said.
He said, 'Show me one!'
So we showed him *Meet Me In St Louis*. When Judy Garland came on the screen, he said, 'She's great! Who's that?'

JANE: Oh no!

BETTE MIDLER: Once I saw that, I just wanted to bang my head on the table. But I gave it a good shot and I had a great run. I don't resent anybody; I've made peace with myself. You have to. The girls who are now forty will be joining me very soon at the other end of the spectrum. It's a big shock when they say, 'It's time for you to play the mom.' So you play the mom and then you play grandma and then you're in the wheelbarrow!

JACKIE: Do you think that you can have it all in your business, including a love life? You hear about a lot of people who've given up their career for family.

BETTE MIDLER: I think it depends on who you are, what your skills are and whether you have some support – a great family or mom and dad or husband who helps you. You cannot do it all alone.

JACKIE: You were very driven until you met your husband, weren't you?

BETTE MIDLER: And I was driven after I met my husband. I'm driven, driven, driven and I sometimes think that a lot of it is hormonal. I think it's just what's in the DNA. Eventually as you age and you go through the menopause —

JACKIE: Don't say that word in front of Carol!

CAROL: Noooo! I haven't had it yet!

BETTE MIDLER: Oh, you haven't? It's hell! I'm passed it. I don't care any more. No, it's not so bad. It's not so good, but it's not so bad.

JANE: Did you make a conscious decision to back off your career a little bit to put some energy into your relationship?

BETTE MIDLER: I was very lucky that I met my husband when I did. He'd come out of a failed marriage. It was the time, the 1980s, and we were looking for love in all the wrong places. But somehow we met and we clicked, but you know what? It's not so easy. You have to compromise every damn day. But you know, when you get the picture and compromise, you go along to get along and it can be kind of fabulous.

CAROL: Are you listening, Jane?

JANE: Yes.

CAROL: We had this conversation last week about prioritising things in your life and Jane's very clear on it, aren't you? Jane cannot put anyone or anything before her career.

BETTE MIDLER: How interesting, and she admits that? Oh my God, I'm shocked! Well, how are you going to get laid that way? Are you the one who didn't have sex for seven years?

CAROL: No, that's me!

Hollywood actress and comedienne, the wonderful Whoopi Goldberg, came by to be an honorary Loose Woman for the day and to talk about the West End musical stage version of her film *Sister Act*.

JACKIE: The big question is, why are you not on the stage?

WHOOPI GOLDBERG: Because I'm too old.

COLEEN: No!

WHOOPI GOLDBERG: Yes, honey, eight shows a week? Are you mad?

JANE: Which do you prefer, producing or being in front of the cameras?

WHOOPI GOLDBERG: I like it all, especially when the cheque doesn't bounce!

DENISE: Has there been a global search to find the lead character?

WHOOPI GOLDBERG: I think they went partially global, but they found this wonderful young girl. I think they've been trying to figure out how to do this for the last five or six years and it just occurred to the new folks who have taken over, the people I'm working with, that you can't look for me. There's just not another one.

JACKIE: That's a good thing!

WHOOPI GOLDBERG: Well, some people think it's a good thing. Some people are really glad there's only one! But once these very smart producers figured that out, it got a lot easier. So they have this wonderful young lady who's twenty-three, tall, statuesque and beautiful, as I was in my youth . . .

JACKIE: Exactly!

WHOOPI GOLDBERG: She's fantastic and she can sing. The movie originally was written for Bette Midler, so Deloris was originally supposed to be a great singer. Then when I got the part, we had to make some adjustments!

JACKIE: Was that the first time you'd sung in a role?

WHOOPI GOLDBERG: On film, in front of people? Yes.

JACKIE: And it was all your voice . . .

WHOOPI GOLDBERG: That was all me.

JACKIE. No cheating?

WHOOPI GOLDBERG: No cheating.

COLEEN: So is the musical based on the film?

WHOOPI GOLDBERG: Well, here's the thing. If you're going to look for me, I'm not there. If you're going to look for the Motown music, it's not there, because Motown has its own revue that it's been working on, and so they didn't want to split it up. So Alan Menken, who has won a million Oscars and Tonys, has written the score. It's all about the 1980s, because Patina Miller, the young lady playing the Deloris part, is so much younger that we have to put her at the beginning of her career. So it takes place in the 1980s and the music is all that fabulous disco music. You think you know the songs, but they're all new. So it's really cool and exciting. It's a great way for this to happen. This is the second movie of mine that this has happened with; they made a musical of *The Color Purple*, and it irritated me.

JACKIE: Really?

WHOOPI GOLDBERG: Yeah! It was *mine* and they got some young girl doing it.

JACKIE: Is there talk of them doing a musical of *Ghost*?

WHOOPI GOLDBERG: Yes!!!! I wonder why! It's wonderful, actually.

JACKIE: So you don't feel territorial watching the new Deloris do her thing?

WHOOPI GOLDBERG: I say it in jest, but you do these pieces and time goes by. You have to release when you get to a certain age.

JACKIE: So why is it hard to release *The Color Purple*?

WHOOPI GOLDBERG: Because that was my first film and I didn't anticipate it becoming a musical.

JACKIE: It's a little incongruous . . .

WHOOPI GOLDBERG: Well, you know: [sings] 'Mister, you took my baby!'

JANE: You were a really serious actress when you made that film. What made you go into comedy?

WHOOPI GOLDBERG: I was always a straight actor, but people assumed that I was a stand-up, because I always did characters.

DENISE: That was a Steven Spielberg film, wasn't it? So how did you get that part?

WHOOPI GOLDBERG: Well, I'd been doing a one-woman show. I'd written it mostly so that people would know I could act, because I'd go up for a part and people would say, 'Come on!'
I'd say, 'What?'
'Have you looked in the mirror?' they'd ask, because I looked unusual. Now, everyone's used to dreads, but when I started wearing them, they were different. People said, 'We're not putting you in a Shakespearean play looking like that!'

JACKIE: So Spielberg saw you in that one-woman show?

WHOOPI GOLDBERG: No, he heard about it. Also, I had written to Alice Walker, who wrote *The Color Purple*, to tell her that my daughter and I had heard her reading it on National Public Radio and if they ever made a movie of it, I would like to play the dirt on the floor.

JACKIE: You'd like to play anything!

WHOOPI GOLDBERG: Yes! Then I got an invitation to go back to New York to do a performance of a piece that I'd been doing, but nobody came to see it. There were people looking at me with the fish eye and I felt bad, because nobody knew who I was. Then a gentleman from the *New York Times* came and wrote a review that, even if I had married this guy and made all his dreams come true, I would not have been able to get a better review. Next thing I knew, there were people everywhere and suddenly they started calling and saying, 'Can you do this? 'Would you be interested in this?' We got a call saying, 'Steven Spielberg wants to know if you would come to California and perform at his place?'
'Yes, sure!' I said. But it turns out that he was quite serious.

JACKIE: I heard a story that you were table reading with him and you suddenly looked up and realised that you were reading in front of Steven Spielberg. You couldn't stop laughing for half an hour after that. Is that right?

WHOOPI GOLDBERG: Actually, I'd already gotten the job and it was the very first day of the shoot, for me. I'd never made a movie and I thought it would be just like a show, as in, you do it in a night and it's done. They're like, 'No. It's going to take three months.'

'Why?' I asked.

'Just do it, you'll see how it works.'

So I was sitting there, watching all these people buzzing around and I suddenly saw Steven behind the camera, looking at me. And I started laughing, because I thought, Oh my God! *Oh my God!* Argh! All I could do was shake with laughter.

'Are you OK?' he said.

'Yes, yes, I'm cool!' I said, still shaking.

'What's the matter?'

I pointed at him and the set. 'I'm making a movie!' I said.

'Well, that's what we do here, babe,' he said.

JACKIE: The other guy that you have a lot to thank for, for another film that brought you so much attention, is Patrick Swayze. Basically he said, 'If you don't get this woman to play this part in *Ghost*, I'm not doing the movie.'

WHOOPI GOLDBERG: Actually, what happened was this: a friend of mine came to my house – another actress – and she was chatting away. Then I heard her say, 'And every black actress and their mother has been up for this part.'

What part? I thought. I haven't heard about it. But you don't want to say that, because you don't want to sound like you're going to snatch it away. After she left, I called my agent and said, 'Is there a movie being made out there with a black woman? Is it possible to get an audition?'

'No,' he said.

'Oh, OK,' I said. 'Why not?'

'Because they don't want you,' he said.

'All right. Why not?'

'Because you're too famous and they're afraid that you will pull people out of the movie.'

I wish I'd said, 'OK, you mean like Marlon Brando did in every film he ever made?' but I didn't think of that until much later! Soon after that, I went down to Montgomery, Alabama to make a film with Sissy Spacek called *Long Walk Home*. Three weeks later, I got a phone call from my agent. 'Do you remember that movie they don't want you for? Well, they would like to come down to Alabama and audition you.'

'OK,' I said.

'With Patrick Swayze,' he said.

'Why Patrick Swayze? That's a funny choice,' I said.

'Because they gave him the job!'

'Oh, OK!' I said. I was thinking that maybe they just called him and said, 'Hey, do you want to go down to Alabama?' Sometimes I'm just not the brightest bulb!

So Patrick came down. He'd asked them, 'Who's playing Oda Mae?' And they said they hadn't found anyone, so he said, 'Has that Whoopi Goldberg girl said no?' They said they hadn't asked me. 'Why not?' he said. They said they didn't want me. 'Listen, you have to at least audition her, because if you don't audition her, I'm not doing this.'

So he came down and we had just a blast being ridiculous. He went back saying, 'Bye, nice to meet you, really good!' And I went back to walking the long walk.

A week later, they said, 'You got the job!' Then I got the Oscar, which was quite fantastic!

JACKIE: We are especially honoured to have you here today because you have not travelled overseas very often, because you have had a chronic fear of flying, but you were cured on television . . .

WHOOPI GOLDBERG: Cured-ish.

JACKIE: . . . by having aversion therapy?

WHOOPI GOLDBERG: Virgin Airlines does this thing only here in the UK, where they have a ten-hour course, which has a pilot, a psychologist and someone who has also had the same fear. I spent five hours with them, because they flew to the US to do this with me. The pilot was extraordinary. I like the psychology, but you know, tell me what's happening with the plane! That's really what I want to know.

DENISE: Was yours a fear of the claustrophobia of flying or a fear of crashing?

WHOOPI GOLDBERG: Mid-air collision, which is something I had seen in San Diego in 1978. So these guys got all the information on that particular collision and the pilot took me through all the things that the plane can do. I knew a lot of it, but what I didn't know was that in the last three years, every plane that is in the sky has a piece of machinery on it that will never allow a mid-air collision to happen again, ever, and no plane can go up without it. If the plane does not have it, they do not let the plane fly.

JACKIE: Do you believe him, or is he just telling you that?

WHOOPI GOLDBERG: Well, actually, I asked around, and all commercial airlines and private jets have to have it, and there are six or seven fail-safes for everything that goes wrong on a plane now. This didn't exist when I saw the collision. So the idea that

I no longer had to worry about this happening was incredible. I can't even explain it. Am I really over it? It's still not my favourite thing to do, but I got on the plane here. Now, will I use a little something . . . something to help me?

JACKIE: To take the edge off?

WHOOPI GOLDBERG: Yes, and let's face it, a free high is a free high! Sorry, sorry, I just remembered that there are kids watching. Children, don't listen to me!

JACKIE: Whoopi's high on life.

WHOOPI GOLDBERG: That's right; way high on Easter eggo!

COLEEN: Today we've been talking about hunky men. Do you like a hunky man or a skinny man?

WHOOPI GOLDBERG: I like a *man*. I don't like boys.

COLEEN: Oh, well, you wouldn't get on with Carol McGiffin, then!

WHOOPI GOLDBERG: I just feel like I don't want to raise anybody else. I have a thirty-five-year-old daughter. If I have to guide you and tell you what to do, you're not worth the time. You need to know what you're doing when you get there!

COLEEN: I'm with you on that!

THAT'S ALL FOLKS!

Ah, we've sadly reached the end of this latest magical mystery tour through the lives and loves of the Loose Women. We hope you've enjoyed our year round survival guide, and hopefully you've managed to salvage one or two nuggets of wisdom and if not, fingers crossed you've at least had a laugh along the way!

Love the Loose Women xx

Picture Acknowledgements

Getty Images: 6 above, 6 below (FilmMagic). ITV/Kent News and Pictures Ltd: 1 above left, 1 below left. Courtesy ITV Studios Limited: 2, 3, 4, 5. Rex Features: 8 above (Jonathan Hordie), 1 above right (ITV), 1 below right (Ken Mckay), 7 below (J. Ritchie), 7 above, 8 below (Richard Young).